THE ARTS IN A
NEW MILLENNIUM

THE ARTS IN A
NEW MILLENNIUM

Research and the Arts Sector

Edited by Valerie B. Morris and David B. Pankratz

Westport, Connecticut
London

Library of Congress Cataloging-in-Publication Data

The arts in a new millennium: research and the arts sector / edited by Valerie B. Morris and David B. Pankratz.

    p. cm.

  Includes bibliographical references and index.

  ISBN 0–275–97013–2 (alk. paper)

    1. Arts—Research—United States. 2. United States—Cultural policy. 3. Arts and society—United States. I. Morris, Valerie B. II. Pankratz, David B.

NX705.5 U6 A755 2003

306.4'89—dc21   2002070897

British Library Cataloguing in Publication Data is available.

Library of Congress Catalog Card Number: 2002070897

ISBN: 0–275–97013–2

First published in 2003

Praeger Publishers, 88 Post Road West, Westport, CT 06881

An imprint of Greenwood Publishing Group, Inc.

www.praeger.com

Printed in the United States of America

The paper used in this book complies with the Permanent Paper Standard issued by the National Information Standards Organization (Z39.48–1984).

10 9 8 7 6 5 4 3 2 1

Contents

Tables

Acknowledgments

The editors would like to thank a number of persons who contributed to the production of this volume. We were prompted to publish this book by members of the Association of Arts Administration Educators, several of whom had used our previous coedited book *The Future of the Arts* in teaching arts policy and administration courses. They sought an updated discussion of issues and trends in the arts and wanted a new bibliography reflecting the flurry of arts research over the past decade. We hope arts administration educators, along with policy-makers, arts and culture leaders, managers, and researchers, find this volume a success on both scores.

We express our most sincere, heartfelt gratitude to those accomplished professionals who contributed chapters to *The Arts in a New Millennium*. The contributors are nationally prominent leaders in the conduct, support, and dissemination of arts research. We are grateful for the time they took out of their busy schedules to write chapters for this book. We also thank them for their patience during the long process of production from initial invitations to write to the appearance of their words in print. Production of this book would not have been possible without the excellent assistance of Greg Eck, a graduate student in English at the College of Charleston. Greg managed all technical aspects of preparing this volume for final publication. Thanks also to Chris Burgess who assembled the bibliography for the book and to Boris Bohun-Chudyniv for a final edit of the manuscript. Finally, we thank James Sabin of Praeger for his early acceptance of our prospectus and his consistent support throughout the book's development. We are pleased to present this sequel to our 1990 volume *The Future of the Arts*, and to once again work with Praeger.

Introduction

Valerie B. Morris

In 1990, David B. Pankratz and Valerie B. Morris coedited a volume of essays titled *The Future of the Arts: Public Policy and Arts Research.* The 1990 volume was organized around one basic question: What role can social science research play in the formulation of public policy, which can address serious issues confronting the future of the arts in the United States? The chapters sought to answer three main questions that seemed to naturally follow from the organizing question: (1) What was the state of arts research at that time? (2) What problems and opportunities characterized public arts policy? and (3) What key issues would shape the future of the arts in the United States?

A decade later, the editors recontacted many of the contributors to the original volume and asked them to respond to essentially the same organizing question and to the three main questions: (1) What is the current state of arts research and how has it changed over the last decade? (2) What problems and opportunities characterize public arts policy today? and (3) What key issues will shape the future of the arts in the United States and how will they differ from the issues identified in the previous volume?

THE CURRENT STATE OF ARTS RESEARCH

In the 1980s, arts research could, perhaps optimistically, be described as a "developing" study area. A core of dedicated researchers, most of whom knew each other, labored away in a field that brought them little academic recognition and almost no research funds. Then, along with the Robert Mapplethorpe and Andres Serrano controversies and the end of the Cold War, came the period of the "culture wars," when what little funding there had been, was threatened. Scholars dedicated themselves to (1) preserving and/or restoring the concept of public support and funding for the arts, (2) arguing for the development of a new paradigm for arts support in this country, or (3) explaining why the time for federal arts support had passed.

Several worthwhile reports were issued during this time, including the Report of the Independent Commission set up to evaluate the National Endowment for the Arts (NEA), issued in 1990, and the somewhat controversial American Canvas Report, issued in 1997. Also in 1997, the American Assembly in New York convened its significant "Arts and Public Purpose" Forum.

Arts research then began to occupy an important position within the funding agenda of several of the larger charitable foundations, particularly the Pew Charitable Trust, the Leila Wallace Reader's Digest Fund, and the Ford and Rockefeller Foundations. By the late 1990s, several new arts research centers had been established, including the Center for Arts and Culture, a think tank created by several of the major foundations in Washington, DC, and research centers located at universities throughout the country such as Princeton, Ohio State, Columbia, Carnegie Mellon, Virginia Tech, and Northeastern.

By the end of the 1990s, arts research capabilities had progressed measurably. This progression held significant implications for defining and implementing arts policy.

PUBLIC ARTS POLICY IN THE UNITED STATES

The past decade has been a significant one in the public arts policy arena. The official arts policy of the United States is still represented by the claim that there is no official arts policy in the United States. Events during the past decade have, however, raised a national debate over the worth, or lack thereof, of such a policy. The culture war "scandals" of the 1990s raised some of the very same issues that had been feared during the mid-1960s' discussions that led to the formation of the NEA, when many artists felt that public funding would of necessity lead to undue censorship and politicization, while many political and religious leaders felt that publicly funded art would result inevitably in publicly funded endorsement of sin!

Ironically perhaps, the resulting national debate has had a positive outcome for arts researchers, lifting the topic of public arts policy from the very "back burner" of the national agenda to the "front burner," even though in a somewhat antagonistic way. Arts policy now has become a creditable area for academic research, or at least a more creditable area than it was in the 1980s.

KEY ISSUES FOR THE FUTURE

Prior to the publication of this volume, the world was dramatically changed by the terrorist event that demolished the World Trade Center towers in New

York on September 11, 2001. How this event will impact the arts is a topic that is now widely debated in academic and arts policy circles, with no clear answer yet emerging.

How will new technologies affect the arts? Several chapters in this volume address this issue. Ten to twelve years ago, technology concerns centered around the growing network of cable television and the envisioned positive and negative effects of that network on live, visual, and performing arts programming. Hardly foreseen at that time was the enormous impact the Internet, fax machines, and cell telephones would have, enabling instantaneous worldwide communication. Will the arts need to change radically to encompass these new technologies? How can the arts use these technologies to best advantage?

In the 1990s, the growing importance of the nonprofit sector was acknowledged, with the separations between the nonprofit and for-profit sectors and the noncommercial and commercial seen as crucial. Today, researchers are interested in exploring where the nonprofit and for-profit intersect, or even perhaps merge.

Some of our old, tried and true issues remain: How does U.S. cultural policy compare, contrast, and relate to worldwide cultural policies? Should our stance toward government subsidy more closely match that of other Western cultures? Or, in fact, are the cultural policies of other nations being remodeled to more closely match ours? What is the economic impact of the arts, internationally, nationally, and locally? Are we losing our audiences to technology, to aging, to boredom? What is the role of marketing in the arts?

The NEA has now survived the culture wars unleashed on it by the religious and political right. It has been downsized and restructured. Can it survive? Will it survive?

Finally, in the past decade we have seen a tremendous growth in the occupation called "arts administration." Will there be a greater emphasis on the use of arts administrators in the future? Will these trained arts administrators have a helpful or a harmful impact on the future of the arts? Will they streamline arts bureaucracy to good effect, or will they sacrifice artistic quality in search of the ever-elusive "bottom line"?

The chapters in this volume, written by many of the country's most important arts researchers, explore a wide range of arts policy issues and topics. In our previous volume, we stated that "understanding and interpretation of current conditions is a necessary prelude to developing sound arts policy for the future." This present volume, written a decade later, continues us on that path.

I

The Production, Dissemination, and Utilization of Research

Values and Policy Paradigms:
Foundations for Research on the Arts Sector

David B. Pankratz

In the 1990 publication "Arts Policy Research for the 1990s and Beyond," Milton Cummings, Monnie Peters, Richard Swaim, Margaret Wyszomirski and myself wrote:

Despite its short history, arts policy research has made substantive contributions to our understanding of many specific topics: rationales for public support of the arts, historical and cross-national trends in government arts policy, controversies in policymaking, interrelationships between public and private support for the arts, leadership styles in public arts agencies, the implications of tax regulations for arts organizations as well as private arts patrons, and many others. But even a sympathetic observer would be hard-pressed to conclude, as the 1990s begin, that arts policy research is a healthy enterprise. Many issues remain uninvestigated, alternative research methods go underutilized, researchers struggle amidst limited support systems, and arts policymakers treat research with relative indifference, when they are aware of it at all. The time for stock-taking, then, is overdue.[1]

The start of the new millennium, and the passage of a decade, represents a new opportunity for taking stock. This section will address two key questions: (1) What has changed or improved in the production, dissemination, and utilization of research on the arts sector over the past decade? and (2) Are there keys to improving the production, dissemination, and utilization of research on the arts sector in the next decade and beyond? To answer these questions, this chapter will first identify notable changes and persistent problems in arts research in the last ten years. Chapters on change initiatives underway to improve arts research now and in the future follow.

THE CHANGING CONTEXT OF RESEARCH
ON THE ARTS SECTOR

While acknowledging the extensive, substantive work done by arts researchers prior to the 1990s, the extract at the beginning of this chapter also notes that many research issues had not been investigated. Explanations for this deficit, in "Arts Policy Research for the 1990s and Beyond," focused on problems with data collection in the arts, the conditions of researchers, the training of future researchers, and the relative lack of interest by the public in the arts as a policy area. But additional factors shaped choices of topics for inquiry made by university-based and independent researchers and their public arts agency and foundation sponsors. Of particular impact was the prevailing "arts policy paradigm" of the 1980s and early 1990s, a paradigm with two key features: (1) the belief that public support for the arts is warranted and that the primary beneficiaries of such support are nonprofit arts organizations and individual artists; and (2) strategies by public arts agencies to both insulate them from politics and to broaden their political bases of support.

This "arts policy paradigm" was a response of supporters of public arts funding to pressures to reduce the vulnerability of public agencies as political targets, to safeguard and maximize budgets, and to meet the claims of an expanding base of constituents. At the same time, the paradigm shaped the production of arts research (and its utilization) in significant ways. Several kinds of research that served as *political ammunition*, by contributing to case statements for increased funding, were favored by sponsors and arts advocates. These included opinion polls, economic impact studies, cross-national comparisons, and audience surveys.[2]

As the culture wars of the early 1990s clearly demonstrated, however, the predominant "arts policy paradigm" did not insulate public arts agencies and their advocates from conflict and criticism on religious, political, and administrative grounds. Furthermore, when confronted with calls for reorganization of the National Endowment for the Arts (NEA), budget reductions and redistribution of its funds to the states, or its elimination, *political ammunition* research proved inadequate. Without a research tradition to foster systematic examination of and diverse perspectives on arts policy alternatives, research-based scenarios to revise existing policies, to formulate new ones, or to alter decision-making processes and structures were not available.

The congressionally mandated report by the Independent Commission on the National Endowment for the Arts, issued in 1990, was a flash point in a process of revising the predominant arts policy paradigm. Most significantly, the commission report called for a shift in values. It argued that "the Endowment exists to bring the benefits of the arts to the American people.... [T]he NEA must not operate solely in the interest of its direct beneficiaries—[artists and arts organizations]."[3]

In the mid-1990s, policy analysts explored how the role of research might be reconstituted in the arts policy world, in part, by calling for development of an arts policy community.[4] These analysts pointed to the experience of policy communities outside the arts, in which research, policy dialogue, issue identification, and option development occur in multiple venues and are ongoing. Generating alternatives and proposals in policy communities have been likened to "policy primeval soup."[5] In such processes, successful new policy ideas do not just happen—they are the fruits of extensive thought and effort by fertile, interactive, and context-sensitive policy communities.

The mid-1990s arts policy community, in contrast, was seen as fragmented, incomplete in its core resources of data, evaluation, and analysis, and uncoordinated with few opportunities for arts policy actors to interact. Such fragmentation had left the arts with:

1. an inability to analyze the relative merits of programs across disciplines or to anticipate the range of implications of their actions;
2. few mechanisms to resolve policy conflicts and to cultivate common outlooks, values, and new policy options; and
3. instability and vulnerability in the face of change or crises borne of shifting public perceptions, program flaws, or unstable leadership.

But many leaders, as will be seen, have addressed this problem and devised initiatives to build an effective arts policy community, including:

1. forums to promote the expansion of policy dialogue;
2. establishment of arts policy research centers;
3. improvement of research brokerage functions;
4. investing in the arts policy infrastructure through support of better information, communication, analysis, and evaluation; and
5. supporting projects that foster a supportive public and expand relations between the arts and other communities.

INITIATIVES TO CHANGE RESEARCH ON THE ARTS SECTOR

Policy Forums

The 1997 "The Arts and the Public Purpose" forum convened by the American Assembly, following the President's Committee on the Arts and Humanities' *Creative America* report,[6] represented a sea change in thinking about the arts, policy, and research. The forum's final report articulated a new vision and values paradigm to reorient arts policy development and research.[7] It made a case that the arts are not the province only of arts organizations and artists, but that the arts can uniquely serve a broad range of public purposes rooted in enduring American values of security, community, prosperity, quality of life, and democracy. The report also reaffirmed that the United States' pluralistic system of public, private, and market support of the arts, in contrast to oft-envied centralized systems of arts support, is both consistent with American values of democracy and, on balance, provides an effective means of encouraging and rewarding initiative and entrepreneurship.

"The Arts and the Public Purpose" also called for a broader definition of the arts sector, one that includes the nonprofit, commercial, and unincorporated (amateur and avocational) arts. Its final report proposed new and expanded cross-sector collaborations arguing that the arts sector as a whole, through collaborative activities, will be better able to serve public purposes in U.S. society.

By offering a new values paradigm for arts policy and a broadened vision of the arts sector, "The Arts and the Public Purpose" has spurred new forms of inquiry. These include increased attention to the ends of arts policy—such as how to serve public purposes—as well as the final stages of policies—impacts and outcomes. Forms of outcomes analysis, in an environment of increased accountability requirements by public and private funders, measure how program and policy initiatives are met and the processes and obstacles they face in the pursuit of goals.[8] Finally, the American Assembly has stimulated research on interactions between the for-profit and nonprofit arts. Examples include case studies of cross-sector collaborations and analysis of the legal, regulatory, and tax constraints and opportunities of those and future collaborations, the impacts of corporate structures and new technologies on cross-sector activities, and research on the cross-sector trajectories of artist careers.[9] Also, research on the unincorporated sector is expanding.[10]

Research Centers

The mid-1990s have marked the establishment of new research and policy centers in the arts and culture field. Among these are university-based centers such as the Arts Policy and Administration Program at Ohio State University, the Princeton University Center for the Arts and Cultural Policy Studies, and the Cultural and Arts Policy Research Institute at Northeastern University. These groups, and the continuing work of the Research Center on Arts and Culture at Columbia University, are focused on training future cultural policy scholars and developing significant research initiatives. The independent Washington, DC–based Center for Arts and Culture, among its many activities, has created a Web-based Cultural Policy Inventory of cultural policy scholars and a searchable bibliography of research, as well as the Cultural Policy Network, a network of twenty-five university sites whose representatives discuss questions and share strategies in cultural policy research.

Research Brokers and Convenings

These research centers also serve as research brokers by convening arts professionals, policy makers, artists, and leaders in the nonprofit, business, and political sectors to discuss research findings and emerging policy issues in the cultural sector. The Center for Arts and Culture presents six or more convenings per year in its *Calling the Question* series. The series has expanded arts and culture policy dialogue to include issues in the humanities and technology, and trends such as the globalization of culture. The Center also briefs foundations (the J. Paul Getty Trust) and service organizations (such as Grantmakers in the Arts). Every two years the Ohio State University's Arts Policy and Administration Program presents the Barnett Symposium on the Arts and Public Policy. Other efforts include the Americans for the Arts' National Policy Board and, at the regional level, the cultural policy convenings of the Western States Arts Federation. A local example is ARTS, Inc.'s *Issues and Opportunities* series of public forums in Los Angeles. The work of these brokers includes on-line readings and research summaries before and after convenings, as well as opportunities for on-line dialogue. Finally, the NEA makes many of its research reports as well as special research notes available on-line, the American Arts Alliance features legislative updates on cultural policy issues on-line, and the Arts Education Partnership has an extensive Web site with research reports and policy task force papers.

Investments in Research on the Arts Sector

The mid-1990s has seen a dramatic resurgence of foundation support for policy dialogue, research infrastructure, and research in the arts sector. This activity is predicated on the belief that improvements in the nation's cultural life are contingent on a strengthened cultural policy community, and that foundations are well situated to provide such support. Examples are numerous. In the policy dialogue area, foundations providing major funding for the 1997 American Assembly were Ford, Rockefeller, Robert Sterling Clark, Getty, and Luce, while Ford was joined by the AT&T Foundation and the Kenan Institute of the Arts in follow-up assemblies.

As for research infrastructure, foundations providing ongoing support for the Center for Arts and Culture include Gillman and Rockefeller, while Pew and the Kenan Institute funded the Center's on-line Cultural Policy Inventory. Center for Arts and Culture project donors include Robert Sterling Clark, Nathan Cummings, Ford, Getty, Kenan, Luce, Packard, and Pew. Furthermore, the Pew Charitable Trusts established the National Arts Journalism Program at Columbia University and the Rockefeller Foundation has funded the Social Science Research Council Program on the Arts. Finally, numerous arts research projects have received foundation support:

1. Data on Arts Organizations by the Princeton Center for Arts and Cultural Policy Studies (Nathan Cummings, Mellon, and NEA Research Division);
2. National and Local Profiles of Cultural Support, a study to map the cultural communities and sources of support in ten cities, in collaboration with Americans for the Arts and the Ohio State Arts Policy and Administration Program (Pew);

3. Arts and Culture Indicators in Community Building Project by the Urban Institute (Rockefeller);

4. John S. and James L. Knight Foundation, Community Indicators Project;

5. the Henry R. Luce Foundation project on Art and Religion in American Life;

6. An Integrated Assessment of the Arts Sector by the RAND Corporation (Pew);

7. Mapping the Associational Infrastructure of the Arts and Culture Sector by the Ohio State Arts Policy and Administration Program (Ford);

8. a RAND Corporation study of strategic and policy dimensions of audience decision making in the arts (Lila Wallace Reader's Digest Fund); and

9. the James Irvine Foundation and Americans for the Arts are in the planning phase of developing a quantitative Arts Performance Index on the nonprofit arts industry.

Furthermore, the Pew Charitable Trusts has initiated Optimizing America's Cultural Resources, a five-year, multimillion-dollar project to improve and develop cultural polices in the United States through research, communications, and institutional effectiveness programs.

Finally, support for research projects has also come from the NEA and arts service organizations, especially in the area of audience development and access to the arts. For example, the NEA, every five years, has replicated its ongoing Survey of Public Participation in the Arts project and has sponsored specialized studies based on the survey. Publications by arts service organizations include: *For the Record: Documenting Arts Audience Development Initiatives* (Arts Presenters); *Invitation to the Dance: Audience Development of the Next Century* (Dance/USA); and *The Guiding Principles of Audience Development* (Opera America). The NEA Research Division also provided funding for the Unified Database of Arts Organizations project, led by the Urban Institute's National Center for Charitable Statistics.

PROJECTS TO FOSTER A SUPPORTIVE PUBLIC AND EXPAND RELATIONS OUTSIDE THE ARTS

A notable example in this area is Animating Democracy: Strengthening the Role of the Arts in Civic Dialogue, a four-year initiative of Americans for the Arts, with support from the Ford Foundation. The purpose of the initiative is to foster artistic activity that encourages civic dialogue on contemporary issues. The project will encourage experimentation and the testing of approaches to arts-based civic dialogue, documentation of those approaches, and scholarly research and writing to provide contextual understanding. The National Arts Journalism Program is aimed at increasing the amount and quality of coverage of the arts and readers' knowledge of the importance of culture. Furthermore, as part of its Optimizing America's Cultural Resources project, the Pew Charitable Trusts will encourage development of arts and culture programming on diverse broadcasting venues and will train spokespersons to communicate positive messages about culture to policy makers, funders, and the media.

CONCLUSION: PERSISTENT PROBLEMS
AND FUTURE PROSPECTS

The many initiatives cited earlier are positive indicators that a mature, effective policy community in the arts and culture is developing. To these indicators must be added the ongoing vitality of interdisciplinary gatherings such as the annual Conference on Social Theory, Politics, and the Arts (which in 1999 celebrated its twenty-fifth anniversary) and the semiannual International Association for Cultural Economics, as well as the *Journal of Arts Management, Law, and Society*, all of which serve as outlets and communications for researchers and policy makers in the arts and culture.

But the promise of a policy community that can foster systematic examination of arts policy alternatives and develop research-based scenarios to revise existing policies and to formulate new ones is muted somewhat by persistent problems.

Problems in data collection in the arts identified in the early 1990s continue. In a review of data collection systems by government agencies, public arts agencies, and arts service organizations, researchers concluded that "none of the data sources we reviewed met the standards of policy-relevant information— technical quality and reliability, comprehensiveness of coverage, comparability across disciplines and over time, and easy accessibility to researchers."[11] As a result, the testing and refinement of theories to explain and predict phenomena in the arts is severely compromised, while special studies and surveys lose some of their value if they are not grounded in comprehensive data sets. That said, arts data collection is improving. For example, the National and Local Profiles of Cultural Support project will yield benchmark data on arts support systems, while the Urban Institute is working on taxonomies of arts and culture organizations and the integration of arts databases.

Furthermore, the growing policy community in the arts and culture has yet to:

1. conduct studies on the infrastructure of policy in the arts and culture that can identify factors to further strengthen the arts research enterprise;
2. develop a comprehensive research agenda of topics that researchers can explore on a systemic, coordinated basis; and
3. educate policy makers and administrators about the many purposes research can serve beyond political ammunition.

The arts and culture policy community is still confronted with the myth that its primary agenda is to maximize federal support for nonprofit arts organizations and artists. In contrast, it seems fair to say that as this policy community has developed, its operating premises have included a commitment to policy research and dialogue on (1) the full arts sector as it interacts with the humanities, new technologies, telecommunications, and U.S. society as a whole, (2) policies in both public and private entities, and (3) policies in federal, regional, state, local, and international contexts. Furthermore, the arts and culture policy community is highly inclusive, including congressional staff, academics, consultants, foundation program officers, cultural administrators, artists, community members, and representatives of the political, nonprofit, and commercial sectors.

These and related issues are addressed in the chapters that follow. The chapters discuss significant change agents from diverse sectors with interests in arts and culture research—a national think tank on cultural policy, a major foundation's cultural policy initiative, a university-based policy center, and a national nonpartisan forum on policy issues. Each chapter, in its own way, will be central in any stock-taking of research on the arts sector done in the future, especially after the new millennium's first decade.

NOTES

1. David B. Pankratz et al., "Arts Policy Research for the 1990s and Beyond," in *The Future of the Arts: Public Policy and Arts Research,* ed. David B. Pankratz and Valerie B. Morris (New York: Praeger, 1990), 263.

2. For further discussion of such research, see Pankratz et al., "Arts Policy Research."

3. Independent Commission, *A Report to Congress on the National Endowment for the Arts* (Washington, DC: Independent Commission, 1990), 2.

4. See Margaret Jane Wyszomirski, "Policy Communities and Policy Influence: Securing a Government Role in Cultural Policy for the 21st Century," *Journal of Arts Management, Law, and Society* 25, no. 3 (fall 1995): 192–205; reprinted in Gigi Bradford, Michael Gary, and Glenn Wallach, eds., *The Politics of Culture: Policy Perspectives for Individuals, Institutions, and Communities* (New York: New Press, 2000).

5. See John Kingdon, *Agendas, Alternatives, and Public Policies,* 2nd ed. (New York: HarperCollins, 1995).

6. President's Committee on the Arts and Humanities, *Creative America: A Report to the President* (Washington, DC: President's Committee on the Arts and Humanities, 1997).

7. American Assembly, *The Arts and the Public Purpose* (New York: American Assembly, Columbia University, 1997).

8. See Margaret Jane Wyszomirski, "The Arts and Performance Review, Policy Assessment, and Program Evaluation: Focusing on the Ends of the Policy Cycle," *Journal of Arts Management, Law, and Society* 28, no. 3 (fall 1998): 191–200.

9. See American Assembly, *Deals and Ideals: For-Profit and Not-for-Profit Arts Connections* (New York: American Assembly, Columbia University, 1999).

10. For example, see Monnie Peters and Joni Maya Cherbo, "The Missing Sector: The Unincorporated Arts," *Journal of Arts Management, Law, and Society* 28, no. 2 (summer 1998): 115–28.

11. Deborah A. Kaple et al., *Data on Arts Organizations: A Review and Needs Assessment, with Design Implications* (Princeton, NJ: Center for Arts and Cultural Policy Studies, Princeton University, 1996), 4.

2

Promoting Research and Building a Cultural Policy Community: The Experience of the Center for Arts and Culture in Washington, D.C.

Gigi Bradford and Glenn Wallach

Something like the Center for Arts and Culture existed as an intriguing idea for some years before it emerged as a living entity in 1997. Initiatives at several foundations in the 1980s and 1990s had explored ways to bring together policy and the arts. In the world of scholarly research, meanwhile, David B. Pankratz and his coauthors in 1990 discussed the prospects for "an arts policy research center" that would be "a coordinating organization to foster interactive networks and shared undertakings and to stimulate a collective research agenda for the arts and arts policy." They concluded, though, that "arts policy research does not yet have a critical mass of researchers or the widespread public interest necessary to support the establishment of a freestanding think tank."[1]

Throughout the twentieth century, policy research institutions organized ideas so that decision makers could evaluate fundamental shifts in society and politics—from the Progressive Era quest for efficiency, through the Cold War complexities of nuclear strategy, to more recent challenges in environmental, economic, and social policy.[2] Recent flux in the cultural sphere brought a renewed intensity to the search for nonpartisan and independent policy development in arts and culture for the new century.

Conflicts that rumbled through U.S. cultural institutions and legislative halls in the first years of the 1990s, now dubbed the "culture wars," narrowed the national conversation about culture to a debate over a few allegedly controversial federal grants. The commotion also obscured a recognition by scholars and others that the policy terrain had expanded and embraced more than the issues in the traditional "arts policy paradigm."

In the new millennium, policy makers and practitioners will need to understand the implications of a complex cultural sector driven by the power of creativity and innovation in a global economy. The President's Committee on the Arts and Humanities' *Creative America* and the American Assembly's *The Arts and the Public Purpose* each played a critical role in describing the nature of this sector. The explosion in the significance of cultural content in new information technologies and an international discussion that linked culture to development strategies, heritage, and promoting "cultural and linguistic diversity in an information society" further expanded the range of potential issues.[3]

While Pankratz et al. had expected universities to be the most likely source for a policy research center, the first independent think tank on the arts and culture emerged from the world of private foundations. Leaders from the Nathan Cummings Foundation, Howard Gilman Foundation, Thomas S. Kenan Institute for the Arts, Rockefeller Foundation, and Andy Warhol Foundation for the Visual Arts, among others, took a bold step to create an institution named Center for Arts and Culture, devoted to research, convening, policy development, and communication, that would raise the level of thought and discourse surrounding cultural issues above partisan and ideologically charged debates.

As noted in Chapter 1, serious consideration of cultural concerns must be rooted in a community capable of sustained research, generating and testing new ideas. An impulse for coordinated approaches and collective solutions, however, can appear to participants in the field to be an attempt to direct their activity. One of the center's initial tasks, therefore, has been to act as a catalyst for a new kind of policy community that acknowledges the traditional independence of practitioners and scholars of the arts.

The center has worked to build a critical mass of both inquiry and action, to investigate the new policy environment in arts and culture, and to find the best means to foster networks that span disciplinary and professional lines. With the advice of a distinguished panel of scholars, its Research Task Force, it developed programs directed less at particular policy questions and more at creating mechanisms that foster access to information and constructing an intellectual infrastructure to promote research throughout the field.[4]

The center compiled and organized disparate information into a reliable and accessible resource: the Cultural Policy Inventory. The inventory, created with the support of the Pew Charitable Trusts, includes facts and statistics on the cultural sector; a resource bank of more than one hundred scholars and their work in cultural policy; a guide to organizations, institutions, events, and opportunities; an on-line bibliography of more than two thousand cultural policy publications; a collection of university course syllabi in cultural policy; and a report on newspaper arts coverage (as part of a collaboration with the National Arts Journalism Program at Columbia University). Information is updated regularly and has been integrated into a searchable and user-friendly interface on the center's web site: <http://www.culturalpolicy.org>.[5]

Because the center is not associated with a single academic institution or discipline, it pursues partnerships across the spectrum of the emerging cultural sector—from university classrooms and artists' studios to the offices of both policy and arts professionals. As a way to connect the important scholarly work underway on many campuses and at the university-based policy centers described in Chapter 1, it created the Cultural Policy Network (with the support of the Ford Foundation). The network held an initial series of meetings in 1999 that gathered scholars—historians, sociologists, arts educators, cultural economists, and arts policy experts—from more than twenty-five academic institutions to identify current research in the field, form alliances across and beyond university walls, and create an efficient mechanism for scholarly exchange.

Rather than impose a research agenda on the network, the center provides opportunities for academic insight to become applied policy research through research grants to faculty and graduate students, and network scholars' participation in the center projects; creates structures for curriculum development with targeted meetings and the bank of syllabi on the web; and provides an arena for sharing research and planning new initiatives in the virtual (on-line discussion forum) and the actual world (periodic conferences for network representatives).

Raising public awareness is a critical dimension in building a new policy field. The center sponsors a series of public programs addressing critical issues in the cultural sector entitled *Calling the Question*. These events open a dialogue with national and international leaders and identify future areas for center research and recommendations. In 1999, one series explored the cultural sector in the twenty-first century and another examined globalization and its impact on culture. In the spring of 2000, three panels investigated technology's effects on the cultural sector.

To set some preliminary boundaries for the policy discussions that lie ahead and reflect various styles of cultural policy inquiry, the center published a collection of essays *The Politics of Culture: Policy Perspectives for Individuals, Institutions, and Communities*.[6] The volume's contributors argue that policy makers need to redefine "cultural policy" to mean more than arts funding policies and must recognize the ways in which the production of ideas and content will drive domestic and international arrangements. The volume was the first in a series of publications that will track the growth of this realm. With the Henry R. Luce Foundation, the center will produce *Crossroads of the Spirit*, a book on the relationship of art and religion in American life.[7]

After several years of work to connect members of the field, provide critical information, and create opportunities for new research, the center was prepared to embark on a major initiative with concrete policy impact. Art, Culture, and the National Agenda is a project to conduct research and produce briefing papers and a collected volume on critical issues in arts and culture facing the presidential administration and Congress.

While recommendations about the future of several individual disciplines in the arts had appeared before, particularly during the 1960s, there had been little comprehensive assessment of issues facing the sector.[8] The Independent Committee on Arts Policy in 1988 made an important contribution in "The Nation and the Arts: A Presidential Briefing Paper,"[9] but no similar initiative had analyzed the broad implications of the new policy environment in culture for decision makers and the interested public.

Through a series of public events, policy papers, and digital and print publications, the center will endeavor to order seemingly disparate questions into a coherent set of cultural policy concerns and demonstrate why and how this cluster of issues belongs on the public agenda. It will provide the cultural sector, the public, and the next administration with the data and analysis it needs to make informed decisions about these issues. Release of the briefing papers and the completed volume will be coordinated with a series of meetings for officials and staffs of the administration and Congress, opinion leaders, journalists, and policy makers in the private sector.

Art, Culture, and the National Agenda follows in the tradition of the Brookings Institution's *Setting National Priorities* and the Heritage Foundation's *Mandate for Leadership.* Just as those think tanks created documents that provided Americans with an enduring vocabulary to discuss subjects ranging from health care and the environment, to economics and defense throughout the 1970s and 1980s, this project will set the terms for informed discussions of arts and culture for the twenty-first century. As recognition of the fundamental place of culture in a global economy based on creativity and innovation grows, the policy community in arts and culture will continue its evolution to meet a growing need for research and analysis. The alliances that link independent research centers, the academy, foundations, policy makers, and the public will increase in their richness and complexity.

NOTES

1. David B. Pankratz et al., "Arts Policy Research for the 1990s and Beyond," in *The Future of the Arts: Public Policy and Arts Research,* ed. David B. Pankratz and Valerie B. Morris (New York: Praeger, 1990), 280, 282.

2. To trace this history, see James Allen Smith, *The Idea Brokers: Think Tanks and the Rise of the New Policy Elite* (New York: The Free Press, 1991).

3. Excerpts from both of these reports and further assessment of the changing cultural sector are in Gigi Bradford, Michael Gary, and Glenn Wallach, eds., *The Politics of Culture: Policy Perspectives for Individuals, Institutions, and Communities* (New York: New Press, 2000); UNESCO, *Final Report: Intergovernmental Conference on Cultural Policies for Development, Stockholm Sweden, March 30–April 2, 1998* (Paris: UNESCO 1998), 14–174.

4. Founding Research Task Force members in 1998 were: Alberta Arthurs, Milton Cummings Jr., William Glade, Stanley N. Katz, Ruth Ann Stewart, and Margaret Wyszomirski.

5. Center for Arts and Culture, <http://www.culturalpolicy.org>.

6. Bradford, Gary, and Wallach, *Politics of Culture.*

7. *Crossroads of the Spirit.*

8. For example, see Samuel B. Gould, *The Arts and Education: A New Beginning in Higher Education* (New York: Rockefeller Brothers Fund, 1968); United States Conference of Mayors Special Committee on Historic Preservation, *With Heritage So Rich* (New York: Random House, 1966); Rockefeller Panel Report, *The Performing Arts: Problems and Prospects—Rockefeller Panel Report on the Future of Theatre, Dance, Music in America* (New York: McGraw-Hill, 1965); United States Department of State, *International Understanding through the Performing Arts: A Report on the Cultural Presentations Program* (Washington, DC: U.S. Government Printing Office, 1965); Commission on the Humanities, *Report* (New York: American Council of Learned Societies, 1964).

9. Independent Committee on Arts Policy, *The Nation and the Arts: A Presidential Briefing Paper* (New York: Independent Committee on Arts Policy, 1988).

3

The Role of Research in the Cultural Policy Matrix

Marian A. Godfrey

In Chapter 1, David B. Pankratz summarizes some of the cultural research projects and initiatives that have been undertaken in the last three to five years. As he points out, this new research is not happening in a vacuum. It is sustained by a matrix of individual, institutional, and financial resources and activities and is part of a conscious effort to build a cultural policy infrastructure in the United States. During the 1990s, increasing numbers of cultural leaders, funders, advocates, and policy makers became interested in building the capacity of the cultural sector to analyze existing policies, to develop new policies for the benefit of artists, cultural institutions, and cultural audiences, and to broaden the public constituency for arts and culture. As is the case for any policy community, access to reliable and useful data and information is a priority and consequently significant new financial and human resources have recently been devoted to policy-relevant cultural research.

The 1997 American Assembly meeting "The Arts and the Public Purpose" was a catalytic moment in this effort in several ways. The representatives of the cultural sector present at that meeting engaged in what turned out to be an anxiety-provoking but fruitful effort to create new and more inclusive definitions of "arts" and "culture." This process, which resulted in the meeting report's inclusion of commercial culture and avocational or "unincorporated" cultural activities under the same rubric as the professional nonprofit arts, raised important and difficult challenges for funders, policy makers, practitioners, and scholars alike. If the arts are to be considered an integrated sector including these three subsectors, how can the economic dynamics linking for-profit and nonprofit arts be understood? How does the concept of "participation" change when avocational or community-based as well as professional activities are considered, and what are the implications of a more capacious definition of participation? How can we even count cultural organizations, according to the American Assembly's more inclusive description of the sector? Embedded in the meeting report was an implicit research agenda to answer these and other questions.

In addition to a series of follow-up meetings convened by the American Assembly, other meetings and discussions spun off from the 1997 gathering. Later that summer, as a direct result of the American Assembly, the Pew Charitable Trusts and the Howard Gilman Foundation coconvened at the White Oak Conference Center a small group of researchers, practitioners, policy entrepreneurs, and funders to discuss—to imagine—what a cultural policy community might look like and what research and other activities it might undertake. At that meeting, they studied how other policy communities had been formed and developed a rough draft of a matrix and action plan for a cultural policy infrastructure. The proposed infrastructure would consist of individual and institutional players (academic research centers, independent think tanks, artists and cultural leaders, cultural organizations and associations, advocates, scholars, cultural journalists, funders, and policy makers), categories of activities (research and the building of the intellectual framework for the sector; data collection and the building of information on the sector; convening and discourse; and dissemination and public affairs), and short-, medium-, and long-term goals.

The 1997 White Oak meeting played a critical formative role in the Pew Charitable Trusts' development of a major multiyear national initiative whose goal is to strengthen financial and policy support for U.S. arts and culture through research and advocacy activities. (Since that time, Pew has invested $11 million in research and media initiatives designed to advance knowledge and understanding of the arts.) The action plan developed at the meeting helped frame Pew's cultural research and information initiatives and began an ongoing process of communications among a number of key participants in the developing cultural policy community, many of whom are represented in this publication.

At White Oak, as at the American Assembly, participants struggled mightily with problems of definition and description. "Cultural policy," as well as the "cultural sector" itself, cried out to be parsed, and they talked about local, state, regional, and federal public policies; philanthropic policies; public policies in other sectors (e.g., education) that affected the arts; and the policies set by national associations for their memberships and by cultural boards for their own institutions.

The discussion about the cultural sector has by now moved from rhetoric to reality testing. A number of research projects, including the Pew-funded National and Local Profiles of Cultural Support (conducted jointly by Americans for the Arts and Ohio State University) and RAND's Integrated Assessment of the Arts Sector (funded by Pew and the Rockefeller Foundation), which is developing a compendium of data and information about the visual, performing, literary, and media arts, have operationalized definitions of the cultural sector, and when their research findings are published those definitions can be scrutinized, challenged, and revised if need be. The Urban Institute's National Center for Charitable Statistics and the National Endowment for the Arts Research Division, along with the National Assembly of State Arts Agencies, have embarked on the creation of a Unified National Database of arts, cultural, and humanities organizations. This database, although initially restricted to those independent cultural organizations with operating budgets of more than $25,000 that file IRS Form 990s, will be built up with the addition of information on other cultural organizations from the profiles project and other research initiatives.

The RAND study and a number of other studies currently underway are first steps in the development of the comprehensive research agenda that will be so necessary to guide the nascent cultural policy community's broader efforts. The Social Science Research Council (SSRC) has established a Program on the Arts, with funding from Rockefeller, to develop a research agenda on how arts matter in people's lives. The SSRC seeks to launch a field of scholarly inquiry and to integrate the arts into social science debates. The Urban Institute has undertaken a Research Study on the Support System for American Artists, with grants from a broad consortium led by the Ford Foundation, which will help define an agenda for further research on artists, as well as provide guidance about how support systems for artists might be strengthened.

Another area of current activity that should prove fertile both for future scholarly efforts and for arts advocates and practitioners is research on various types of cultural indicators and on the social impact of the arts.[1] The Rockefeller Foundation has played a significant leadership role here by supporting the Fordham Institute for Innovation in Social Policy to include the arts and culture in its work on Social Indicators and the Nation's Social Health, and the Urban Institute to develop Arts and Culture Indicators in Community Building. The John S. and James L. Knight Foundation has developed a Community Indicators Project to develop information in all seven priority areas of its funding, including arts and culture, in the twenty-six communities in which it makes local grants. The James Irvine Foundation has made a grant to Americans for the Arts to explore the potential for developing an Arts Performance Index—a Dow Jones Index for the arts, if you will. In Philadelphia, the Social Impact of the Arts Project at the University of Pennsylvania, with support from Pew and the William Penn Foundation among others, has produced a series of studies mapping and analyzing cultural resources and cultural networks throughout the city.

With research at its core, a picture of the emergent cultural policy matrix begins to come into focus. It includes a growing number of academic policy research centers led by the Princeton Center for Arts and Cultural Policy Studies and Ohio State University's Arts Policy and Arts Administration Program; independent arts think tanks, most notably the Center for Arts and Culture, along with fast-developing arts research capacity in other institutes such as RAND, the Urban Institute, Fordham, and the SSRC; and arts funders, who demonstrably are leading this work through their grant making. It also includes arts associations and arts advocacy organizations that are both increasing their own information efforts and becoming an important market for the research findings of others. Examples are Americans for the Arts, the American Arts Alliance, and other advocacy organizations; the National Assembly of States Arts Agencies; discipline-based national service and membership organizations (e.g., OPERA America, Theatre Communications Group, Dance/USA, the American Symphony Orchestra League, and the Association of Performing Arts Presenters, which are working together with funding from Pew to develop comparable data about their members); regional organizations such as the New England Foundation for the Arts, which is building a regional database of cultural organizations, and organizations such as New York City's Alliance for the Arts, which is building local databases; Grantmakers in the Arts, which has conducted a ten-year series of arts funding studies and has recently expanded its research and publication efforts; and the National Arts Journalism Program, established by the Pew Charitable Trusts and based at Columbia University's School of Journalism, which conducts research on how the arts are covered in the media.

This matrix also includes data and research repositories and portals such as the Center for Arts and Culture's Cultural Policy Inventory and Americans for the Arts' National Arts Policy, and the publications and convenings through which both research results and policy ideas are disseminated to the arts community, the media, and policy makers. As the cultural policy community matures, the new supply of cultural research and information will find users on the "demand side": advocates, journalists, funders (who need it to guide their own policies as much as to inform public policies), and practitioners. Advocacy activities and policy innovations will accelerate, and the general public's as well as policy makers' understanding of and commitment to the arts will increase.

NOTE

1. Brief descriptions of cultural indicator research projects were prepared by Christine Dwyer of RMC Research as part of a chart presented at the Grantmakers in the Arts annual conference in November 1999.

4

The Vital Border of Cultural Policy Studies

Paul DiMaggio

In Chapter 1, David B. Pankratz provides an excellent synopsis of the growth of the field of arts and cultural policy studies over the past decade. Among other things, it updates the map of terrain he and a distinguished set of colleagues first visited more than a decade ago in the conclusion to this volume's predecessor.[1] No one could fail to be struck by the rapid institutional development of cultural policy research over the past decade. More than one-third of a century after the publication of William J. Baumol and William G. Bowen's *Performing Arts: The Economic Dilemma*,[2] and more than twenty-five years after the creation of the National Endowment for the Arts (NEA) Research Division, arts policy researchers and their supporters can take satisfaction in the fact that the field has reached critical mass.

To be sure, we must not take the field's vitality for granted. But perhaps we can afford to avert our eyes from the heartland of arts policy research at least briefly and focus, as I shall do in this chapter, on its borders, where students of cultural policy mingle with scholars working in other traditions. For research fields, no less than nation-states, urban neighborhoods, or natural ecological zones have border areas in which processes of cultural exchange, intergroup abrasion, and interspecies mating often generate surprising creativity and innovation. As Paul Starr points out, the border that separates two research fields can also be the cutting edge of each.[3]

FINDING ORGANIZATIONS AND PEOPLE

Few problems in arts policy research are as basic as the difficulty of finding the organizations and people that policies are meant to affect. This is true of many kinds of arts presenters, especially in the "unincorporated" sector, who may be evanescent, too small to file IRS Form 990s, or embedded in some larger entity like a church, university, or community organization.[4] It is also true of artists in almost every sector, especially those who work by themselves. This is a problem because to the extent that the kinds of artists and organizations we study differ from those that policy is meant to research, our research will not serve policy makers' needs.

Solutions come from two different neighborhoods way out on the outskirts of cultural policy studies: one from students of organizations and management, and one from researchers who study the AIDS epidemic. Students of organizations have developed a method called hypernetwork sampling that permits one to create a representative sample of organizations (an unknown population) based on a survey of people (a population that social scientists are good at sampling). Sociologist J. Miller McPherson pioneered this approach in a study of how voluntary associations compete for members.[5] A National Science Foundation–sponsored study of changing employment conditions used this approach to identify a national sample of employers.[6] By analogy, one could identify a sample of arts presenters by surveying community members about the venues in which they encounter the arts. For presenters that serve large local publics, this approach can also produce rough estimates of the kinds of people they serve.

Research on artists presents an analogous problem. There is no master list of artists from which one can select a sample. Successful artists are easy to find, of course. But many public policies aim to provide resources like working space or health benefits to artists who are starting out, sporadically employed, or averse to joining organizations. Studies of artists' needs that exclude the least successful or most isolated may teach policy makers the wrong lessons.

This problem seemed insoluble until arts researchers came into contact with students of the AIDS epidemic, for whom finding reliable samples is literally a matter of life and death. Douglas D. Heckathorn, one such researcher, developed an approach called "respondent-driven sampling" that uses referral networks to estimate the size and characteristics of unknown populations. Even though the mathematics and the technique are too complex to go into here,[7] the important thing is that an approach capable of identifying reliable samples from groups like HIV–positive intravenous drug users, who have good reason *not* to be found, should work at least as well with unknown populations that do not bear such stigmata. Presently, Joan Jeffri of Columbia University's Research Center for Arts and Culture is collaborating with Heckathorn on an NEA–sponsored study of jazz artists in five metropolitan areas that may serve as a model for the field.[8]

STUDYING CONNECTIONS

The "network" is a powerful and culturally salient image. Social scientists are using it to understand everything from globalization to civic virtue.[9] Increasingly, they have come to believe that the way people or organizations behave has more to do with the *relationships* they have with one another than with purely individual characteristics. This is at least as true in culture, where creative people must collaborate to produce their work, as it is in other fields.

Network analysts—such as sociologists, anthropologists, political scientists, and even engineers—who undertake formal analyses of network data, have created one of the few truly interdisciplinary research communities outside of the natural sciences. In addition to having a great metaphor, they have developed data-analytic methods that allow one to calculate the centrality of any one person or organization in a network of relations; to depict the informal structure of relationships within groups that lack formal organization; and to estimate the "vulnerability" of the network as a whole to the departure of key members.[10] Clearly, such information is relevant to policy makers who hope to enhance the stability of or propagate new management approaches throughout the arts community in a metropolitan area.

Students of social welfare policy were among the first to use network models in their work. Motivated by the aims of doing more with less and overcoming the fragmentation clients faced in assembling services from multiple, independent providers, they used network methods to study social service delivery networks in the 1970s.[11] This work found its way into the language of arts policy in the late 1970s, when people in Washington sometimes spoke of the "arts-service delivery system." But it has only recently entered cultural policy research, most notably in Mark J. Stern and Susan C. Seifert's work on the rich variety of relationships between arts groups and other organizations in their communities.[12]

The network studies of the 1970s usually examined formal linkages between organizations, thereby missing important connections that occur at the person-to-person level. Recent studies by business-school researchers have emphasized how individuals use their personal networks to make their organizations more effective. One recent study, for example, reported that hotel managers who have dense and trusting relationships with their counterparts in other hotels run more profitable and highly reputed establishments than those who lack such ties. Such connections are both valuable sources of information about the business environment *and* a way to solve problems (as when they make it possible to relocate a guest to a satisfactory location when the hotel has overbooked).[13]

If this is true of hotels, it must be doubly so of the arts, for staff of museums and performing arts organizations often rely on informal relationships to find artworks for retrospective exhibits, fill out a subscription season when an anticipated booking falls through, or find performance or gallery space to mount a program. Network analysis promises a way to better understand how these processes operate. And if researchers can do that, policy makers may be able to intervene to make them more effective.

POPULATION ECOLOGY

So far I have emphasized borders that cultural policy research shares with other policy sciences. But the border between the social and natural sciences has also provided a source of valuable tools. Of these, none is more valuable than the methods and perspectives of population ecology, which have been influential among students of organizations in recent years.[14] If we think of particular types of organizations—such as performing arts centers, craft artists' cooperatives, or chamber quartets—as analogous to species, we can use well-developed methods from population biology to understand the factors that make their populations rise and fall.

The potential policy payoffs are great. For one thing, this perspective jogs our thinking about what makes fields healthy, because it requires that we think separately about the influence and determinants of birth rates and death rates. Most arts policy focuses on keeping death rates low by sustaining existing organizations. In some fields, however, it may be just as important to reduce barriers to entry and make birth rates high. Population models give us a way to talk about such matters.

Second, population ecology provides a neutral analytic approach to an important topic that makes many people in the arts community uncomfortable—*how many arts organizations are enough?* Population biology cannot help us with the normative side of this question. But population models can help us identify natural limits to growth, above which sustaining a field will require extraordinary investments and difficult trade-offs with other objectives. This is information that most policy makers would like to have.

Third, models from population biology provide a natural way of studying the interdependence of the nonprofit and commercial cultural sectors, for example by modeling the effect of nonprofit theater activity on the number of commercial productions over time. Sometimes such connections are unexpected. In a study of the beer industry (if we may consider beer making an art form), Glenn Carroll discovered a causal link between the oligopolization of the industry in the 1970s and the rise of microbreweries in the 1980s. Rather than driving out quality as many feared, the big national beer companies eliminated the midsized regional producers, thereby creating a variety of niches too small for the Coorses and Budweisers to bother with, but just right for the Samuel Adamses and Anchor Steams.[15] Although the answers might be very different, one could easily apply this type of analysis to the vital question of how concentration in publishing and book selling are shaping the long-term prospects of small presses and independent bookstores.

Finally, if we can pretend that types of organizations are like biological species, we can do the same for kinds of art—to understand, for example, shifts between easel painting and prints, or between musicals and dramatic productions. Although arts researchers have a general idea of the economic factors involved in such trade-offs, population models can provide precision of the sort that could inform policy design.

One final point: There is a natural complementarity between network analyses, which provide insight into relationships and structures, and population models, which explain the emergence and decline of the organizations that networks comprise. One could combine these tools to gain a sophisticated understanding of *how art worlds operate as systems*. For example, we might learn how unincorporated, nonprofit, and commercial arts organizations influence one another; how opportunities for young artists to learn their crafts shape the environment for arts presenters; or how demographic changes influence potential audiences and open up opportunities for cultural entrepreneurs.

With such information, it may not be completely fantastic to imagine that local grant makers could learn to fine-tune the systems they support with surgical interventions. Indeed, one day our children may play *Sim Artworld* at their computers, using policy research to develop programs of investment and philanthropy that turn imaginary metropolises into models of cultural abundance.

DANGEROUS BORDERS

Borders can be dangerous places. If the right analogy can open our eyes, the wrong one can close them. Effective border workers must be able to know when an analogy expands one's vision and when it constrains it.

The cases of productive borrowing I have described are diverse, but they have one thing in common. In each case, arts researchers have imported not just a compelling trope or a technically sophisticated method, but also the *combination* of the two: an analogy that enables them to see familiar problems in new ways combined with a method that permits them to use that insight to produce usable knowledge.

Borrowing the vision without the technique is a little like buying a sports car without an engine: It looks great sitting in the driveway, but it won't get you anywhere. Technique without vision too often generates answers to policy questions that no one has asked. Value lies in the combination of the two.

INCREASING TRANSBORDER TRAFFIC

How can the policy community—grant makers, researchers, and policy makers—enhance the process by which innovations in other research fields inform studies of arts policy?

First, arts researchers need solid training in a social science or humanities discipline, to which they maintain strong ties throughout their careers. Scholars with such connections are in the best position to learn about work from other areas, assess it critically, and use it appropriately.

Second, and equally important, we must maintain a strong interdisciplinary commons in which students of cultural policy studies can interact. It is through this infrastructure that arts policy researchers can share new ideas and approaches with colleagues who share their substantive concerns.

Third, in planning conferences and meetings around research themes, we should routinely anticipate fruitful analogies and import participants from across relevant borders. A conference on how grant makers evaluate artists, for example, might benefit from the contributions of a sociologist who has studied peer review in the hard sciences, an economist who knows how the investment market rates equities, or a historian who understands the dynamics of historical reputation. In my experience, the cultural policy field has a great advantage in doing this because most scholars in other areas find the arts intrinsically interesting, sometimes more so than whatever they happen to be studying.

CONCLUSION

All this is premised on the belief that the arts policy research enterprise is moving ahead swiftly and soundly. Interacting with other research fields is not an alternative to developing one's own, but rather part of the natural development of any thriving intellectual enterprise.

Government and foundations have invested more heavily over many years in research infrastructure in other policy fields, so it is natural that scholars in these fields have had the time and means to address problems that arts policy researchers are only just encountering. But the real value of intellectual border crossing is in the insights that the right analogy can provoke.

My first employer in graduate school was a visionary information scientist who used to advise librarians to file books by the color of their spines. The juxtapositions browsers encountered, he reasoned, would set off the kinds of intellectual chain reactions of which scientific progress is made. I suspect that no librarian ever took his advice; regardless, we can create those chain reactions for ourselves by exploring the borders that separate arts policy researchers from our intellectual neighbors.

NOTES

1. David B. Pankratz et al., "Arts Policy Research for the 1990s and Beyond," in *The Future of the Arts: Public Policy and Arts Research,* ed. David B. Pankratz and Valerie B. Morris (New York: Praeger, 1990).

2. William J. Baumol and William G. Bowen, *Performing Arts: The Economic Dilemma* (Cambridge: MIT Press, 1966).

3. Paul Starr, "The Edge of Social Science," *Harvard Educational Review* 44 (1974): 393–415.

4. Deborah Kaple et al., "Comparing Sample Frames for Research on Arts Organizations: Results of a Study in Three Metropolitan Areas," *Journal of Arts Management,*

Law, and Society 28 (1998): 41–66; American Assembly, *The Arts and the Public Purpose* (New York: American Assembly, Columbia University, 1997).

5. J. Miller McPherson, "An Ecology of Affiliation," *American Sociological Review* 48 (1983): 519–32.

6. Arne J. Kalleberg et al., *Organizations in America: Analyzing Their Structures and Human Resource Practices* (Thousand Oaks, CA: Sage, 1996).

7. Douglas D. Heckathorn, "Respondent Driven Sampling: A New Approach to the Study of Hidden Populations," *Social Problems* 44 (1997): 174–99.

8. Douglas D. Heckathorn and Joan Jeffri, "Finding the Beat: Using Respondent-Driven Sampling to Study Jazz Musicians," *Poetics* (November 2000).

9. Manuel Castells, *The Rise of the Network Society,* vol. 1, *The Information Age: Economy, Society and Culture,* 3 vols. (Berkeley: University of California Press, 1996); Robert D. Putnam, *Bowling Alone: The Collapse and Revival of American Community* (New York: Simon and Schuster, 2000).

10. Stanley Wasserman and Katherine Faust, *Social Network Analysis: Methods and Applications* (New York: Cambridge University Press, 1994).

11. James Lincoln, "Intra- and Inter-organizational Networks," *Research in the Sociology of Organizations* 1 (1982): 1–38.

12. Mark J. Stern and Susan C. Seifert, *Cultural Organizations in the Network Society,* Working Paper no. 11, Social Impact of the Arts Project, University of Pennsylvania School of Social Work, February 2000.

13. Paul Ingram and Peter W. Roberts, "Friendships among Competitors in the Sydney Hotel Industry," *American Journal of Sociology* (2000).

14. Jitendra V. Singh, *Organizational Evolution: New Directions* (Newbury Park, CA: Sage, 1990); Michael Hannan and Glenn Carroll, *Organizational Demography* (Princeton, NJ: Princeton University Press, 2000).

15. Glenn R. Carroll, "Concentration and Specialization: Dynamics of Niche Width in Populations of Organizations," *American Journal of Sociology* 90 (1985): 1262–83.

5

Arts Research: From the Hill to the 'Hood

Alberta Arthurs

Within the last two years, the country's cultural professionals have been witnessing a remarkable surge of interest in policy thinking and policy research in their field. To these professionals, who work in and worry about the arts and humanities, this interest in policy is remarkable because it is so rapid, so strenuous, and so promising. A long-standing policy vacuum has existed in U.S. cultural life. Today, there is a growing acknowledgment among scholars and practitioners that policy discussion, articulation, research, and action are important to the future of the arts and humanities. The policy challenge posed by several major foundations, recent convenings, new centers, and cultural organizations have been stimulating—progress is being made on understanding the cultural conditions and the cultural options for the United States in the twenty-first century.

Within just the past three years, there has been a substantial development in structures for the creation of cultural knowledge. Databases new to the field are in development at the RAND Corporation, Ohio State University, and Americans for the Arts. Scholars are being connected in research networks, on-line, and face-to-face by the Center for Arts and Culture in Washington, DC. Graduate students are being schooled in steadily—if slowly—growing numbers in cultural policy courses at Princeton, Rutgers, and other research institutions. Research projects funded by several national foundations are in place at the Urban Institute, the Social Science Research Council, the American Academy of Arts and Sciences, and other institutions of the broader society, institutions that would not have countenanced arts subjects until recently. Anthologies of essays and ideas are being released by the New Press, the *Journal of Arts Management, Law, and Society,* Rutgers University, Temple University, and Greenwood Presses; and a rush of reports from the American Assembly, the National Arts Journalism Program, and the President's Committee on the Arts and Humanities have had unusually broad circulation. Without being overly optimistic, it is possible to say that the arts are beginning to claim the academic resources, the intellectual energy, and the infrastructure essential to an emerging field of policy study and theory.

The opening chapter in this volume, by David B. Pankratz, describes these developments well. But the chapter also articulates the challenges that face this changing, growing field—the "persistent problems" that continue to plague cultural policy formation. Specifically, many point to problems in data collection in the arts and culture, which do not yet meet the "standards of policy-relevant information." There is work to be done to ensure that cultural policy research is as thorough, as comprehensive and reliable, and as accessible as it can be. Pankratz's chapter also speaks to the field's failure so far to build a comprehensive research agenda of topics and subspecialties that could, then, be more systematically studied and reported. We are also far behind in our efforts to educate policy makers and other leaders in society about the practical uses of research in the arts and culture. And we need to better understand and coordinate the emerging cultural policy infrastructure to strengthen the linkages of policy centers, policy convenings, and policy scholars.

In my view, however, the most important "persistent problem" for the field is the perceived target for policy. The extant arts and cultural policy community, as Pankratz writes, has long perceived that "its primary agenda is to maximize federal support for nonprofit arts organizations and artists." Certainly, the significance and appropriateness of federal support should never escape us as a policy concern: The realities of that support and the arguments and the achievements enlivened by federal attention, its precedents, processes, and principles are important in the arts and culture—just as important as those same factors are in considerations of, for instance, the country's highways, parks, student aid, health and safety guidelines, security and exchange regulations, or the hundreds of other policy arenas in which the federal government functions. We must document and monitor federal support for the arts and the humanities. But we should do so—and this is the point—as one part of a much broader mandate for cultural policy, out of a much broader sense of engagement by the cultural policy community.

I like to think that a reason that transportation policy in this country has been so widely debated, so intensely subscribed as a priority, and so successful in getting Americans and their products around and moving is because so many of us share in that policy in so many ways. Automobile owners, straphangers, soccer moms and dads, truck drivers, construction workers, landscape architects, business travelers, tourists, travel agents, farmers, and factory owners all know that transportation affects their lives. Every American realizes the necessity and the value of transportation, so policy debates and decisions that relate to vehicle manufacture, schedules, reliability, safety, prices, imports, and even the placement of bridges and bike lanes are the policy concerns of every single American. Furthermore, Americans know that their transportation concerns are addressed locally and regionally, in workplaces and at tollbooths, in tire stores and at ticket counters everywhere. No American waits for Washington before deciding where he or she has got to go or before developing an opinion about how to get there.

My point, of course, is that in focusing policy attention as we have on federal funding of the arts and culture, and on the small (though critically important) nonprofit segment of the arts sector, we have managed to lose that same sense that the arts are every American's business. We have failed to engage the attention of the citizenry, by whom and for whom policies are made. We have managed to make it seem as though the arts are remote and irrelevant to the everyday concerns of Americans (when this is demonstrably not true). We have managed to make it seem as though the arts are needy, rather than needed. It's time that we made it clear that the arts and arts policy, like transportation and transportation policy, are every American's business.

In short, the target—or one target—for cultural policy research should be the U.S. public. And there is reason to think that much research currently underway serves to mirror the true cultural involvements of the U.S. public and documents those involvements. As Pankratz's chapter also points out, the recent and dramatic "resurgence" in policy formation is "predicated on the belief that improvements in the nation's cultural life are contingent on a strengthened cultural policy community." The relationship between research and public purposes and realities is being made by the researchers themselves; the public interest is explicit in much of their research.

For instance, by looking at lists of current research projects the connections between cultural research and the interests of Americans begin to clarify and impress. The Henry R. Luce Foundation, after some years of concern about the subject, has mounted studies and community-based projects that examine relationships between the arts and religion in American life. The studies trace the history, the shared and severed attitudes between the two domains, and the reactions of leaders in arts and religion toward each other. This is an aspect of the American experience that has not been examined before, and one that relates specifically to citizen interests. Several research efforts, sponsored by several foundations—such as Rockefeller, Knight, Irvine, and Kenan—are finding ways of assessing the impact of the arts on community life and values in U.S. neighborhoods. The assumption in these studies is that the arts are indicators as important in their communities as are the more usual indicators: economics, health, education, and family structure. This is a big step forward in the siting of the arts in American life. A Ford Foundation–Americans for the Arts initiative is intended to stimulate as well as measure civic exchange and dialogue through the arts in U.S. communities. The Pew Charitable Trusts have undertaken several efforts to assess and improve the media's coverage of the arts and culture, aiming to move that coverage from entertainment pages to news pages, from reviews to public interest coverage. Thirty foundations are working together to fund a massive national effort to locate artists as citizens in American life—their work patterns, lifestyles, connections to institutional life, and support systems. Other efforts are tracking the for-profit–nonprofit connections in the arts as they are trying to see the movement of artists and audiences across the whole sector to understand the ties and trends that bind the cultural, the commercial, and the avocational in the arts. Clearly, in such projects as these the policy target is not limited to federal funding or to the federal role in the arts and culture; rather, the goals of such research are to discover the dimensions of the arts and their meaningfulness in American life much more generally.

What Americans need, if they are to see the pervasiveness, the value, and the reality of the arts in their lives, are facts—facts about the nature and kind of the arts they experience, the role of the arts in advancing public purposes, the significance of expressivity to "Americanness," the uses of the arts in individual and community lives, and the quantitative facts about the arts in the U.S. economy. These and many other "facts"—researched substantively—will surprise, instruct, inspire, and, hopefully, provide alternatives to the ephemeral reviews, sensational headlines, and "leisure-time" emphases that currently pass for public information about arts and culture.

In actual fact, the cultural policy community will wind up addressing the question of federal support for the arts more effectively, with greater directness and assurance, by producing its work in this broader context. To the extent that many Americans are engaged and arts-mindful, the arts will more successfully appeal for a full measure of government support. To the extent that the arts are perceived as an essential of American life, Americans will make the case for them, as they have for other requirements of their existence, from highways to health care to holidays. And to the extent that these factors influence the federal debates and decisions, they will equally influence the policy environment that dictates other public support—regional, state, local, and private—for the arts and culture. Ironically enough, with good facts and solid findings routinely provided to the public, the job of fostering federal interest may be far easier in the future. When "cultural" is taken to mean only the nonprofit, and "policy" is taken to refer only to the National Endowment for the Arts, the target for cultural policy is both limited and limiting.

The rising climate for cultural research, the increasing infrastructure of scholars and institutions, and the new findings are heartening in many ways, but certainly in this respect, in particular, they give us the chance to move the country's cultural geography from war zones to policy fields, from the Hill to the 'Hood.

II

New Paradigms for Research on the Arts Sector

6

Care and Feeding of Calliope and Her Friends: The Production Perspective in Arts Research

Richard A. Peterson

Arts advocates and researchers share a passion for one or more of the arts that motivates their work. As essential as such passion clearly is, it is vital, nonetheless, to regularly step back and look at the art world in which one works, because in order to be effective one needs to understand how artwork is conserved, created, and appreciated. To put it crudely, to be an effective player, you need to know how the game is played and you need to know the score.

Two generations ago, any comparison between the arts and a game evoked dismissive snorts of contempt. The arts were seen as a world apart, artists were expected to starve while feeding their passion, and connoisseurs were expected to be obeisant in the presence of their genius. These were not new ideas in the United States of the 1950s.

In the 1950s, attempts to understand the arts world as a social system were seen as sacrilegious, and terms like "art market," "art career," and "arts administration" were unknown. Before World War II, the fine arts were seen as morally uplifting and their purity as essential to the advance of civilization. For social aspirants, support of the arts, whether genuine or pretended, was deemed necessary for acceptance in the more powerful circles of society. The arts, as then conceived, were promoted as the symbolic representation of all that was beautiful, uplifting, and worthy of support in the struggle to stave off the onslaught of "inferior," "mass," and "brutal" culture.[1]

Given such a mind-set, it was possible for arts advocates to successfully garner financial and political support with appeals to saving the fine arts from the onslaughts of "mass" culture. This strategy of garnering money for the arts worked for most of the twentieth century, but it is no longer effective for two distinct reasons. First, the appeal has all too often been used to serve philistine civic, corporate, and national pride. What starts as arts advocacy becomes a defense of lists of the "great works" and "genius artists," so for all too many people painting becomes the *Mona Lisa*, a late Rembrandt, Edgar Degas's dancers, a Vincent van Gogh landscape, an expressive Pablo Picasso, and a pleasant Jackson Pollock. Opera is all ABC—*Aïda, La Bohème,* and *Carmen*—with a dash of Valkyries, and classical music becomes a hit parade of perhaps twenty oft-played pieces. Brilliant as these works surely are, most were made over a hundred years ago and all are by white men now dead. Audiences can easily conclude that the fine arts happened a long time ago and that there is no need to attend to contemporary art or support living artists. In such an environment, the only creativity that is valorized is the interpretation of canonical works.

The second reason the alarmist appeal to saving the best of the fine arts from crass commercial culture is now foredoomed is that people increasingly find aesthetic and moral value in diverse elements of popular and folk culture. Rather than singling out the fine arts as valuable—and shunning all popular, folk, and non-Western art as vulgar—an increasing number of people now find value in learning to understand and appreciate in its own terms a wide range of symbolic activities.

It is not at all surprising that such cosmopolitan omnivorousness should be emerging now. Earlier generations understood that their popular culture was youthful entertainment to be abandoned when they grew up, settled down, and became adults. However, those born after World War II, the period of the generation gap, learned that their popular culture had a message that had to be taken seriously. As their pop lyrics said, "Roll over Beethoven, give Tchaikovsky the news," "The times are a-changing," "We are the Woodstock generation."

As "[v]ideo killed the radio star" and as they get older, baby boomers have not forsaken the idols of their youth so much as they have learned how to appreciate their culture in the broader context where all kinds of cultural expressions are valorized. Thus, while their parents gained status by being able to discriminate the best of traditional art from the dross of popular and middlebrow culture, boomers show their sophistication by being able to smoothly code-shift from Bach to the Beach Boys, from the Beatles to Fat Boy Slim, bocce, baseball, Bangra, and Brecht.[2] It is easy to see why narrow appeals to "saving the arts" now commonly fall on deaf ears.

To save the arts among a vibrant array of aesthetically shaped cultural activities, we need, like human anatomists, to unblinkingly examine in mundane detail what gives Calliope and the other eight muses life and sustains their creativity. One of the essential tools for this task is what has come to be called the "production of culture perspective."

THE PRODUCTION PERSPECTIVE

The production perspective is centered in the assertion that the social arrangements used in making symbolic elements of culture significantly shape the nature and content of the cultural elements that are produced.[3] Thus, the production perspective focuses on how the content of culture is influenced by the milieu in which it is created, distributed, evaluated, taught, and preserved. Research in the production perspective freely draws on the theories, methods, and concepts developed in other branches of sociology. It is, however, distinctive in focusing on the consequences of social activities in the production system for culture. This sounds simple enough, so let's illustrate what people mean by the "production system" and just how it influences the arts. We focus briefly on five examples.

The Pianoforte and Genius[4]

Creativity in the arts depends on genius, and a few people seem to have markedly more than the rest. Whether that genius is expressed and is recognized as creativity rather than as eccentricity or madness, however, depends on the conditions in the particular art field at the time. Mozart and Beethoven were keyboard players who began their careers in the latter decades of the eighteenth century. Their acclaim as uniquely gifted genius composers depends, however, on the development of a new musical machine, the pianoforte. Its name clearly suggests its advantage over harpsichords and the other keyboard instruments of the time. It had a profoundly wider dynamic range; it could be played softly or, unlike a harpsichord, it could be played loud, and it could be played rapidly, or, unlike a harpsichord, it could be played slowly while the sound still resonated.

Over the years of the eighteenth century from its invention in the Medici workshops, the pianoforte became hugely popular among those in European fashionable society. Its popularity was based on the fact that it was easy to play tolerably well and that it complemented other instruments and yet could be pleasurable played on its own. It was the ideal accompaniment for the human voice. Pianos didn't need to be retuned every time they were used, the small square Zumpe models were affordable by the rising bourgeois middle class, and a woman could play a piano as easily as a man while still looking "ladylike." Understandably, the demand for compositions created expressly to take advantage of the piano's flexibility and dynamic range soon proved insatiable.

As the instruments were improved, and as the piano became the emblematic parlor room instrument and the focus of evening entertainment, professional keyboard performers like Mozart and Beethoven increasingly turned from the harpsichord and the organ to explore the possibilities of the pianoforte. Generations of pianists were able to showcase their resourcefulness and improvisational skills. Beethoven's notoriety as a performer sustained him for a decade while he was developing his compositional skills.

Finally, because of its wide range and its ability to sound a number of notes simultaneously, other composers, following Beethoven's lead, rapidly made the piano the instrument of choice for composing large orchestral works. The influence of the piano on composition in the nineteenth century was so great that

Howard Goodall says, "the structure of a vast amount of *orchestral* music owes its shape to the mindset of the piano."[5]

It is simplistic to say we know of Beethoven as a composer of genius today simply because he worked in the generation following the invention of the piano machine. This was essential, but other factors were vital as well. He came from a family of professional musicians, early in his career he received aristocratic patronage, he was an innovator in the practice of sustaining himself from subscription concerts, and the heroic style of his mature composition captured the modernist mood of the nineteenth century.

Patronage, Organizational Structure, and Creativity[6]

The 2000 Oscar for Best Foreign Film was won by the Spanish film director Pedro Almodóvar for his *All About My Mother*. No newcomer to filmmaking, Almodóvar has been celebrated throughout his career as a fiercely independent artist who would not compromise his standards for commercial success. That he has been fiercely independent, there is no doubt, and still he has been able to make increasingly ambitious feature-length films without participating in the large-studio Hollywood system of production and distribution and having his creativity compromised in so doing. Unlike the crop of other young creative Spanish would-be filmmakers before and since his time, Almodóvar has been able to maintain his creative independence for two distinct but interrelated reasons.

First, in 1985 at exactly the time when Almodóvar having worked on five films was at a point in his career to venture out as an independent film director, the Spanish government was offering start-up film production companies the financial backing necessary to complete a modest film. Other young Spaniards who were awarded grants either blew off the money without completing their project or used the grant money to make an introspective symbolic work that enjoyed a narrow critical acclaim in Madrid or Barcelona and had no great box office success. Almodóvar used the grant to make a compelling story film that was both critically acclaimed and a moderate box office success. The government, concerned about the money that others had wasted, determined in its bureaucratic wisdom to stem the highly narcissistic and morally "questionable" plots and increased its own control over artistic factors with more restrictions imposed on how grant funds could be spent. The predictable result was a higher project completion rate and uniformly mediocre films. The surviving film directors became complacent with the conclusion that the Spanish film industry could not survive without continuing support and fell into what is called the "subsidy trap."

The second reason for Almodóvar's success was that, largely through the efforts of his brother Augustín, he was able to avoid the subsidy trap. Their film company was formed jointly by the brothers with Pedro focusing completely on the process of "direction," while Augustín devoted his efforts to what is called the "production" side involving financial and administrative matters. In an industry where egos feed on how much money can be spent, Pedro focused on parsimoniously fulfilling his filmic vision and Augustín economized wherever possible to build for the future while protecting his brother from all outside pressures and concerns. Based on his success, Pedro has been offered a great deal of money in recent years to come to Hollywood. He has declined because he would have to lose the protection provided by Augustín and the clarity of his artistic vision would be lost to the Hollywood machine system of production.

If Pedro had come to maturity even five years before or after 1985, and if Augustín had not organized the financial and organization support, *All About My Mother* would not have won the Oscar in 2000. Again, we see that genius is necessary but, without the appropriate production system, it is not sufficient.

The Vagaries of Legal Protection[7]

U.S. and English literary critics have long noted that acclaimed nineteenth-century American novels dealt with themes quite different from those of their contemporary British counterparts. The British were most successful writing novels of manners, strong women, imprudent passion, failed marriage, and bourgeois domestic life set in the home. In marked contrast, leading American-novelists spotlighted the primitive man-child, estranged from society and caught in mortal combat with forces of nature, the supernatural, and other primitives. Generations of literary critics and U.S. studies scholars have interpreted this contrast as demonstrating a difference between American and British values and character.

Wendy Griswold notes, however, that until 1891 U.S. law protected the work of American authors but provided no copyright protection to books by their foreign counterparts. In practice, this meant that American publishers had to pay no copyright fees to English authors and publishers and they could offer British novels at a much lower price than those by American authors. Consequently, British novels on love and domestic life were immediately reprinted in the United States. In practice, the competition for these works was so great that rival American publishers would buy copies on the day of their release in London for shipment to the United States. In order to tempt American publishers to bring out their own works under these conditions, American authors had to eschew plots of morals and manners and exploit themes the British were not treating.

Two independent lines of evidence give weight to Griswold's interpretation. First, contemporary novels of morals and manners always sold better in the United States than did *Moby Dick, Last of the Mohicans,* and the like. Thus, the preferences of American readers were not so different from their English counterparts. Second, if the workings of copyright law were so consequential, then the themes treated by American and British authors should have converged rapidly after 1891 when the U.S. government recognized international copyright agreements. Just such a convergence has been noted by various commentators. However, in line with their earlier reading, they point to global changes, including the closing of the American frontier, America "coming of age," or a rapid increase in the cosmopolitan tastes of the U.S. reading public. Perhaps more to the point, the example illustrates the power of altering mundane legal regulations in shaping artwork.[8]

Art-Shaping Consequences of Professionalizing Arts Management[9]

At the beginning of the twentieth century, the major arts organizations in the United States were directed by a set of long-serving "larger than life" cultural impresarios who shaped their museum collections or performance presentations around their own vision of art and public interest. By the beginning of the twentieth-first century, in marked contrast, arts administrators, as they had come to be called, regularly job-hopped from one arts organization to another.

General Luigi Palma di Cesnola, the first full-time director of the New York Metropolitan Museum of Art, served in that capacity for twenty-five years. Cesnola, like other impresarios, exhibited a commanding and flamboyant style, flattering wealthy patrons and tyrannizing subordinates, but relating to all on a personal individualistic basis. In this he combined the appearance of selfless devotion to art with attention to the most mundane detail, thus embodying the museum.

In contrast, contemporary arts managers come to their jobs from formal university training where they have generally concentrated in arts management, accounting, and marketing, and prove themselves by serving in a sequence of evermore responsible administrative jobs. Whereas the job of each long-serving impresario became highly individualized, contemporary job-hopping administrators become interchangeable parts filling positions that are evermore bureaucratically circumscribed and alike from organization to organization. While the impresario was personally responsible to a circumscribed board of governors, the arts administrator is formally accountable to a number of constituencies, each with its distinct interests and expectations. Thus, in concert with his most powerful patrons, the impresario was free to express his own long-term vision. In contrast, the arts administrator, focused on short-term career goals and the constraints of diverse constituencies, laws, and regulations, plays it safe and stays in step with current museum world fashion and practice. This shift in management style surely helps to account for the fact that the presentations of the major orchestras, museums, and performance companies have become both more like each other and rapidly changing along the same lines.

Generations of Audience Come and Go[10]

Audiences, it goes without saying, are vital to the vibrant development of the arts, and, given the facts of life, they have to be reproduced from generation to generation. At first glance, the experience of the recent past is encouraging because the audiences for most arts forms are at least as large as ever, and, if self-report surveys are to be believed, a wider range of people participate than ever before. Yet, the observations of many long-time observers suggest that an ever-increasing proportion of the audience have gray hair, blue hair, or no hair at all. Surveys conducted for the National Endowment for the Arts (NEA) in 1982, 1992, and 1997 confirm that audiences are aging, even after adjustments for the fact that the U.S. population is aging. Looking at information for the seven art forms regularly tracked by the NEA, the average age of audiences for five of the forms was at least marginally younger than the whole sampled population. The opera audience was the oldest in 1982, but by 1997 its audience alone among the arts had aged no faster than the population as a whole. By 1997, only one art form, jazz, had an audience younger than the population as a whole, and its audience had aged faster than that of any other discipline.

Further analysis of these data show that these age-cohort differences reflect remarkably great differences in the attendance patterns of individuals born following World War II, the baby boomers, with those born before. The best demographic predictors of arts attendance are education, occupation, income, urban residence, being female, and not having dependent children. When compared with older cohorts, baby boomers are generally "better off" in each of these measures, meaning that arts attendance should have exploded in the fifteen years between 1982 and 1997, but it has gone up only modestly. In other words, as they mature, individuals in the recent birth cohorts most likely to participate in the fine arts do not share the orientation to the arts of their comparably advantaged elders. Since comparable postboomers share the boomer take-it-or-leave-it attitude to the arts, the size of arts audiences, if nothing is done, will ebb as the large cohort of boomers become history.

SIX FACETS OF THE PRODUCTION PERSPECTIVE

Arts production is a single, if complex, process as the five previous examples clearly suggest, but it has proven useful to see it as having six facets. The six include: technology, law, industry structure, organization structure, occupational careers, and market. The first three—law, technology, and industry structure—largely set the conditions within which the other three—organization structure, occupational careers, and market—operate, though over time, each affects all of the others. No one of these is outside the dynamic system thus created. So, for example, law is not simply imposed from outside because many within the culture field devote a great deal of energy to shaping laws in ways congenial to their own interests.[11] Study in the production perspective, including future study, must come to terms with each of the constraints and understand how they operate in concert in shaping the content of the arts.

Technology

We like to think that changes in technology don't greatly affect artists' work, but the effects can be profound. The development of photography, for example, profoundly affected both the subjects and the styles of painting in the century from 1850 to 1950, as painters were liberated from the need to make representational works. Photography also made all of the world's great art available to everyone interested. The development of premixed oil paints in standard colors just before that time freed painters from the need to understand practical chemistry, and the provision of these paints in metal tubes freed painters from their studios and facilitated painting in the field. The impact on landscapes was profound as artists introduced the tones they were actually seeing rather than the remembered conventional landscape colors. Likewise, the development of recording and broadcast technologies has completely changed the way that music is appreciated. Before 1900, experiencing classical music was a rare and privileged experience, as performers and connoisseurs had to travel to the place where music was being performed. As importantly, the music disappeared forever as it was being created. Now, Allison Krauss sings as I am writing this, and the other compact discs cued to be played include Hildegard von Bingen, Carlos Santana, Charles Mingus, Queen, Fat Boy Slim, the Kronos Quartet, and George Philipp Telemann. The effects of this change on composition, performance, music appreciation, and taste are yet to be fully explored.

The development of a new music-making machine is, of course, at the heart of our first illustration earlier that focused on the role of the pianoforte in Beethoven's emergence and success. The availability of cheaper, more portable filmmaking and editing machinery might also have been mentioned as a factor in Almodóvar's ability to work independently of the large established film studios. Turning to the example of contemporary audience dynamics, the development of cheap high-speed digital computers was essential in making this analysis possible. Such changes in technology are often triggers to ongoing systematic change.

Law and Regulation

The laws governing political and moral propriety importantly shape artistic expression, and many of the arts' most profound expressions (in the West at least) have been made in an effort to push the boundary of what is allowed. Tax regulations, grant-giving rules, and government initiatives of all sorts foster some arts activities and inhibit others. Of all the arts, dance in the United States, for example, was probably shaped the most by federal government incentives during the NEA era. There have been many studies of the British Broadcasting Corporation (BBC) of course, but none has analyzed the impact of the BBC on music in Britain. Once an art-music backwater, the musical scene seems vibrant there. Law governing the conversion of creative activity into property is the other great category of law that shapes artistic activity. A prime example of its power is seen in explaining the difference between the themes of nineteenth-century British and American novels as shown in the above case study, and Vera L. Zolberg shows the profound consequences that differing patterns of ownership of works have in the visual arts as compared with classical music.[12] The impact of copyright law administration was at least as important in shaping popular music in the middle quarters of the twentieth century;[13] the laws of intellectual property are likely to be at least as important in the twenty-first century. Meanwhile, two competing tendencies seem apparent. On the one hand, even the genetic code of human life is asserted to be private property, and at the same time, innovations are being superseded so rapidly in the computer software generation that it may become meaningless to enforce exclusive rights.

Industry Structure

The creation of art, as Howard Becker has so eloquently shown,[14] is a collective activity and can be organized in numerous quite distinct ways, each of which has consequences for the art that is made. Perhaps the most influential early study exemplifying the power of the production perspective was Harrison C. White and Cynthia A. White's 1965 study of the changes in the French art world that turned in the nineteenth century from a tightly bound academic system, to a highly dynamic market system organized around entrepreneurial dealers and critics that in a matter of decades fundamentally altered the opportunities for aesthetic innovation.[15] More recently, Charles R. Simpson has studied the production system underlying the explosion of innovative painting in New York following World War II,[16] Liah Greenfeld has shown the existence of two quite different visual arts worlds in Israel,[17] and Samuel Gilmore has described three quite differently structured classical music worlds operating on Manhattan Island in the 1980s, each of which produced a quite distinct type of music.[18]

These studies all contrast industries structured by academic standards and subsidized by private persons or government agencies with industries more nearly driven by open market competition. This contrast figures in the cases developed earlier, most notably the rapidly changing art world of Beethoven's time, the emergence of professional arts management, and the dynamics of the contemporary film industry that made Almodóvar's work possible, which, like the contemporary popular music industry, is a dynamic mix of small and large firms.[19]

Organization Structure

Production organizations are more or less bureaucratic. At issue are the number of levels of authority in the organization, the degree to which different aspects of the task are performed by separate departments, and the degree to which all of the production functions are performed in the organization or are contracted for on a job-by-job basis. Compare, for example, the organization of the highly labored French academic art world with that of the market system of the Impressionist period, or indeed, think of the difference for the art produced of the contrasting organization structure of a modern dance company as compared with a classical ballet troupe. In the film production company of Pedro and Augustín Almodóvar, coworkers all have distinct roles on paper, but like the Motown Recording company in its explosively creative period people act like a team, facilitating each other's work to achieve the common goal, while Hollywood studio departments often compete with each other for recognition and power in filmmaking. Finally, Hollywood studios generally have as many functions as possible performed by studio departments themselves, while the Almodóvars contract out on a job-by-job basis many of the activities necessary to making a film.

Occupational Careers

The art world career of each participant is unique, and yet the nature of the organizational structure, as well as the production facets just described, dramatically condition the career chances of those working in arts worlds in ways totally independent of their own talent or effort. Consider, for example, the differences in the career paths of a dancer in a classical ballet company and that of a modern dance performer. When the classical ballerina is no longer able to go on dancing, the only job for which she may be qualified is teaching the next generation of ballet aspirants.

Modern dancers are more likely to be recruited in their teens from gymnastics or athletic competition, and through high school, at least, their schooling and experience is much like that of others their age. Even their dance training is likely to be more diverse so that they are able to work in a range of dance styles and have a wider range of postdance job options open to them, from jobs in the sports industry to arts administration.

As the comparison made earlier between the impresario and the arts administrator suggests, the working conditions and careers readily available for arts managers has changed dramatically over the years. As the case described earlier suggests, Beethoven's unique talents and skills could not have flourished under the court composer-as-Kapellmeister system that nourished several generations of innovative musicians before him. Like Pedro and Augustín Almodóvar after him, the expression of his genius depended on the career opportunities uniquely available in his lifetime.

Market

The market comprises the audience as seen from the perspective of the industry. Ironically, even the most experienced actors in the industry can never fully understand their audiences because their knowledge is based on samplings of information, and what they see is dependent on how the market has been conceptualized and how it is measured.[20] Indeed, what they know from long experience typically becomes increasingly out of date as audience tastes change. The negative consequences of long and successful experience can be observed in the rise and passing of art dealerships. During their careers, successful dealers who begin as champions of an avant-garde tendency, become, with the art they champion, established as promoters of a dominant trend in the visual arts, and finally, if they cleave to what they have learned over the years, become defenders of the dernier garde.[21]

THE FACETS COMPRISE A GEM: ART

In concluding, one final point needs to be made. While we have taken pains to isolate each of the six facets of the production perspective in turn and to look at them separately, perhaps the most important consequence of separating them analytically is the ability to understand better how they work in concert. The five illustrations with which we began this chapter focused on a different facet, but in each case the consequences of change had compounding consequences for each of the other facets and for the arts as a whole.[22]

NOTES

1. Lawrence Levine charts the causes and consequences of the rise of fine arts–popular culture distinction in the nineteenth century in *Highbrow/Lowbrow: The Emergence of Cultural Hierarchy in America* (Cambridge, MA: Harvard University Press, 1988). Paul J. DiMaggio makes a detailed analysis of how the rising Boston elite of that time cultivated the high-brow, low-brow distinction in support of their own class interests in "Cultural Entrepreneurship in Nineteenth-Century Boston, Part II: The Classification and Framing of American Art," *Media, Culture and Society* 4 (1982): 303–22. Herbert J. Gans shows how and why several generations of academic scholars worshiped at the altar of the elite fine arts in *Popular Culture and High Culture: An Analysis and Evaluation of Taste* (New York: Basic, 1999).

2. To see the dynamics of the shift, see Richard A. Peterson, "The Rise and Fall of Highbrow Snobbery As a Status Marker," *Poetics* 25 (1997): 75–92; Richard A. Peterson and Roger Kern, "Changing High-Brow Taste: From Snob to Omnivore," *American Sociological Review* 61: 900–7 (1996); Richard A. Peterson, "Snob to Omnivore: The Implication of Shifting Tastes for the Arts and Cultural Industries" (paper presented at the Long-Term Developments in the Fine Arts and Culture Industries Conference, Rotterdam, 2000).

3. For general works explicitly devoted to exploring the production perspective, see Richard A. Peterson, "The Production of Culture: A Prolegomenon," in *The Production*

of Culture, ed. Richard A. Peterson (Beverly Hills, CA: Sage, 1976), 7–22; Richard A. Peterson, "Culture Studies through the Production Perspective," in *Emerging Theoretical Perspectives in the Sociology of Culture,* ed. Diana Crane (London: Blackwell, 1994), 162–89; Richard A. Peterson, "Globalization and Communalization of Popular Music in the Production Perspective," in *The Globalization of Popular Music,* ed. Andreas Gebesmair (forthcoming); Diana Crane, *The Transformation of the Avant-Garde: The New York Art World, 1940–1985* (Chicago: University of Chicago Press, 1987); Harrison C. White, *Careers and Creativity: Social Forces in the Arts* (Boulder, CO: Westview, 1993); John Ryan and William M. Wentworth, *Media and Society: The Production of Culture in the Mass Media* (Boston: Allyn and Bacon, 1999).

4. This section is based primarily on Tia DeNora, *Beethoven and the Construction of Genius: Musical Politics in Vienna, 1792–1803* (Berkeley: University of California Press, 1995); David W. Jones, *The Life of Beethoven* (Cambridge: Cambridge University Press, 1998); Howard Goodall, *Big Bangs: The Story of Five Discoveries that Changed Music History* (London: Ghatto and Windus, 2000).

5. Goodall, *Big Bangs,* 175.

6. This section is based on Jose Louis Alvarez and Silviya Svejenova, "Symbolic Careers in Movie Making: Pedro and Augustin Almodovar" (paper presented at the Creative Careers Conference of the London Business School, March 2000); Martin Dale, *The Movie Game: The Film Business in Britain, Europe and America* (London: Casell, 1997).

7. This section is based on Wendy Griswold, "American Character and the American Novel," *American Journal of Sociology* 86 (1981): 740–65; Wendy Griswold, *Renaissance Revivals: City Comedy and Revenge Tragedy in the London Theatre, 1576–1980* (Chicago: University of Chicago Press, 1986); Wendy Griswold, "The Writing on the Mud Wall: Nigerian Novels and the Imaginary Village," *American Sociological Review* 57 (1992): 709–24.

8. Richard A. Peterson, "Six Constraints on the Production of Literary Works," *Poetics* 14 (1985): 45–67.

9. This section is based on Richard A. Peterson, "From Impresario to Arts Administrator: Formal Accountability in Nonprofit Cultural Organizations," in *Nonprofit Enterprise in the Arts,* ed. Paul DiMaggio (New York: Oxford University Press, 1986), supplemented by decades of association with the NEA and the Tennessee Arts Commission.

10. This section is based on Richard A. Peterson, Pamela Hull, and Roger Kern, *Aging Arts Audiences* (Santa Ana, CA: Seven Locks, 2000).

11. Kim L. Scheppele, *Legal Secrets: Equality and Efficiency in the Common Law* (Chicago: University of Chicago Press, 1988).

12. Vera L. Zolberg, *Constructing a Sociology of the Arts* (New York: Cambridge University Press, 1990).

13. John Ryan, *The Production of Culture in the Music Industry* (New York: University Press of America, 1985).

14. Howard Becker, *Art Worlds* (Berkeley: University of California Press, 1982).

15. Harrison C. White and Cynthia A. White, *Canvases and Careers* (New York: Wiley, 1965).

16. Charles R. Simpson, *SoHo: The Artist in the City* (Chicago: University of Chicago Press, 1981).

17. Liah Greenfeld, *Different Worlds* (New York: Cambridge University Press, 1989).

18. Samuel Gilmore, "Schools of Activity and Innovation," *Sociological Quarterly* 29 (1988): 202–19.

19. See Richard A. Peterson and David G. Berger, "Cycles in Symbol Production: The Case of Popular Music," *American Sociological Review* 40 (1975): 158–73; Richard A. Peterson, "Why 1955? Explaining the Advent of Rock Music," *Popular Music* 9 (1990): 97–116; Paul D. Lopes, "Innovation and Diversity in the Popular Music Industry, 1969–1990," *American Sociological Review* 57 (1992): 56–71; N. Anand and Richard A. Peterson, "When Market Information Constitutes Fields: Sensemaking of Markets in the Commercial Music Field," *Organization Science* 11 (2000): 270–84.

20. See Anand and Peterson, "When Market Information Constitutes Fields."

21. See Crane, *Transformation of the Avant-Garde.*

22. The most systematic presentation of the total dynamic of the production perspective is found in the "new institutionalism" of Paul DiMaggio and his associates. For example, see DiMaggio, "Cultural Entrepreneurship, Part II," 303–22; Paul J. DiMaggio, ed., *Nonprofit Enterprise in the Arts: Studies in Mission and Constraint* (New York: Oxford University Press, 1986); Paul J. DiMaggio, "Cultural Boundaries and Structural Change: The Extension of the High Culture Model to Theater, Opera, and the Dance, 1990–1940," in *Cultivating Differences: Symbolic Boundaries and the Making of Inequality,* ed. Michele Lamont and Marcel Fournier (Chicago: University of Chicago Press, 1992), 21–57; Walter W. Powell and Paul J. DiMaggio, eds., *New Institutionalism in Organizational Analysis* (Chicago: University of Chicago Press, 1991).

7

Public Participation in the Arts and Culture

Judith Huggins Balfe

If we are to understand and evaluate the impacts and consequences of both public policy and private commercial activity in the arts and culture, we must first have complete and inclusive models of the total system of cultural production and its correlate, participation.[1] In the last few years, a new paradigm has emerged to provide researchers with general guidance, as well as with enhanced techniques and instruments, for both collecting and interpreting the quantities of data that are being generated. This chapter focuses on only one ingredient in the emerging, inclusive paradigm of arts research: public participation. My purpose is to assess the impacts of that paradigm on our understandings of the scale and range of cultural participation, and then to consider the implications of those findings.

Falling sequentially in the middle of this section of the book, a discussion of participation could well be understood as the result of policy and purpose, which lead to production—and that it, in turn, generates consequences and impacts. However, such an understanding would itself be inadequate, as public participation includes not only consumers via the media and members of the live audience, it also includes those who are involved, by avocation or profession, in policy making and production in every aspect of arts and cultural activity, at the level of individuals, communities, or the nation, and affecting our economic, political, and social quality of life. One *begins* as a consumer or member of the audience before one goes on to become an artist, producer, or cultural analyst; one still *remains* a participant thereafter, albeit at a higher level of motivation, expertise, and perhaps satisfaction. Given this near total *inclusivity* of the category of public participation, then, it becomes all the more important to understand how it might be accurately measured so as to show the *interaction* not only of factors leading to one or another type of participation, but also to demonstrate those leading to *non*participation. Only then can the consequences of either be assessed—and compared. What key concepts might help us in this daunting task?

KEY THEORETICAL CONCEPTS
SHAPING CURRENT RESEARCH

At the core of the new paradigm is the erosion of what had been understood since the late nineteenth century as a vast "divide" between "high" or elite culture and "mass" or popular culture.[2] The most significant finding of the several American Assembly meetings of the last several years is the interaction of the commercial, nonprofit, and "unincorporated" arts in nearly every aspect of the social organization of artists and other production personnel, as well as in the channels of distribution via the media.[3] As a sociologist and also as a participant in many forms and venues of the arts, like most Americans, I find it remarkable that only recently have such integrative "cross-overs" come to be recognized on the "supply side." Most of us on the "demand side" have long and increasingly enjoyed the full range of cultural offerings made available by a vast panoply of producers without regard to whether they were commercial or nonprofit, and even whether or not what they presented was defined as "high" or "mass" in appeal. As consumers or participants, we cross over in practice just as Americans did prior to the "divide" erected between elite and popular arts a century ago. Indeed, in the words of my professional colleague Richard A. Peterson, the American. arts public is no longer split between "the snob and the slob" but rather between the "omnivore" and the "univore."[4] Omnivores are those who participate in genres and venues *across* the "taste cultures" delineated by Herbert J. Gans;[5] univores are identified not as elitist snobs, but typically as "guys driving pick up trucks with gun racks and mangy dogs in the back, who like only Heavy Metal." Such a shift in the cultural practices of the majority of the public affects our conceptual understanding of the entire system in many ways.

For example, specific dimensions of participation must be explored if the promises and challenges of the new, enriched paradigm are to be realized. Foremost among these dimensions are indicators of the *meaning* any such participation may have for those so engaged, as that meaning may link one level and sector of participation with another. How might it be measured with any methodological consistency?

Let's start with the question of the varieties of possible *motivation* for any participation or involvement as a contributing factor to its meanings.[6] *Why* do I participate at all, in what manner and in what art forms, and how do these motives interact with others that aestheticians have not often accepted as legitimate to their inquiries? I may be unavoidably exposed to "easy listening" music in the dentist's office as a kind of "white noise" to blot out the other sensations involved in the encounter, or I may deliberately tune in to a "classic rock" radio station while driving so that I can sing along in order to stay awake. I may take guitar lessons because I really want to immerse myself in that sound for the sheer aesthetic pleasure of it, or because I want to become good enough to join a rock group and find an outlet for my exhibitionist urges. I may go to the ballet on singles nights, when they serve wine and cheese during intermission, in order to meet potential dates, and for the next year I choose the music of Firebird as background to my seductions. I may be asked to serve on the board of the local art museum because I am a lawyer and they need the contribution of my expertise, and I agree because it will raise my standing in the community and attract other clients. If I may experience all of these distinct and changing motivations, so too may every other participant in the arts. Some motives are to experience "art for art's sake"; others are to simply pass the time, to look for entertainment, or to enhance economic or social status. We should not be surprised: such mixed motives have always been present in arts patronage, production, and less intense forms of participation.[7]

Other contributing factors must be assessed as well if the total meaning of participation is to be understood. Among them are the *range* and the *venue* of my involvement across the genres and forms available to me, as potentially one of Peterson's omnivores. Sociologist Judith Blau has shown the geographic distribution of cultural institutions across the United States by the standard metropolitan statistical area, demonstrating that many forms of "high" culture are more available on a per capita basis than some forms of "popular" culture.[8] While this availability certainly affects my participation options as a member of the live audience, at home it has much less effect on what I may consume via the media (radio and recordings, television and video, film and the Internet). It may have a potentially very different effect on where I may go and what I may do as a tourist. But while an art form may be available to me geographically or through the media, there may be barriers of supply in terms of its cost or timing. There may be additional demand-side barriers to my own interest, based on insufficient education or other subcultural factors that preclude my participation in any manner: I may know about the availability of this art form, but I deliberately choose *not* to participate in it. Thus, even my noninvolvement is potentially meaningful.

Perhaps the most critical factor in any adequate assessment of my arts participation is a measure of its *intensity* as this varies across my motives for participation, and the inclusive and interactive range of genres and venues in which it occurs. I can be a completely passive consumer of the arts, as I "channel-surf" while watching television on Friday night after a stressful week at the office. I may suddenly find myself entranced by a taped rerun featuring the dance group Pilobolus. I may then check the listings of local dance performances to see if they are scheduled. Even if they aren't, my curiosity may lead to my attending a few such events as a member of the live audience, as I become increasingly engaged in the field of contemporary dance. I may then go on to become a member of the local arts council, ultimately joining its top rank of patrons. I may become so personally involved that I shift my exercise class to one featuring dance movements, and in time become an accomplished, if amateur, performer. That role may come to serve as the basis of my social identity and my network of friends. Alternately, I may finally shift careers, earn a graduate degree in arts management, and become the marketing director of the local arts center, where I deal with artists and audiences of every conceivable taste, as well as with media coverage—and hang up my dancing shoes.

The mind boggles in anticipation of the effort that will be required—in expertise, time, money, and good will—if research on public participation is to satisfy the new standards based on more inclusive data and *also* on measures or indicators of motivation, range, venue, and intensity. Fortunately, we have an enormous accumulation of data and its analysis from which to start.

CURRENT KNOWLEDGE AND KNOWLEDGE GAPS

The various Surveys of Public Participation in the Arts (SPPAs) sponsored by the National Endowment for the Arts (NEA) and taken at intervals from the mid-1980s on have provided the data on which Peterson and others have come to the conclusion of "omnivorousness" on the part of most arts participants. Many other large surveys, taken over recent years, have provided analysts with extensive supportive material, showing rates of attendance at crafts fairs and sporting events, and participation in gardening, volunteering, or just going fishing.[9] Among the many virtues of such surveys is their intentional replicability, allowing for analysis of changes in patterns of public participation over time. They are typically national in scope and are published with a summary report providing cross-tabulations of participation in various art forms by demographic categories of age, race, education and income level, and the like. For SPPA surveys, the NEA also has commissioned an additional series of analyses of distinct subsets of the data on participation (race, age, socialization patterns, specific art forms, and so on) by social scientists.[10]

However, these survey instruments have usually been formulated under the previous paradigm, when any such data were expected to be used primarily in *advocacy* of public support for the arts and culture by the very agencies that have sponsored the research, especially the NEA. Accordingly, the seven "bench mark" art forms about which participation was asked were primarily those of the so-called fine arts of interest to public arts funding agencies and foundations that are typically nonprofit in organizational structure (classical music, opera, jazz, musicals, nonmusical plays, ballet, and art museums). Over the years, thousands of respondents have been asked questions about "live" participation in these art forms, as members of the audience or as "personal participants" (as amateur or professionals), and also about their similar consumption patterns via the media (radio, recordings, video, and film). Only in this fashion have the commercial media entered the data collection, primarily in terms of their transmission of the high art forms of particular interest to the NEA. To be sure, jazz and musicals are frequently produced in commercial venues, but any consideration of the connections between for-profit and nonprofit cultural organizations were avoided for many years.

Over time, however, questions about a range of "nonarts" leisure activities were added to NEA surveys to flesh out the early findings by social psychologist John Robinson (who devised the first SPPA of 1982), thereby establishing the principle of "the more, the more."[11] "The more" one participates in at least one of the seven bench mark art forms, "the more" one is likely to participate in other activities such as sports, camping, or volunteering for community charities. All of this made the point that those involved in the supposedly "elite" arts are involved in many "nonelite" activities as well. Not surprisingly, education and its correlate, income, are the best—if not the exclusive—predictors of "fine arts" participation, just as they also predict every other form of popular cultural activity, including political participation. Indeed, rates of arts participation exceed rates of voting in many recent national elections: depending on the year of the survey, 40 to 50 percent of the respondents reported live attendance at one of the seven bench mark art forms, and if media participation is included (along with additional forms of cultural activities such as reading books), the rates are reported to be as high as 95 percent.[12]

Nonetheless, while such surveys have provided evidence of cultural tastes and forms of participation outside the expected categories (hence the discovery of omnivores), their summary reports seldom capture the full range of public participation—let alone try to explain important sectors of *nonparticipation*—required for the more inclusive analysis of the new paradigm. In part, this is a result of the sheer expense of commissioning such finely tuned analyses on a consistent basis, precluding a series of multivariate regressions or factor analyses of successive data sets, each involving thousands of cases and over 150 questions. And that is without the inclusion of any indicators of motivation! (Such evidence could sometimes be extracted, with considerable effort, from the raw data of SPPA surveys to support inferences of range, venue, and intensity. However, such inferences are seldom robust enough to be included in the findings.) Now consider the addition to these research instruments the categories used to measure the contribution to the gross national product of the commercial sector, as well as the nonprofits, included by Harry Chartrand in his model of the "culture industry." This separate set of measures from the supply side of production, matched up with the reports of activity on the demand side of participation, provide a sense of the incredible complexity of the research problem.[13]

At the same time, it is increasingly recognized that the more common, manageable, and usually episodic inquiries into audiences for particular art forms or even for particular institutions typically suffer from the lack of generalizability as well as a lack of context. In City X, symphony orchestra A may find its audience to be smaller and also demographically different from that of its neighbor art museum B, with no way to understand why or what to do about it. Museum B is unlikely to want to share its mailing list with orchestra A: however distinct the art forms, each is competing for a share of the audience's limited leisure time and discretionary spending, some of which is devoted to the media.[14] Without a compelling rationale for sharing their findings, each arts provider and producer will fail to understand its participants to the fullest extent. Comparably, arts agency Q will find its data discrepant from those desired by arts funder R, let alone by politician S. Each data collector may have reasons to misrepresent its findings, if only to keep its potential rivals and political antagonists at bay. And the separate researchers who develop the distinct instruments and analyze the resulting data sets will come away with findings of little inherent interest, to say nothing of little utility to anyone trying to develop coherent public policy to enhance the cultural life of City X in which all reside.

EMERGING RESEARCH QUESTIONS, NEEDS, AND OPPORTUNITIES

The inadequacies of national surveys based on the old paradigm driven by arts advocacy, as well as those limited to specific art forms (e.g., opera) or even to particular providers, are well known by now. The new research paradigm provides not merely new demands for a value-neutral analysis (or at very least one with full-disclosure of the interests of the sponsors), it also suggests different ways of acquiring a more extensive and richer understanding of who participates in the arts, how, when, and *why*. Fortunately, technological advances have made it conceivable that these new demands *can* be met, and a number of projects, carefully designed to meet those demands, are currently under way.

The appropriate level for such research—one likely to be most productive in terms of policy outcomes as well as research implications—is increasingly recognized to be that of the community, region, or state. Such an examination is the best way to explore the local *ecology* of the arts and culture at the level of the *participants*.[15] It is also more likely to be funded by local *producers* and *policy makers,* such as the local or state arts agencies and collaborative grantors. Because the latter will have provided some of the questions of greatest immediate concern to themselves, the research findings are more likely to be implemented and have real and not merely academic consequences. At this scale of inquiry, researchers can employ a wider range of techniques, such as focus groups and interviews with key individuals, to assess not just patterns of consumption, attendance, and personal participation, but also to structure their inquiries to explore bottom-up definitions of participatory practices and their related meanings, given by individuals involved. Rather than having respondents check off a list of categories, as in any survey, such research methodologies allow such individuals to provide their own definitions and explanations of

what they do and don't do—and why. What cultural activities do they deliberately avoid or simply remain ignorant of, as well as what do they consume
through the media, attend in person, and otherwise engage in personally? In a
market saturated with arts offerings, what cultural choices do people make?

One of the new projects, funded by the Urban Institute, is discussed in the
next chapter by Maria-Rosario Jackson. Grounded in the new paradigm, it and
other similar projects are synchronized in using the same research instruments
and methodologies, during the same time frame, in a number of different communities. Accordingly, they foster *comparative* analyses across the various
component ecological case studies. Thereby each one acquires more significance
as part of a larger whole, even as the local and regional particularities are illu-
minated. While the findings resulting from these projects are expected to be
utilized by community development advocates as well as arts providers, they
will also have intrinsic interest for academics interested in how cultural forms
are created, perpetuated, and superseded, and in the meanings they communicate among their participants. In time, the lack of generalizability of such local
or regional studies—the defect of their many virtues—can be overcome when
their methodologies and their findings can be distilled to serve as the basis of
national studies now represented only by SPPAs and census surveys.

Given the wholistic and contextual nature of such inquiries, interconnections
can be explored among the commercial and nonprofit arts, considering as well
as media consumption, lighter or heavier levels of live participation, and
personal involvement as amateur or professional. They will also permit explo-
rations of subcultural patterns linking certain forms and venues of participation to the exclusion of others, whether specific to a region or found across
those subcultures, wherever located geographically.

IMPLICATIONS FOR FUTURE RESEARCH

Let me summarize the previous discussion of the new paradigm as it relates
to cultural participation, leading to a discussion of the enormous challenges
faced by contemporary researchers. The new paradigm explores:

1. Comprehensive notions and patterns of participation, beyond mere attendance
2. Broad definitions of the arts and culture in which one may participate
3. Various motives and meanings that add explanatory power to what has been a largely
   descriptive analysis
4. Intervening variables potentially affecting participation (e.g., cost or availability)
5. Patterns of nonparticipation (exclusion and not merely inclusion)

Beyond collection of the data, this new and complex paradigm carries the
methodological mandate of value-neutrality rather than agenda advocacy, be it
for or against public funding of the arts and culture. Difficult as this mandate

may be to implement, perhaps the most important challenge is to produce an analysis that is both complete and clear. The research design may indeed be consistent with these new requirements, the methodologies perfected, the funding sufficient, and the staff well trained in the implementation of the project. Wonderful. But the findings will be ignored if they are badly presented, perhaps overloaded with figures requiring too much prior knowledge to interpret easily (e.g., multiple regressions—however valuable these are otherwise), or reported in a dry, factual, and objective style, with no alternative policy directives even being suggested. Indeed, tables in the same report have too often presented the data in ways that inhibit the reader from making any connection from one set of figures to another, in order to answer a specific research question not included among those of the summary.

Of course, the absence of systematic reporting of summary data is a common and often inadvertent flaw in analyses of quantitative survey research, comparable to selective quotation in reports based on qualitative methodologies. Such flaws become more serious when the sponsor's agenda seems to determine their direction. Consider two examples from reports based on the previous paradigm, with some kind of advocacy or denigration of public support for the arts inherent within the reports. Take the latter example first, from a source with an obvious agenda of "demystifying" the claim that art is somehow "above" or untouched by political power struggles, thereby presenting the counterargument that any public support for the arts is in the interests only of the elites. The report states that the rate of upper-class people who like abstract art is double that of working-class people—so any support for its exhibition is clearly class biased. Only in the fine print is it learned that the actual percentages for each respective category are 4 percent and 2 percent, respectively.[16] Obviously, huge majorities of *both* classes don't like abstract art—a finding with very different implications and contrary to that desired by those who want to find *class bias* in every form of public art support so as to delegitimate it as antidemocratic. If there *is* a bias here, it is not based on class but on taste, a far more elusive concept to assess.

A similarly biased report, sponsored by those advocating rather than denigrating public support, notes in a bold-faced summary that 84 percent of the audience for classical music have had at least some college education. Given the fact that nearly half of the adult population has had such education, that sounds as if an enormous number of people are included here, with implications of vast public support for classical music. However, omitted in that summary is the fact that only 14 percent of those with higher education attended classical music *at all*. Only with some effort can the latter figure be derived from those provided elsewhere in this particular report, although prior analyses of these surveys had made that finding explicit. Why was it deliberately obscured here?[17] This time, the implications are not what advocates for public support may prefer. If 86 percent of those with higher education, like 95 percent of those without it, don't attend classical music, as in the previous example of a biased analysis there may be less of a cultural divide among nonattenders, as demonstrated as well by the omnivore pattern among attenders. The consequences of such an analysis for advocates of public funding of minority tastes—in each example tastes held by a minority even of the most educationally and economically privileged—may be considerable. But so may they be for those who denigrate public funding for the "elite" arts, as they typically oppose the alternative products of "mass" commercial culture as much as to the advocates of public art support.

In any event, the academic researcher, interested in making a correct analysis with plausible conclusions, may have a different understanding of the point of the research than does its sponsor and funder. It then behooves the researcher to explain to the sponsor that even bad news is useful in pointing out the flaws and political problems inherent in any policy that may result. It may be far more important to know one's enemy than to believe one has none. While awareness of all of one's potential political antagonists may lead to paralysis and a refusal to move toward *any* proactive cultural policy, one may become aware of potential allies as well.

Even in contexts less antagonistic than that of contemporary America, seen by some analysts as torn by "culture wars," it is important for policy makers to understand the potential trade-offs and to anticipate who may benefit and who may suffer from their decisions. Making participants in every conceivable arts and cultural practice subject to the same institutional research and analysis, in the interests of multicultural inclusivity (and its frequently intended purpose, community development), may have unintended and negative consequences for some participants. Researchers in public participation should pay particular attention to these concerns. For example, foremost among those who may suffer are the self-conscious elitists who raise the alarm that without public subsidy for the nonprofit "fine arts," only cultural products that are acceptable to the lowest common denominator will survive.[18] However, some who see the creativity and innovation of the arts as their foremost public purpose find that it is precisely these characteristics that are undermined by public arts support, with its inherent requirements of financial accountability.[19] Financially stable institutions, even nonprofit ones, take fewer risks—even as they absorb the majority of public funds, leaving the small, locally based organizations to starve.[20]

Others whose interests are presumably represented in the new paradigm's more inclusive focus may find their own meanings overridden rather than celebrated. Groups of Native Americans are increasingly expressing alarm at the ways objects of their cultural heritage are interpreted in museum settings, torn from the context of their creation and intended use. Religious conservatives are sometimes offended by public funding of artworks that they see as obscene or blasphemous: Should the values they expect to find, as part of the public who participates in the arts and culture, be denied?[21] And in a democracy, how are conflicts between the particular values of cultural minorities and the majority culture to be resolved?

CONCLUSION

While the new paradigm promises to provide an accurate assessment of cultural participation, inclusive of all the forms and contexts in which that participation may take place and also unbiased by political agendas of either the advocates *or* the denigrators of public support for the arts, inevitably there will be unintended consequences as the findings become known. The findings will be used by individual arts and cultural organizations, in internal program evaluation, as well as by politicians and public and private funders as measures of external popularity and success. Immediate market advantages to certain sectors may override the long-term public interest, however that may be defined.[22]

Consider the wider implications of the omnivore thesis. Contrary to the "culture warriors" who have captured so much media attention, as they try to call supporters to the barricades (along with their money and their votes), it appears that the vast majority of the U.S. public is disinterested in such battles when their own lives are as culturally rich as they wish and when other domestic and economic issues are of greater concern. At the same time, the flip side of omnivore participation is not univore cultural isolation, but the likelihood of nonparticipation in any specific art form or cultural genre, even by omnivores. The broader my cultural tastes, the easier it is to replace one item with another as convenience or fashion dictates.[23] Such findings are not likely to be welcomed by the traditional sponsors of research on arts participation, unless they reconceptualize the issues in terms of the new paradigm and consider less the question of public funding for particular fine arts and more the issues of the complexity of the cultural ecology in which participation occurs.

As that reconceptualization is just beginning, the recent development of nonprofit think tanks and research centers provides safe havens where researchers can examine all of the implications of their findings objectively, based on the new, more inclusive research paradigm, as they explore the full significance of the myriad forms of public participation in the arts and culture and the meanings they create and convey to both individuals and to society and to society as a whole.

NOTES

1. The most inclusive model of the arts industry has been developed by cultural economist Harry Chartrand. Its most recent version is: "Toward an American Arts Industry," in *The Public Life of the Arts in America*, ed. Joni Maya Cherbo and Margaret J. Wyszomirski (New Brunswick, NJ: Rutgers University Press, 2000), 22–49.

2. The reasons for and the process of the construction of this "divide" has been analyzed by Paul J. DiMaggio, "Cultural Entrepreneurship in Nineteenth-Century Boston," in *Nonprofit Enterprise in the Arts: Studies in Mission and Constraint*, ed. Paul J. DiMaggio (New York: Oxford University Press, 1986). 41–61; see also Lawrence

Levine, *Highbrow/Lowbrow: The Emergence of Cultural Hierarchy in America* (Cambridge, MA: Harvard University Press, 1988). Herbert J. Gans, in the revised and updated edition of his *Popular Culture and High Culture: An Analysis and Evaluation of Taste* (New York: Basic, 1999), explicates some of the sociological reasons for the recent erosion of this once-formidable divide.

3. Joni Maya Cherbo and Margaret J. Wyszomirski, eds., *The Public Life of the Arts in America* (New Brunswick, NJ: Rutgers University Press, 2000).

4. Richard A Peterson and Albert Simkus, "How Musical Taste Groups Mark Occupational Groups," in *Cultivating Differences: Symbolic Boundaries and the Making of Inequality*, ed. Michele Lamont and Marcel Fournier (Chicago: University of Chicago Press, 1992), 152–68.

5. Gans, *Popular Culture and High Culture*.

6. Judith Huggins Balfe and Monnie Peters: "Public Involvement in the Arts," in *The Public Life of the Arts in America*, ed. Joni Maya Cherbo and Margaret J. Wyszomirski (New Brunswick, NJ: Rutgers University Press, 2000), 81–107.

7. For case studies of such mixed motives, see Judith Huggins Balfe, ed., *Paying the Piper: Causes and Consequences of Art Patronage* (Champaign–Urbana: University of Illinois Press, 1993).

8. Judith Blau, *The Shape of Culture: A Study of Contemporary Cultural Patterns in the United States* (New York: Cambridge University Press, 1986).

9. See Peter V. Marsden and Joseph F. Swingle, "Conceptualizing and Measuring Culture in Surveys: Values, Strategies and Symbols," *Topical Report* no. 26, the National Opinion Research Center (1993), <http://www.icpsr.umich.edu/gss99>. See also the overview of the field by Becky Pettit, Resources for Studying Public Participation in the Arts, and Inventory and Review of Available Survey Data on North Americans' Participation in and Attitudes towards the Arts, Working Paper no. 2 (Princeton, NJ: Princeton University Center for Arts and Cultural Policy Studies, 1997).

10. A complete listing of NEA reports is provided through its Web site: <http://arts.endow.gov/pub/ResearchReports.html>.

11. John P. Robinson, *Arts Participation in America, 1982–1992: A Report for the National Endowment for the Arts*, NEA Report no. 27, prepared by Jack Faucett Associates, October 1993.

12. Caveats should be registered here: These rates are those for the sample of survey respondents, applied to the total population. Ignored even in such "representative samples" are the large numbers living in poverty, who are unlikely to be represented adequately in such surveys despite efforts to make them truly random; also ignored are the large numbers housed in various institutions (prisons, nursing homes, and so on). All such people are unlikely to participate in cultural activities to the same degree as those who agree to talk (at considerable length) with researchers.

13. Chartrand, "Toward an American Arts Industry." Other useful sources include the United States Census Bureau, *Statistical Abstract of the United States, 1999* (Washington, DC: U.S. Government Printing Office, 1999), and various issues of the *Communications Industry Forecast* (New York: Veronis, Suhler and Associates, 1996), as well as arts sector surveys conducted by the American Association of Museums and other com-

parable organizations. See also the useful, if incomplete analysis, Port Authority of New York and New Jersey, *The Arts As an Industry: Their Economic Importance to the New York–New Jersey Metropolitan Region* (New York: Port Authority of New York and New Jersey, 1993).

14. Everette J. Freeman and Neil Bania, "A Different Tempo: African American Attendance at Performances of the Cleveland Orchestra," *Journal of Arts Management, Law, and Society* 25, no. 2 (summer 1995): 127–40.

15. Judith Huggins Balfe and Margaret J. Wyszomirski, "An Ecology of Arts Institutions: A Community Case Study of Montclair NJ, 1985" (unpublished, College of Staten Island, City University of New York); Judith Huggins Balfe and Margaret J. Wyszomirski, "The Arts in New Jersey: Political and Social Issues," *Journal of Regional Cultures* 5, no. 1: 205–22.

16. This particular mistake was committed by preeminent French sociologist of culture Pierre Bourdieu with Alain Darbel, *The Love of Art: European Art Museums and Their Public*, trans. Caroline Beattiie and Nick Merriman (Stanford, CA: Stanford University Press, 1990).

17. The failure of omission is that of the National Endowment for the Arts, "Summary Report," in *1997 Survey of Public Participation in the Arts* (Washington, DC: National Endowment for the Arts,). The rate of participation from among those with college educations was included in the National Endowment for the Arts, "Summary Report," in *1992 Survey of Public Participation in the Arts* (Washington, DC: National Endowment for the Arts).

18. For an overview, see DiMaggio, "Cultural Entrepreneurship in Nineteenth-Century Boston." For a more recent and explicit example, Robert Brustein, theater director and drama critic for the *New Republic*, concludes: "The high arts have become an endangered species in this country, being picked off by a variety of sharp shooters, including commercial producers, politicians, multi-culturalists, middlebrow critics, and, not least of all, the foundations." See Robert Brustein, "Requiem," *New Republic*, 27 March 2000, 29.

19. Joel Bassin, "Dancing with the Devil: An Analysis of the Negative Impact of Federal Arts Support on the American Not-for-Profit Theatre" (Ph.D. diss., City University of New York, 2000).

20. In New York City, for example, over 80 percent of the budget of the Department of Cultural Affairs (DCA) is allocated to some thirty large cultural institutions, usually city-owned, such as the Metropolitan Museum of Art, with the remainder to cover over five hundred smaller and more local arts organizations and the DCA administrative costs as well. During city budget crises, the large institutions survive; the rest flounder. See Judy Levine, "New York City Department of Cultural Affairs: Art As Municipal Service," in *Paying the Piper: Causes and Consequences of Art Patronage*, ed. Judith Huggins Balfe (Champaign–Urbana: University of Illinois Press, 1993), 137–60.

21. A recent case in point was the uproar over the Brooklyn Museum's exhibition of "Sensation" in the fall of 1999, where a mixed-media image of the Virgin Mary, including elephant dung and "crotch-shots" cut out from pornographic magazines to simulate the appearance of butterflies, was attacked by New York City mayor Rudy Giuliani as

"blasphemous." For another example, many Jews deplored the inherent "aestheticization" of the horrific material displayed at the Holocaust Museum in Washington, DC, as thereby preventing full recognition of the consummate evil of the events portrayed.

22. Margaret J. Wyszomirski, "Raison d'Etat, Raisons des Arts: Thinking about Public Purposes," in *The Public Life of the Arts in America*, ed. Joni Maya Cherbo and Margaret J. Wyszomirski (New Brunswick, NJ: Rutgers University Press, 2000), 50–78.

23. Freeman and Bania, "A Different Tempo."

8

Arts and Cultural Participation through a Neighborhood Lens

Maria-Rosario Jackson

Around the country, there are myriad examples of how art and cultural participation are important elements of neighborhood life, particularly as dimensions of community-building processes.[1] However, the specific roles that art and cultural participation play in neighborhoods, for the most part, are not well documented or understood in the arts or community-building related fields. In fact, with the exception of some research on education and economic impacts, there is no real coherent body of well-articulated theory or empirical research about the social impacts of the arts.[2] Without a better grasp of how art and cultural participation (defined broadly) contribute to community-building processes and various types of community improvement strategies, we are disadvantaged in two ways. First, practitioners and policy makers concerned with improving quality of life cannot do their best work because they have neglected to explore the full potential of art as a neighborhood transformation force. Second, the arts field is weakened and left politically and financially vulnerable because the full breadth, depth, and importance of U.S. arts practices cannot be recognized, cultivated, or strategically capitalized.

This chapter seeks to advance our efforts to understand the social impacts of the arts by providing researchers, policy makers, and practitioners with an expanded lens for capturing the presence and value of arts and cultural participation at the neighborhood level, particularly within community-building contexts. The lens is based primarily on field research conducted in numerous urban neighborhoods around the United States. It allows one to capture activity that may be missed using conventional narrow conceptions of arts and cultural participation. Moreover, it alerts the researcher to the possibility that arts and cultural participation may be embedded in and inextricable from other community processes. The field work informing this lens was conducted through two Urban Institute (UI) projects: the Arts and Culture Indicators in Community Building Project (ACIP) supported by the Rockefeller Foundation and the Participation Project: Artists, Communities and Cultural Citizenship carried out by the Getty Research Institute (GRI) in collaboration with the Urban Institute.[3] Having presented a more expansive concept of art and cultural participation, we then discuss the practical implications for developing grounded theory and data on social impacts of the arts and cultural participation at the neighborhood level.

ART AND CULTURAL PARTICIPATION THROUGH A NEIGHBORHOOD LENS

The ability to more adequately capture the presence and value of arts and cultural participation at the neighborhood level is critical to advancing research on social impacts of the arts and to the progress of the arts and community-building related fields. Early research conducted through ACIP and subsequent field work conducted through the Participation Project revealed that too often formal research and data collection (among academic scholars and arts administrators/practitioners alike) rely on narrow definitions of art and cultural participation that do not adequately capture the full breadth or depth of cultural activity at the community level. In-person interviews and focus group discussions with artists, arts practitioners, community builders, and neighborhood residents, as well as observations of community arts practices in a number of urban neighborhoods around the United States suggest that the following guidelines should be taken into consideration when attempting to understand the presence, roles, and value of art and cultural participation in community settings.

First, definitions of "art" and "culture" should be based on the cultural values, preferences, and realities of residents and other stakeholders in a given community. Art and cultural participation at the neighborhood level span a continuum that ranges from amateur to professional activities and often includes the cultural expressions of ethnic, racial, age, and special interest groups that may not be validated or adequately represented in large mainstream cultural institutions. For example, in some neighborhoods residents may value landscaping in private and public gardens, graffiti, gospel choirs, altars, storytelling, local culinary traditions, and various activities related to community festivals as art or arts-related community assets. Correspondingly, the notion of cultural venues must be expanded to include conventional venues such as theaters, auditoriums, or museums as well as community centers, church halls, parks, schools, libraries, and business establishments where art and cultural activities at the neighborhood level take place.

Second, while cultural participation is generally understood as audience participation, often at the community level, people participate in cultural activities in a variety of ways that include, but are not limited to, audience participation. To date, collection of data on audiences has been a priority because the role of audience members as consumers of art is an important factor in determining the fiscal health of cultural organizations (especially presenting organizations) and the arts sector in general. However, people also engage in the arts and cultural activities as artists/creators, students, teachers, judges, advocates, donors, sponsors, and so on. Participation spans many artistic disciplines and can be amateur or professional, active or passive, individual or collective, continuous or episodic, public or private. Moreover, it can be motivated by arts and nonarts specific reasons.

Third, art and culture should be understood as artifacts and processes that carry multiple meanings and purposes simultaneously and therefore rely on arts and nonarts specific sources/systems of support. For example, a dance that is part of a church-based rites of passage program for neighborhood youth (and activity leading to it) can be understood and evaluated for its aesthetic and technical qualities, as a human development mechanism for youth, as a means of expressing or celebrating cultural identity, and/or as a means of bringing families and members of a community together. The art itself is valuable, but it is also important because it is instrumental to and embedded in other social processes. Correspondingly, the youth dance activity is likely to rely on arts and nonarts specific resources: the artists/dancers who teach the art form, the youth development professionals who organize and run the rites of passage program, and the clergy or church leaders who make the facility available to the group, among others from various fields who may have contributed to the program.

ACIP focus group discussions revealed the following community-building related functions attributed to arts and cultural participation:

- Bridge racial/ethnic/cultural divides
- Preserve cultural heritage
- Promote pride in ethnic/cultural identity
- Transmit heritage intergenerationally
- Create group memory and group identity
- Worship
- Interpret or reinterpret present, past, or future environment
- Promote civic participation
- Improve built environment
- Promote ownership and stewardship of place
- Promote public safety
- Encourage economic development
- Develop life skills and problem solving
- Educate[4]

The neighborhood lens discussed here provides researchers and others with an indication of the breadth of arts activity that should be taken into consideration when attempting to examine the social impacts of arts and cultural participation in a community. It also makes the researcher attentive to the possible links between art and other community processes. So, given this more expansive notion of arts and cultural participation, what are the practical implications for developing grounded theory and data on the social impacts of the arts and cultural participation, particularly at the community level?

DEVELOPING GROUNDED THEORY AND DATA ABOUT SOCIAL IMPACTS OF ARTS AND CULTURAL PARTICIPATION

To develop grounded theory and data on the social impacts of the arts at the neighborhood level in ways that incorporate a neighborhood lens, researchers and others concerned with this issue have several tasks before them: (1) democratizing the process of defining art and culture; (2) differentiating various forms of cultural participation and developing corresponding nomenclature; (3) harvesting the wisdom of community arts and community-builder practitioners in the field; and (4) drawing from theoretical and conceptual frameworks in various disciplines (i.e., sociology, political science, community development, community building, youth development, folklore, cultural studies, anthropology, and so on) to craft new tools appropriate for analysis.

Democratizing the Process of Defining Art and Culture

If future research and data collection on the social impacts of the arts are to be relevant to the design of new policies and programs, the types of art and cultural participation studied have to reflect local realities and encompass art presented in large mainstream cultural institutions as well as art and culture produced and experienced at the community level. To incorporate other types of art and forms of cultural participation that currently are absent from most research and data collection efforts, everyday people in communities must have the opportunity to define art and culture for themselves.[5] Incorporating local values into research and data collection design requires a more thorough understanding of the mechanisms and processes by which residents validate artistic and cultural expression in their communities. To this end, emerging ethnographic work such as the Research Study on Informal Arts conducted through the Chicago Center for Arts Policy is likely to provide valuable insights for the design of future research and data collection. The study, conducted in several Chicago neighborhoods, seeks to reveal arts activities and assess the contributions of those activities to individual and community development in ways that reflect the values of residents in the neighborhoods examined. The arts activities identified as well as the value paradigms revealed are likely to provide leads for understanding the similar issues in other communities.

When opening up the definitional process, an inherent consequence is the likelihood that the number of entities included in expanded definitions of "art" and "culture" will be vast. This raises a number of questions for researchers to consider. What forms of art and culture are most important to community members and why? How do these values become part of the equation in establishing research priorities? Researchers are challenged to take into consideration community values in the design of future studies, particularly if the research is to be policy-relevant.

Differentiating Various Forms of Cultural Participation

An expanded notion of cultural participation is essential to a more comprehensive understanding of the investments that people make in the arts as well as to the development of theory about the possible impacts of cultural participation. Certainly, in establishing a base of theory about social impacts of the arts, it is critical to recognize that not all cultural participation will have the same outcomes. Participation in the actual creation of a community mural in collaboration with other people from the same neighborhood over a series of weekends is likely to have different outcomes than participation as an episodic individual museum visitor.

The development of a strong body of theory about the impacts of cultural participation requires that we make some informed assumptions about what kinds of participation are likely to render what kinds of outcomes. As these ideas are formulated, the field must develop the nomenclature that allows one to distinguish one kind of participation from another. Current practice among funders and practitioners alike suggests that "cultural participation" is still largely understood as shorthand for audience participation. Thus, the development of language to reflect the diversity of activity in which we are interested is crucial. Moreover, the continued use of "cultural participation" as an undifferentiated phenomenon militates against a better grasp of the social impacts of the arts.

Harvesting Wisdom from the Field and Culling from Case Studies and Anecdotal Information

While we lack a coherent, well-articulated body of theory and data on the social impacts of arts and culture that can guide useful research, it is important to note that researchers and others concerned with this issue are not exactly starting from scratch. ACIP field research in cities around the country revealed that there is a great deal of wisdom from the field that has not yet been fully harvested. Community arts practice has a long tradition and many practitioners have operated their programs with well-developed assumptions about the impacts of their efforts.[6] However, frequently mired with the tasks of running nonprofit organizations, community arts practitioners seldom have time to reflect on the premises that guide their work. As a result, these assumptions often go unarticulated and they are not codified into theory that can guide research.[7]

In addition to capturing the premises that guide community arts practices, it is worthwhile to pay attention to some of the informal documentation activities carried out in the community arts field.[8] Informal data collection practices, intended to signal the strength and worth of their programs, provide illustrations that can guide theory development and subsequent formal data collection and research designs. For example, one way in which administrators of community arts agencies said that they better understood their role in a neighborhood was through monitoring their relationships with other types of organizations and institutions in the area such as social service organizations, schools, community development organizations, local businesses, churches, and so on. This practice can serve as a basis for more rigorous analysis of the organizational networks of community arts agencies. A better understanding of these networks can reveal important issues related to the social impacts of the arts at the community level.

Case studies and anecdotal information about community arts practices are also valuable sources of information that can help shape the development of theory. Many community arts organizations have come to rely on case studies and anecdotal information to document their practices, and to some extent, the outcomes and impacts of their programs. While useful, as examples of individual community arts practices, too often this documentation exists in isolation. The field would benefit from efforts to assemble and analyze existing case studies and anecdotes to reveal themes and patterns relevant to social impacts. ACIP work in Oakland, California, in collaboration with the East Bay Institute for Urban Arts and other local players involved in art-based youth development have assembled case studies, journals, and a variety of other types of information in an effort to identify patterns and themes related to the connections among arts practices, youth development, and civic participation at the community level. ACIP collaborators in Denver are similarly working toward developing a framework that allows for aggregate analysis of existing case studies of art-based youth programs.

Drawing from Conceptual and Theoretical Frameworks in Other Fields

Conceptual and theoretical frameworks in other fields can be useful in developing analysis tools appropriate for assessing social impacts of the arts. An interdisciplinary approach to analysis of community arts practices is consistent with the understanding that arts and cultural participation are often embedded in other social processes. For example, as part of ACIP fieldwork in several cities, UI staff has developed an arts and community-building conceptual framework to more clearly illustrate the ways in which arts and cultural participation contribute to community-building processes.

The cultural participation examined through ACIP (and the Participation Project) in East Los Angeles provides a useful context to illustrate the framework. Activity in East Los Angeles involves collective art making in preparation for three community celebrations: Día de los Muertos (Day of the Dead), Día de la Virgen de Guadalupe (Day of Our Lady of Guadalupe), and Las Posadas (traditional Mexican Christmas celebrations). All of the celebrations involve the practice and creation of traditional arts through weekly workshops organized by Proyecto Pastoral (a neighborhood development organization) and Self-Help Graphics (an East Los Angeles visual arts organization) over two to three months preceding the celebrations. Arts activities include making decorations from tissue paper through papel picado (chiseled paper techniques), the creation of papier-mâché figures and masks, mural making, Aztec music and dance, the preparation of special holiday treats, processions, theater, and altar making.[9]

The arts and community-building conceptual framework is informed by the field work in East Los Angeles and other places as well as theoretical work on the development of social capital, collective efficacy, and research on community-building practices. The framework supposes that community building—which is broad-based collective action in support of comprehensive neighborhood development—relies on six basic elements that arts practices impact: civic engagement, community ownership/shared memory, relationships, assets, leadership, and strategies.[10]

Civic Engagement

Art and cultural participation are interpreted as civic engagement or catalysts for civic engagement—that is, individual participation that is removed, at least to some extent, from the individual's immediate self-interest. For example, people participating in the creation of a mural to educate others about community issues can be interpreted as a form of civic engagement. Likewise, arts activities can attract people into contexts where other kinds of civic engagement are likely or expected.

Community Ownership/Shared Memory

Art and cultural participation are understood as mechanisms to create, or evidence of, community ownership, shared meaning, or shared identity. Focus group respondents who participated in the art-making workshops and culminating festivals in East Los Angeles indicated that their participation had resulted in feelings of increased pride and ownership in their neighborhood, particularly when the art products they made (murals and other visual pieces) were displayed at the festivals for the whole community to see. Moreover, the art products themselves were interpreted as evidence of some shared identity and bonds that were developed or reinforced through the creative process.

Relationships

Art and cultural participation are interpreted as mechanisms by which relationships among individuals and networks of individuals within and beyond a community are created, affirmed, or extended. As suggested in the previous element, the arts workshops in which focus group respondents participated led to the development and reinforcement of relationships within the community (and beyond). These included intergenerational relationships, relationships among different cultural groups, professional artists and community tradition bearers, as well as residents of East Los Angeles and people from other parts of the city.

Assets

Art and cultural participation are interpreted as community assets as well as specific processes through which community assets are revealed, strengthened, or created. Arts and cultural participation are also evidence of social, human, and cultural capital within a community. The art products developed as part of the workshops were interpreted by focus group participants as community assets because they were not only used for the immediate festivals but are reused for a variety of other community purposes and events including peace walks, political marches, and family celebrations. Respondents said that the process of creating the art also served to reveal and/or develop artistic as well as organizational and leadership skills. Moreover, the art products and cultural participation were viewed by residents as evidence of a community's ability to collaborate.

Leadership

Art and cultural participation are understood as mechanisms through which leadership is exerted and existing relationships among community stakeholders can be appropriated for other purposes (one of which may be art itself). In East Los Angeles, artists and community tradition bearers played important roles as community leaders and organizers in the art-making and teaching processes and in the culminating celebrations. They galvanized the participation of youth groups and members of religious affiliate groups of the local church as well as Chicano activists from local universities and political organizations for the purposes of making art and all of the purposes simultaneously associated with art-making processes (worship, education, recreation, and so on).

Strategies

Art and cultural participation are interpreted as core elements of human, family, physical, economic, political, and cultural neighborhood development strategies. In East Los Angeles, several of the arts practices that were part of the workshops and culminating celebrations were extensions of preexisting art-based neighborhood development strategies. For example, the theater and Aztec dance programs are part of an ongoing youth development strategy. It is also important to note that new neighborhood development strategies sprang from the workshops. The chiseled paper art making was extended beyond the weekend workshops and incorporated into the activities of a women's support group. Also, residents had many ideas about how the crafts they were learning could anchor a number of economic development ventures.

This arts and community-building framework is but one example of ways in which researchers can integrate concepts from other fields with research on arts and cultural participation to create appropriate analytic tools. The development of appropriate analytic tools is crucial to advancing the body of theory on social impacts of arts and cultural participation as well as the design of meaningful data collection, especially at the neighborhood level.

CONCLUSION: TOWARD A STRONG BASE OF POLICY-RELEVANT DATA ON SOCIAL IMPACTS OF ARTS AND CULTURAL PARTICIPATION AT THE NEIGHBORHOOD LEVEL

As noted earlier in this chapter, the current state of research and data on social impacts of the arts, especially at the community level, is very limited. While some promising studies have been launched in recent years, many are still in the early stages.[11] Generally, research and data collection has been funder-driven and until recently not focused on assessing social impacts of the arts. As the need to document social impacts of the arts and cultural participation has become more urgent, researchers and practitioners concerned with addressing this have quickly realized the challenges before them. There is currently scant well-articulated theory on social impacts at the community level to guide research and data collection. Given the sometimes intangible nature of community arts activities and their possible impacts (such as transmittal of heritage, bridging of racial and ethnic divides, promotion of sense of ownership and stewardship of place, and creation of group memory and group identity), documentation, especially quantification, can be difficult. Moreover, there is emerging acknowledgment that social science–based methods alone are perhaps inadequate to capture the complexities of community arts practices.

In addition to taking on the tasks involved in developing grounded theory about social impact of the arts at the neighborhood level, as discussed in this chapter, the field is also charged with developing innovative data collection strategies capable of capturing the complexities of community arts practices. This requires experimenting with traditional social science–based methods as well as incorporating documentation strategies from the humanities and other fields that may be more appropriate for certain aspects of arts practices. Correspondingly, developing the nomenclature that facilitates an interdisciplinary approach to research and data collection is essential. Last, acknowledging that community arts practitioners are important sources and potential users of information about social impacts of the arts, emerging models of data collection should be designed to be sustainable at the local level.

At this point in time, the need to understand arts and cultural participation through a neighborhood lens—providing a more comprehensive grasp of the presence and roles of art and culture in people's lives—is crucial for several reasons. First, in a period when public funding for the arts has diminished and the societal value of the arts has been called into question, the need to more adequately capture the value of art and culture in American life is urgent. Second, in an era characterized by dramatic demographic shifts in many cities around the United States, the increasing racial, ethnic, and political diversity and complexity in many neighborhoods make conventional narrow definitions of "art" and "cultural participation" obsolete. Thus, a neighborhood lens provides a mechanism for expanding definitions of these terms in ways that can capture the values of people who heretofore have not been part of the definitional process. And last, in a political climate in which issues related to urban poverty and urban inequality are more frequently addressed at the local level, the need to strengthen community building and neighborhood development practices is critical. Understanding arts and cultural participation through a neighborhood lens provides valuable insights about the potential of the arts as an important force in neighborhood transformation.

NOTES

I wish to thank Florence Kabwasa-Green, my research associate, for her assistance in the preparation of this chapter.

1. In this chapter, "community building" refers to the creation and reinforcement of social ties, trust, and relationships of reciprocity that allow for broad-based collective action toward comprehensive neighborhood development strategies.

2. According to Margaret Wyszomirski, a noted cultural policy scholar, for the most part existing studies of impacts of the arts have focused primarily on audience impacts, education impacts, economic impacts, and social utility of the arts. To date, theory and research on the social utility of the arts is the area least well developed. See Margaret Wyszomirski, *Revealing the Implicit: Searching for Measures of the Impact of the Arts* (Washington, DC: The Independent Sector Conference on Measuring the Impact of the Non-Profit Sector on Society, 1996).

3. Launched in 1996 with the support of the Rockefeller Foundation, the Arts and Culture Indicators in Community Building Project (ACIP) is an exploratory and experimental effort to develop arts and culture neighborhood indicators—recurrently updated measures that allow one to describe societal conditions, track societal trends, and assess desired outcomes over time at the neighborhood level. The project operates in collaboration with numerous local organizations in seven U.S. cities—Boston; Chicago; Denver; Los Angeles; Oakland, California; Providence, Rhode Island; and Washington, DC—including community-building organizations and local arts agencies. ACIP also operates in collaboration with the Urban Institute's (UI) National Neighborhood Indicators Project, an effort dedicated to creating and improving neighborhood indicator systems around the country. The Participation Project: Artists, Communities and Cultural Citizenship was a research effort launched by the Getty Research Institute (GRI) to explore the relationship between community arts practices and civic engagement. Focused on activity in East Los Angeles, the effort (1997–1998) was a collaboration between the GRI and the UI. Research activities started during the Participation Project have continued under the auspices of ACIP.

4. Maria-Rosario Jackson, *Arts and Culture Indicators in Community Building Project: January 1996–May 1998, a Report to the Rockefeller Foundation* (Washington, DC: Urban Institute, 1998), 40.

5. During ACIP pilot focus group discussions, UI researchers gained important insights into the dynamics of arts and culture definitional processes at the neighborhood level. In pilot discussions, initially, UI researchers asked participants about what examples of "art" and "culture" were present in their neighborhoods. In several instances, residents concluded that there was no "art" because there were no "museums," "theaters," or "galleries." However, when residents were asked to think broadly about the terms "art" and "culture" and to explicitly consider "creative expressions" that they found moving, inspiring, provocative, beautiful, and so on, discussions were rich. UI researchers interpreted the discussion as an indication that there were no mainstream cultural venues, which typically serve to validate objects and activities as legitimate "art." Subsequently, the discussion guide was modified to ask residents about creative expressions first. Once objects and activities were identified, respondents were asked if they would consider these to be art. Most respondents extended the definition of the term to include objects and activities identified. However, in some cases there was animated debate about what did and did not qualify. Another insight gained about the definitional process was that residents must have the opportunity to step outside of their everyday lived experience to reflect on the creative and cultural expressions that exist in their communities. Often, these objects and activities are taken for granted, either because they are embedded in other aspects of community life, or just not thought of as "art" because of their connection to other community processes. To this end, insider and outsider perspectives on a community are useful.

6. For a historical account of the community arts field, see Arlene Goldbard, "Postscripts to the Past: Notes towards a History of Community Arts," *High Performance* 64 (winter 1993); Don Adams and Arlene Goldbard, "Grass Roots Vanguard," *Art in Amer-*

ica 70, no. 4 (April 1982); Arnold Hauser, *The Social History of Art* (New York: Vintage, 1985).

7. To address this, ACIP is taking steps toward documenting and codifying theories of practice through in-person interviews and focus-group discussions with community artists and community arts administrators. In ACIP field work, researchers have structured their inquiry with community arts practitioners in a way that allows the practitioner to have a sounding board and opportunity for reflection. In most cases, respondents said that they found the experience to be valuable.

8. In-person interviews with community arts administrators conducted through ACIP revealed that, for the most part, formal data collection is driven by funders. For organizations that received "arts" funds, data collection requirements typically included audience counts, budgetary information, and in some cases number of performances. For agencies that were undertaking arts and culture-related activity with funds earmarked for direct service provision or physical development, funders were concerned with the number of clients served and/or the number of physical improvements or new units of construction completed. For more discussion about formal data collection practices among arts administrators, see Christine M. Dwyer and Susan L. Frankel, *Reconnaissance Report of Existing and Potential Uses of Arts and Culture Data: A Product of the Arts and Culture Indicators in Community Building Project* (Washington, DC: Urban Institute, 1997).

9. For the workshops, professional artists and neighborhood residents who are recognized by their neighbors as masters of their crafts are enlisted to teach and/or assist with teaching during the weekly sessions. All workshops are free of charge and open to the public.

10. The framework draws from the work of James B. Hyman, *Exploring Social Capital through a Proposed Collective Efficacy Framework: A Concept Paper* (Washington, DC: Urban Institute, 2000), which in turn is informed by Robert Putnam, James Coleman, and Alejandro Portes.

11. Studies contributing to understanding social impacts of the arts at the neighborhood level include the Ford Foundation's Community Development Corporation Arts Resource Initiative; the Social Impacts of the Arts Project at the University of Pennsylvania School of Social Work; and the Chicago Center for Arts Policy's Social Impact of the Informal Arts Study. Additionally, the societal impacts of the arts (although not exclusively at the community level) have been addressed in a number of policy and academic forums, including the American Assembly's "The Arts and the Public Purpose" (1997); the President's Committee on the Arts and Humanities (1999); and the "Saguaro Seminar: Civic Engagement in America at Harvard University" (1999).

9

Beyond Economic Impact

Bruce A. Seaman

The notion that there is merit in moving "beyond economic impact" is meaningless without a clarification of terminology. It has always been the case that a legitimate "economic impact study" of any project, public expenditure, institution, or event requires a comprehensive cost-benefit analysis. Whether the object of the analysis is the arts industry in New York City, the Atlanta Olympics of 1996, or the Salzburg Festival in 2000, such an analysis requires an exploration of the following basic equation:

(1) Net benefits = (consumption value) − (capital costs + operating costs)
− (environmental, congestion, public safety, and other costs) + (increases
in local productivity and long-run economic growth and development) +
(increases in short-run net local income)[1]

"Traditional" economic impact studies have actually been incomplete versions of equation (1), focusing solely on the very last term of the equation: increases in short-run net local income. As such, those "aggregate spending flow studies" have generated useful but incomplete and misleading results that are limited as a guide to rational public policy making, especially regarding public funding of the arts.[2] This chapter focuses on what we know about moving "beyond" such limited studies to develop an approach to more accurately assess the "real" economic impact of specific institutions and events. The focus is on the other components of equation (1), especially the consumption value and the long-run economic growth and development issues, that are normally left out of the aggregate spending flow studies.[3]

Thus, the meaning in this context of moving "beyond economic impact" is not to substitute "noneconomic" for "economic" analysis. Moving beyond economic impact means exploring what we know, or possibly can know, about the more accurate and comprehensive *economic* impact of the arts.

LIMITATIONS OF AGGREGATE SPENDING FLOW ANALYSIS: A BRIEF REVIEW

The component of equation (1) called "increases in net local income" is essentially a "demand-side" analysis of two issues: (1) injections of aggregate net spending into some definition of the "local economy"; and (2) the relevant "induced" further spending effects of that initial net "injection" of spending, as captured by some "multiplier." Such studies when properly done can clarify the interdependence regarding income and jobs of different sectors of the local economy and provide a convenient (although typically noncomparative[4]) bench mark for measuring the "rate of return" from any public funds invested in the relevant institution or event.

However, because it is possible to confuse "net injections" of spending with mere "diversions" of spending from other sectors, many traditional economic impact studies greatly overstate the importance of any one industry or event to the local economy by failing to answer the question: Would the elimination of this industry, project, or event really cause the local economy to decline by the $X of "economic impact" identified in the study?

This overstatement is compounded by the potential misuse of "multiplier" magnitudes—which conceptually should be fairly low in those very geographical regions where net injections might be large (smaller, less self-sufficient versions of the "local economy"), and should be higher in those very geographical regions where spending flows are more likely to be diversions rather than net injections (larger, more self-sufficient versions of the "local economy"). Since these two effects tend to be counterbalancing, the "accurate" spending flow versions of local economic impact are capable of being smaller than the often quite sizeable impacts typically claimed by the sponsors of such studies.

Because of these and more fundamental conceptual weaknesses, critics of such studies often recommend a more "supply-side" approach that shifts the focus from interregional "zero-sum game" export demand shifts, to intraregional changes in resource allocation. A focus on such "nonexport" related intraregional issues would stress the potential effects of industries, projects, and events on: (1) providing more balanced and sustainable growth to the entire region by strengthening the weaker areas, such as central cities relative to suburbs and nearby "edge cities"; (2) improving the transportation, educational, and services infrastructure, productivity of the labor force, and value of urban "amenities" that enhance the ability of the local region to supply valuable products and services to its own residents, as well as serving to "shift" the supply of talented workers and other productive resources to the region; and (3) directly providing consumption benefits from projects, events, and institutions in the form of both "use" or "nonuse" value, including "option" and "existence" values.[5]

A focus on these intraregional issues is reminiscent of the often-ignored subtle distinction between "economic growth" and "economic development." According to Charles P. Kindleberger and Bruce Herrick, "economic growth means more output, while economic development implies both more output and changes in the technical and institutional arrangements by which it is produced and distributed; to emphasize development draws attention to changes in functional capacities—in physical coordination, for example, or learning capacity (or ability of the economy to adapt)."[6] Thus, economic development might be viewed as a longer-term increase in the capacity of a local economy to increase the quality of life to its residents, which requires increases in human productivity and a balance among its component subregions that enhances its ability to coordinate economic activity and adapt to changing circumstances.

AN EXAMPLE: THE 1996 ATLANTA SUMMER OLYMPICS

A good example of the limitations of aggregate spending flow analysis is provided by the Atlanta Olympics.[7] Extensive efforts were made to carefully estimate the economic impact of the Olympics on Metro Atlanta and the state of Georgia, which was estimated to be $5.062 billion from 1991 to 1997.[8]

In reality, this average of about $723 million per year for seven years was an overestimate. This was due largely to a number of understandable miscalculations of the eventual magnitude of "net aggregate injections" into the region: the surprising number of people driving to Atlanta and staying with friends rather than in hotels (which also limited some other ancillary spending); the more than anticipated diversion of other tourist visits and spending by local residents away from Atlanta before and during the event due to fear of local congestion and high prices; and the unrealistically high expectations of revenues to local homeowners from the rental of their houses (in fact, less than 10 percent of the housing stock "listed" for such purposes was ever rented at all, and some who had established special real estate agencies to facilitate such transactions suffered considerable losses).

Despite such complications, the Atlanta Olympics generated at least a $4.5 billion seven-year aggregate economic impact to the state of Georgia (substantial to be sure, but still less than 1 percent of the state gross domestic product for any *one* year). More importantly, it is widely and correctly viewed as having been critical to the long-run economic future of Atlanta, and hence of the entire state. The reason for this enthusiasm is simple: The most important economic impact of the Olympics was not captured by the aggregate short-run impact measured by the interregional "export" based study. As fully recognized by Jeffrey M. Humphreys and Michael K. Plummer, "hosting the Olympic games will increase the economic vitality of the state in other long run, but ad-mittedly less measurable, ways."[9] They specifically cited "reputation effects" as the city and the state become better known on the world stage, and future trade and investment opportunities created by interpersonal contacts made due to the Olympics that would not otherwise have occurred.

But perhaps the most important longer-run effect they cited was the essen-tial financial leverage provided to existing businesses and start-up companies for future expansion that would not have developed until much later, if at all. This hints at the possibility that the primary effects of the Olympics in Atlanta are those linked to potentially dramatic reallocations of resources *within* the metro area—reallocations that were related to, but not adequately measured by traditional impact studies.

By the spring of 2000, the degree to which these "less measurable" effects had changed the Atlanta landscape were evident. Metro Atlanta had been grow-ing very rapidly since 1980 (hitting 3.5 million in 1996), with the second high-est population growth rate of any of the largest twenty Metropolitan Statistical Areas (MSAs) in the United States from 1990 to 1996 (19.7 percent, second only to Phoenix-Mesa's 22.7 percent). And its 32.5 percent population growth was near the top of national growth rates from 1980 to 1990 (tying Dallas–Ft. Worth, and trailing only San Diego and Phoenix-Mesa).[10]

But such growth was extremely uneven. Some Atlanta metro counties were literally the most rapidly growing in the country, while within the narrow con-fines of the city of Atlanta itself, population and housing starts were actually declining (with population hitting a low point of 394,000 in 1990 before climb-ing to 404,000 in 1998—but still lower than the 425,000 of 1980).[11] This famil-iar U.S. urban pattern created serious concerns for the quality of life and longer-run attractiveness of the region due to ever-lengthening commuting times and related environmental problems. International attention on Atlanta as the next "Los Angeles" created a feared image of the city as the "poster-child of urban sprawl." A nascent "back to the city" movement emerged.

Hence, there could be no more opportune timing than the 1990s' buildup to the 1996 Olympics (including the related activities of the "Cultural Olympics"). Superimposed on the modest trend away from limitless suburban growth, the attention and real economic resources focused on the central city and the other urban residential and mixed-use neighborhoods by a business community and a population determined to show a vibrant city to the world moved existing trends dramatically forward. This shift in intraregional eco-nomic activity included important changes in the very perceptions of the cen-tral city among a metro population including an astonishing number of people who told interviewers that they had literally not visited downtown or midtown in recent memory. In the fairly restricted area known as Downtown Atlanta, es-timates of the amount of housing were typically in the range of five hundred units. But lofts and upper levels of storefronts began being converted in time to house visitors to the Olympics. Once those temporary guests left after about one month, such conversions and new building for permanent residents continued at a dramatic pace. Since January 1999 alone, 1,000 condominium units and 754 apartments have been completed, with 2,742 units planned for completion by the end of 2000 along with 4,511 apartments, and more than 750 condominiums and 600 apartments planned for 2001. As noted by staff writer John McCosh, "much of the new housing is a direct legacy of the 1996 Games, particularly the area around Centennial Olympic Park." And quoting David Martin of the Legacy Group of developers responsible for a ninety-five-unit project right next to the park: "We tried to get the deal done before the Olympics and had a great deal of difficulty; the interest in downtown between the time we purchased the property in 1994 and 1999 has turned to the positive, dramatically."[12]

Also, it was clear that the expanding "agglomeration" of downtown housing and entertainment options (including an expanding array of art galleries, a renovated center for the performing arts linked to an expanding Georgia State University, and the conversion of the "Tabernacle" into an Olympic era "House of Blues" and later a permanent music venue as part of a future-planned downtown "cultural district") was one of the factors convincing Turner Broadcasting to work with the city and state to keep the basketball and hockey teams downtown in the new high-tech Philips Arena (also home to the first ever major commissioned piece of art to be displayed in a sports arena, when regional artist Thornton Dial created the mixed media piece "Flying Out" for the Atlanta Hawks basketball team—which has drawn large crowds at open house showings as well as enthusiastic responses from sports fans). In turn, the new arena combined with the other downtown sports facilities to enhance the viability of yet more housing and entertainment projects—thus further creating the "virtuous cycle" of in-town rejuvenation so prized by "balanced growth" advocates.

And just 1.5 to 2.5 miles north of downtown, the already stable midtown neighborhood (home to the "establishment" arts community including the High Museum, the Atlanta Symphony Orchestra, the Alliance Theater, the Fox Theater, and the Atlanta College of Art) has combined the momentum from the Olympics with a budding mini-Silicon Valley to become one of the hottest commercial and residential real estate markets in the country. There are no fewer than fifty-three commercial and residential projects either recently completed or under construction, along with three thousand new residences in the process of being built right in the commercial core of the area—with twice as many office towers under construction on only one street in midtown as there are in the entire area of the wealthy showcase district of Buckhead.[13]

It is important to emphasize that while injections of funding from the "outside" linked to the Olympics provided critical leverage to fragile city projects, and that the unique attention focused on the inner city added respectability to future related projects, it was ultimately the reallocation of local resources from the other thriving parts of the metro area into the weaker areas that has driven these changes. Real estate developers that had only done suburban projects have now shifted their attention to the city. And while the Philips Arena (and its sports franchises and very popular music concert facilities) was always going to stay within metro Atlanta, there had been a serious question of whether it would replace the previous Omni Arena in its original downtown location, or further add to the dispersion of economic activity away from the city. It was thus intraregional spending flows, even more than interregional aggregate net injections, that have been most important to this significant change in the pattern of economic activity in metro Atlanta.[14]

IMPLICATIONS AND RESEARCH QUESTIONS

Rather than being too idiosyncratic to offer general lessons, this particular local sports/arts example illustrates the critical notion that traditional impact studies fail to address the more important "internal" resource allocation issues that may affect the longer-term economic development potential of a region. It also directly raises the question: What do we really know about the importance of "balanced growth" to a region or the degree to which central city vitality is critical to the long-term future of an entire metro area? There is no question that most arts advocates (especially when arguing for enhanced public support) presume the legitimacy of the following syllogism:

1. A healthy urban core is essential for the long-run economic health of the entire metro area and larger region
2. Arts institutions and individual creative artists typically play important roles in preserving and rejuvenating central cities and core urban neighborhoods
3. Therefore, arts institutions and individual artists are essential for the long-run economic health of the entire metro area and larger region

But what empirical evidence exists for the first two critical propositions in this argument? The first of these might be called the "balanced growth hypothesis." It has enormous casual support well beyond arts advocates and scholars and is part of the general intellectual challenge to the evils of "urban sprawl."[15]

But efforts to rigorously confirm the balanced growth hypothesis have been rare or have yielded mixed results. In a study originally conducted in 1994 for the National Urban Policy Report of the U.S. Department of Housing and Urban Development, Keith Ihlanfeldt addresses "The Importance of the Central City to the Regional and National Economy: A Review of the Arguments and Empirical Evidence."[16] He identifies five major "sources of interdependence that allegedly link the economies of central cities and their surrounding suburbs": (1) perceptions of the entire region that cannot easily be distinguished from perceptions of the central city (the quintessential U.S. example being Detroit); (2) location specific and historically unique amenities in the central cities that are valued throughout the entire region; (3) the related notion that central cities provide a "sense of place" that is highly valued not only by central city residents, but also by others living in the metro area who "identify" in some way with those things that make, say, Chicago a unique place to live; (4) fiscal interdependence that creates a potential future tax liability to richer suburban areas as a result of eroding tax bases in the central city (which could include consequent reduced abilities of those poorer areas to bear their portion of regional burdens for such services as indigent care public hospitals); and (5) the "traditional" concept that central cities offer unique "agglomeration economies" that provide a specialized role for the central city even in an ever-decentralizing regional economy.

He concludes that there is no empirical evidence on the quantitative signifi-cance of "perceived image" or "sense of place" effects (numbers [1] and [3] of the major "sources of interdependence"), although he cites some research that is suggestive of how this might be done. He argues that the best way to measure the importance of unique central city amenities would be via "inter-area hedonic wage or housing equations," but notes that this has not been done. Willingness-to-pay and contingent valuation studies are alternative ap-proaches to measuring these economic impacts (discussed later in this chapter). And he cites studies that have confirmed that higher state and local taxes dis-courage economic growth (especially if there is no demonstrable increase in the quality of local services and "infrastructure"), but does not link this common finding in a systematic way to the proposition that weak central cities inhibit regional growth.

Finally, after a detailed analysis of the "agglomeration economies" issue, he does find some empirical support for the proposition that "information ex-change can occur more efficiently in dense urban environments" and that "spa-tial concentration of economic activity is related to technological progress." However, he concludes that "there is no empirical research that has focused ex-plicitly on central cities as possible 'engines of growth,'" and argues that "the most promising area for future inquiry would be to focus explicitly on the relationship(s) between central city decline and metropolitan or suburban growth." Such research would build on tentative findings that demonstrate a strong effect of city income growth on suburban income, housing values, and population growth, but that fail to sufficiently isolate the direction of causality for these important variables between central city and suburban regions.[17]

This direction of causality ambiguity is a critical limitation to our current understanding of the role of central cities in regional development, and greatly limits our ability to draw strong inferences from "simple" tests of the balanced growth hypothesis such as studies of correlations between central city and sub-urban economic and demographic variables. Thus, while Richard P. Voith finds that, for example, the correlation between city and suburban population growth was actually negative for the 1960s (−.57), it was positive for both the 1970s and 1980s (.57 and .51, respectively).[18] Tempting as it is to conclude that this indicates a strong and increasing dependency of suburban growth on the general vitality of the entire region, including the central city, such correlations not only fail to clarify the relative strength of the direction of causality between the economic fortunes of cities and suburbs, but they also do not eliminate the possible interpretation of increasingly independent suburbs (operating as "substitute" central cities) that are merely influenced by the same external events as those affecting the "independent" central cities.[19]

Therefore, the first proposition in the syllogism remains a quite plausible, but only weakly empirically confirmed link in the long-run economic development impact of an expanded arts sector (the fourth component of equation [1] as applied to the arts). But what about the second proposition that identifies artistic institutions and artists as playing important roles in central city rejuvenation, and more generally in better balancing the distribution of economic activity between "north and south" within most metro regions?

The evidence here is empirically stronger, although still largely anecdotal and subject to clarifications regarding the direction of causality between artistic activity and neighborhood revitalization. Perhaps the most extensive effort to move our knowledge beyond "urban folklore" is the Social Impact of the Arts Project (SIAP) of the University of Pennsylvania School of Social Work, directed by Mark J. Stern.[20]

Of course, despite the general concentration of arts facilities in urban neighborhoods and the existence of "designated cultural districts" of various types in the city cores of thirty U.S. metro areas, it should always be remembered that a full accounting of "noncommercial arts and cultural providers" (broadly defined) would find a much less centralized location for such organizations.[21] For example, Stern identifies more than one thousand "arts and cultural providers" in the five-county metro Philadelphia region, with "well over 80%" located outside of center city.[22] And the "north–south" urban dichotomy can hardly be "rectified" by high profile arts institutions located in the wealthier "north," even if those downtown locations are on the "southern boundary" of those northern sectors (e.g., arts rich midtown is north of the I-20 metro Atlanta "demographic boundary," even though it is most definitely south of the dramatically growing wealthy northern suburbs).

But despite those caveats, Stern's findings are potentially path breaking. In brief, he finds that in Philadelphia a "block group" (i.e., a specific measure of neighborhood) "with many arts groups per capita had a 10% chance of revitalizing, about twice the citywide average." By comparison, in Chicago and Atlanta the percentages are somewhat lower at 7.6 percent and 7.9 percent, respectively, but still "about fifty percent higher than the citywide average." More modestly, in San Francisco "5% of high arts block groups revitalized, compared to 3.3% of all block groups."[23]

Of course, as Stern fully recognizes, the causality question remains a significant challenge to this and future research. Thus, he further explores the relationship between nonarts institutions and neighborhood revitalization, and finds that the arts generally are not unique in their revitalization impact: "In Philadelphia, a neighborhood with many non-arts groups was nearly twice as likely to revitalize, a result that was duplicated in Atlanta.... [But] in Chicago ... neighborhoods with fewer non-arts groups were actually more likely to revitalize than those with many organizations."[24] And using sophisticated multivariate techniques, he finds that the most important independent variable "explaining" revitalization (among "ethnic composition," economic "status" including measures of "economic diversity," the number of "accessible" arts and cultural organizations per capita, and metropolitan area) is the variable economic diversity. Economic diversity has a fascinating meaning in this study: a block group is economically diverse if its "poverty rate was above 17% and more than 21% of the labor force were professionals and managers"—simplified as "pov-prof," or neighborhoods with both significant poverty as well as significant professional success.[25]

He concludes: "Across the four cities, economically diverse neighborhoods were more than five times as likely to revitalize as neighborhoods with low poverty." Furthermore, "ethnically diverse neighborhoods' odds of revitalizing were more than twice as high as African American neighborhoods and just below those of white neighborhoods."[26]

Yet, even after statistically controlling for these other determinants, arts and cultural organizations have had an important independent effect on neighborhood revitalization: "Compared to neighborhoods with the fewest arts organizations ... neighborhoods with many arts and cultural organizations ... were more than twice as likely to revitalize."[27] Clearly, further work is needed to clarify the independent effects of arts organizations and "artistic density" on revitalization, especially as it contributes to more balanced growth and a lessening of the urban and regional north–south divide.

Mere correlations are inadequate, but they do raise fascinating questions about the potential economic developmental role of the arts. For example, of the nineteen most rapidly growing U.S. metropolitan areas (i.e., those with population growth above 10 percent from 1990 to 1996), only seven of them (36.8 percent) were within the top forty "arts and culture ranking for MSAs" as compiled by *Money Magazine*.[28] By contrast, eleven of those metro areas (57.8 percent) were in the top twenty-five ranked by "% of adults with bachelor's degree or higher."[29] However, of those nineteen fastest growing metro areas, fully thirteen of them (68.4 percent) had "designated cultural districts" (although Dallas, whose cultural district is widely perceived to have had very limited "success," had population growth of 13.3 percent, while the widely lauded cultural district of Philadelphia is part of a metro area that grew at the paltry rate of only .6 percent over that time period—an obvious reminder of the distinction between correlation and causality). Also, of twelve major metro areas projected to have job growth above 5 percent by 2002, seven of them (58.3 percent) were in the top forty *Money Magazine* arts and culture ranking (but of the top three in projected job growth—Phoenix, Atlanta, and Austin—only Atlanta made the art and culture ranking at number thirty-two). Since such correlations raise more questions than they answer, it is clear that more sophisticated research such as that begun by the SIAP would be extremely productive.

In summary, the syllogism linking the arts to metro regional development via balanced growth has modest empirical support and cannot be dismissed. However, many of the identified gaps in our knowledge from William S. Henden's 1980 *Arts and Urban Development* monograph have yet to be filled, including a fuller understanding of the dynamic processes and historical contexts that would affect the "incremental contribution" of additional artists and arts institutions to the local "social and economic capital infrastructure," and the unique role of "spatial balance" in long-run regional economic development.[30] But progress is being made in clarifying this fourth component of the "net benefits" of equation (1).

ECONOMIC IMPACT VIA CONSUMPTIVE VALUE

The most important economic impact of the arts has always been their "consumption" value (the first of the components of the "net benefits" of equation [1]). However, this value is not limited to the directly observable ticket expenditures for performances and exhibits, but conceptually includes the "consumer surplus" to direct consumers (someone spending $200 for five orchestra performances who would pay as much as $500 rather than consume no performances has $300 in consumer surplus), as well as possible consumption values to nonusers via "option" or "existence" demands (the "public goods" component of consumption value, which might also include separate "bequest," "prestige," and "educational" values). But these more "fundamental" concepts of economic impact are not as easy to derive as the more measurable short-run aggregate monetary measures addressed by conventional economic impact studies. Consumer surplus measurement requires more precise information about consumers' "demand curves," in contrast to the more observable single points on those curves revealed as particular quantities demanded by different people at particular prices.[31] And obtaining unbiased estimates of the magnitude of the various components of the "nonmarket public goods" component of consumption value is inherently problematic. In fact, one of the great motivations for conventional economic impact studies has been the seeming relative ease of deriving short-run aggregate spending measures, despite their conceptual flaws as a guide to public subsidy policy, and the fact that they are only one component of the fuller cost-benefit equation (1). Since the early focus of much of arts economics research was an evaluation of "the public goods case for arts subsidy," a call now for "going beyond economic impact" is more accurately a call for a "return to before economic impact," but with a more sophisticated approach to the measurement of the public goods component of consumption value.

Approaches to measuring these nonmarket values include (1) "hedonic" estimates of changes in housing prices or wage differentials as a function of proximity to cultural resources, (2) travel cost estimates of consumers' "willingness to pay" for the consumption of cultural facilities and events, and (3) "contingent valuation surveys" that have been applied extensively to environmental public goods such as "another clean lake" or an "unobstructed view of a mountain" (with bibliographies identifying over fifteen hundred entries). There have been only limited applications of these techniques to the arts and culture, although contingent valuation studies (which raise very controversial methodological issues of their own) applied to the arts threaten to become as common as conventional economic impact studies were at their peak.[32] Interestingly, there have been efforts in the arts case to measure another important dimension of nonmarket value based on the economic contributions of volunteers to arts organizations, using the well-established "opportunity cost approach," the "value-added approach," and the "market price equivalency model."[33]

Any approach to deriving economic impact as the consumption values of primarily local residents differs fundamentally from the export-based tourism focus of short-run spending impact studies. Such alternatives, however, suffer as a guide for public investment policy from the same lack of full comparisons among other types of "public goods" that plague traditional impact studies (e.g., are the contingent values from keeping a professional sports franchise larger than those from building a new symphony hall?). Also, such studies do not always distinguish between measures of willingness-to-pay out of private user consumer surplus, which would justify higher ticket prices and more creative "price discrimination" schemes (e.g., the Tiziana Cuccia and Giovanni Signorello study focuses on the possible establishment of an "access user fee" to be charged to tourists entering the city of Noto, Italy, but that could also be used to justify higher user fees to local visitors of museums), and the willingness-to-pay of primarily local nonusers who perceive public benefits from the "option" to consume in the future, or from the "existence" and "prestige" public benefits of the "cultural infrastructure" that could justify tax-financed public subsidies (the Robert Kling et al. study of the salvation and restoration of the landmark Northern Hotel in downtown Ft. Collins, Colorado, specifically focuses on public benefits that would justify tax-financed public investment).

In any case, it is clear that such nonmarket values can be substantial. For example, Kling et al. derives the value of the public good aspect of the $10 million hotel restoration project, $670,000 of which is to be provided by the city government, at between $2.5 million and $13 million—from 3.7 to 19.4 times the amount of tax funds committed to the project. As another example, Trine Bille-Hansen remarkably finds that the nonusers' portion of the total willingness-to-pay for the Royal Theatre in Copenhagen was about 82 percent—dramatically confirming the importance of the "option," "existence," "prestige," and "bequest" values of such cultural institutions.

Anecdotal evidence of the importance of such nonuser consumption values is evident in the example of Atlanta residents and corporations suddenly being willing to commit funds to street sculptures and other aspects of the cultural infrastructure on the eve of the 1996 Olympics. And a recent history of public funding of the arts in South Korea shows that the public budget for the Korean Culture and Arts Foundation grew 400 percent over the period just prior to the Asian Games in 1986 and the 1988 Seoul Olympics, with more recent consecutive two-year 40 percent increases in the budget for the arts and culture for the 2000 Asia and Europe Meeting for heads of states, and for the World Cup Football Games scheduled in 2002.[34] But further research using contingent valuation and other techniques to carefully measure and isolate such nonmarket values and to compare them more accurately with the nonmarket values from other claims on public resources are essential elements of using the economic impact measured by the consumption value in sophisticated public policy analysis.

CONCLUSION

Constructive research cannot be limited to identifying the failings of traditional economic impact studies (which are limited to addressing only one of five relevant issues in a full cost-benefit analysis), but must move to clarify all of the components of the "net benefits" of equation (1). Much remains to be learned regarding the consumption value and the long-run economic growth and development components of that equation as applied to the arts and culture. However, there is progress and an agenda for future research that will allow scholars and policy makers to move "beyond economic impact."

NOTES

1. While this type of equation is quite general, a good discussion of its application to sports teams and stadiums is provided in Roger G. Noll and Andrew Zimbalist, "The Economic Impact of Sports Teams and Facilities," in *Sports, Jobs and Taxes,* ed. Roger G. Noll and Andrew Zimbalist (Washington, DC: Brookings Institution Press, 1997), 55–91, especially 74.

2. For a fuller critique of "traditional" economic impact studies, see Dennis Zimmerman, "Subsidizing Stadiums: Who Benefits, Who Pays?," in *Sports, Jobs and Taxes,* ed. Roger G. Noll and Andrew Zimbalist (Washington, DC: Brookings Institution Press, 1997), Chapter 4; Bruce A. Seaman, "Arts Impact Studies: A Fashionable Excess," in *Economic Impact of the Arts: A Sourcebook,* ed. Anthony J. Radich (Denver: National Conference of State Legislators, 1987), 44–75. For a good comparison of different evaluation methodologies for evaluating "cultural property," see Bruno S. Frey, "Evaluating Cul-

tural Property: The Economic Approach," *International Journal of Cultural Property* 6, no. 2 (1997): 231–46.

3. The *Journal of Arts Management, Law, and Society* devoted an entire issue to the topic "Beyond Economic Impact," focusing on the increasing demands of private contributors and government funding agencies for increased accountability from nonprofit arts and cultural organizations. See Louise K. Stevens, "Impacts, Measurement, and Art Policy: Starting the Change Process," *Journal of Arts Management, Law, and Society* 28, no. 3 (fall 1998): 225–28; Eric C. Thompson, "Contingent Valuation in Arts Impact Studies," *Journal of Arts Management, Law, and Society* 28, no. 3 (fall 1998): 206–10; Margaret Jane Wyszomirski, "The Arts and Performance Review, Policy Assessment, and Program Evaluation: Focusing on the Ends of the Policy Cycle," *Journal of Arts Management, Law, and Society* 28, no. 3 (fall 1998): 191–200. The question of how to evaluate the "output" and the "performance" of such organizations leads some authors to make stray references to the "increasingly apparent ... analytical weaknesses" of "familiar approaches such as economic impact studies" (see Wyszomirski, "Arts and Performance Review," 197), and the need for efforts to "move beyond simply counting people served by the programs to include measures of other possible impacts" (see Maria-Rosario Jackson, *Arts and Culture Indicators in Community Building Project: January 1996–May 1998, a Report to the Rockefeller Foundation* [Washington, DC: Urban Institute, 1998], 204). However, only Thompson directly addresses the inadequacy of "conventional economic impact analysis" to "consider how the arts influence the economy by affecting local residents" and enhancing the "quality of life of local residents," instead of focusing on "cultural tourism or other out-of-area support for the arts" (207). He calls for the use of the "contingent valuation method along with conventional economic impact analysis" to make impact analysis more "comprehensive" and to "more closely reflect the primary reasons that states, cities, and private patrons support the arts" (209–10).

4. While such comparisons are rare among public policy makers and advocates who use impact studies, there have been research efforts to make such comparisons. See James H. Gapinski, "Economic Structure and Impact of the Arts: Comparisons with the Nonarts," in *Economic Impact of the Arts: A Sourcebook*, ed. Anthony J. Radich (Denver: National Conference of State Legislators, 1987), 185–228.

5. The importance of focusing on intraregional issues has long been recognized. In 1980, William S. Hendon concluded: "There seems to be general agreement that impacts should be examined and are more likely to be found by looking within a particular city than in comparing cities [using] the export-base notions." See William S. Hendon, *The Arts and Urban Development: Critical Comment and Discussion*, Monograph Series in Public and International Affairs no. 12, Center for Urban Studies, University of Akron, August 1980. A recent renewal of the call for this shift in emphasis toward intraregional productivity and amenity analysis can be found in Ann Markusen, "Should We Target Occupations Rather Than Industries? An Illustration from the Arts" (paper presented at the Eleventh Biennial Conference of the Association for Cultural Economics, International, Minneapolis, Minnesota, May 28–31, 2000).

6. From Charles P. Kindleberger and Bruce Herrick, *Economic Development*, International student ed. (London: McGraw-Hill, 1977), 3; see also the excellent survey by Harold Wolman and David Spitzley, "The Politics of Local Economic Development," *Economic Development Quarterly* 10, no. 2 (May 1996): 115–50.

7. A more recent example of the arts and sports connection is the cooperation between the two communities in Atlanta in promoting the 2000 major league baseball all-star game. Impressed by the successful "street cow sculpture" programs in Zurich and Chicago, local Atlanta corporations and artists (chosen from a list of southern artists who either worked for a commission or donated their talents) decorated up to five hundred large six-foot diameter, thirty-six-square-feet baseballs (some signed by baseball players) that were displayed throughout the city for six months. The first thirty-one giant baseballs (the number of major league franchises plus one) were sold for $27,000 as part of a package including game tickets, while most of the others were donated back by the corporations for a charity sale via the Internet and at a black tie gala for $5,000 per ball. See Erin Moriaty, "Teamwork: Sports and Arts; City Makes Big Pitch with All-Star Game Promotion," *Atlanta Business Chronicle*, 28 April–4 May 2000, 3A, 21A.

8. See Jeffrey M. Humphreys and Michael K. Plummer, *The Economic Impact on the State of Georgia of Hosting the 1996 Olympic Games*, prepared for the Atlanta Committee for the Olympic Games, University of Georgia, August 1992.

9. Ibid., 9.

10. United States Census Bureau, *Statistical Abstract of the United States, 1999* (Washington, DC: U.S. Government Printing Office, 1999), Table 43.

11. Ibid., Table 48.

12. John McCosh, "Downtown Atlanta Gets Boost," *Atlanta Journal-Constitution*, 27 April 2000, E1, E4.

13. *Atlanta Journal-Constitution*, 28 April 2000, F1, F5.

14. As Edward Goetz and Terrence Kayser note: "Although much of the extant literature on public sector competition for economic development is set at the state level or examines the competition between major cities, the fiercest competition for private investment is often between neighboring cities or cities within the same region." See Edward Goetz and Terrence Kayser, "Competition and Cooperation in Economic Development: A Study of the Twin Cities Metropolitan Area," *Economic Development Quarterly* 7, no. 1 (1993): 63. Interestingly, despite the element of a "zero-sum game" to these competing intraregional efforts, about 80 percent of the responding officials perceived benefits to the entire Twin Cities region from their localized developmental strategies, which might be especially likely if such efforts create more "balanced growth" in the region, as addressed in the following section of this book.

15. For example, the *Atlanta Business Chronicle* supported business and government financial assistance to downtown arts institutions to create a "cultural district" because "a more economically vigorous downtown, attracting new in-town residents will yield a handsome return for business." And in a survey of the enduring division between the wealthier "north" and poorer "south" sides of many U.S. metro areas (including Philadelphia, Boston, Chicago, Los Angeles, Seattle, San Diego, Indianapolis, Dallas, Houston, and Atlanta, but with notable exceptions such as Washington, DC,

Denver, and Birmingham), Dan Chapman notes that most pundits offer the antidote of "resolve the inequities by bolstering the downtrodden cores of American cities; the billions spent on barrier-building, sprawl-inducing road projects should now be spent cultivating urban back yards." See Dan Chapman, *Atlanta Journal-Constitution*, 9 April 2000, C1–C2.

16. Keith Ihlanfeldt, "The Importance of the Central City to the Regional and National Economy: A Review of the Arguments and Empirical Evidence," *Cityscape: A Journal of Policy, Development and Research* 1, no. 2 (August 1995): 125–50.

17. Richard P. Voith, Does City Income Growth Increase Suburban Income Growth, House Value Appreciation, and Population Growth?, Working Paper no. 93–27, Federal Reserve Bank of Philadelphia, 1993.

18. Richard P. Voith, "City and Suburban Growth: Substitutes or Complements?," *Business Review* (Federal Reserve Bank of Philadelphia) (September–October 1992): 21–33.

19. An examination of Tables 43 and 48 in United States Census Bureau, *Statistical Abstract of the United States, 1999,* will confirm that in general this positive correlation between population growth of cities and metro areas has continued through the 1990s up to 1998, with those major metro areas suffering from weak growth (3 percent or lower population growth) also generally having central cities with 3 percent or lower, often negative, population growth rates. However, there are important exceptions beyond Atlanta, even to this limited correlation evidence: metro Cincinnati grew at 5.7 percent while the city declined by 7.6 percent; metro Miami grew at about 10 percent while the city grew at only 2.8 percent; metro Minneapolis–St. Paul grew at 8.9 percent, while the cities of Minneapolis and St. Paul both declined by about 5 percent; and the Washington, DC–Baltimore consolidated metro area grew at 6.5 percent despite population declines in the District of Columbia of 13.8 percent and in Baltimore of 12.3 percent.

20. See especially Mark J. Stern, Is All the World Philadelphia? A Multi-city Study of Arts and Cultural Organizations, Diversity and Urban Revitalization, Working Paper no. 9, Social Impact of the Arts Project, University of Pennsylvania School of Social Work, May 1999.

21. For a list of these cities, see Arthur Brooks and Roland Kushner, *A Cultural District for Downtown Atlanta* (Atlanta: Research Atlanta, Inc., Georgia State University, 2000), Table A11, 48. For a European perspective on "cultural districts," see Walter Santagata, "Cultural Districts for Sustainable Economic Growth" (paper presented at the Eleventh Biennial Conference of the Association for Cultural Economics, International, Minneapolis, Minnesota, May 28–31, 2000).

22. Stern, Is All the World Philadelphia?, 1.

23. Ibid., Figure 3, 37.

24. Ibid.

25. Ibid., 17.

26. Ibid., 37–38.

27. Ibid.

28. This comparison can be made by examining Brooks and Kushner, *Cultural District for Downtown Atlanta*, Tables A.1, A.3, 43, 44

29. Ibid., Table A.8, 46. Job growth data is provided in Table A.2.

30. For example, see John M. Quigley, "Urban Diversity and Economic Growth," *Journal of Economic Perspective* 12, no. 2 (spring 1998); Edward L. Glaeser, "Are Cities Dying?," *Journal of Economic Perspective* 12, no. 2 (spring 1998); Paul Krugman, "Space: The Final Frontier," *Journal of Economic Perspective* 12, no. 2 (spring 1998).

31. See William S. Hendon's useful review of these concepts in "Evaluating Cultural Policy through Benefit-Cost Analysis," in *Economic Impact of the Arts: A Sourcebook*, ed. Anthony J. Radich (Denver: National Conference of State Legislators, 1987), 159–84.

32. The two early fairly nontechnical studies not related to any particular arts project were David C. Throsby and Glenn A. Withers, "Measuring the Demand for the Arts As a Public Good: Theory and Empirical Results," in *Economics of Cultural Decision*, ed. William S. Hendon and James L Shanahan (Cambridge, MA: Abt Associates, 1983), 177–91; William G. Morrison and Edwin G. West, "Subsidies for the Performing Arts: Evidence on Voter Preferences," *Journal of Behavioral Economics* 15 (fall 1986): 57–72. The only published studies of specific "cultural objects" citing the technical contingent valuation literature are Trine Bille-Hansen, "The Willingness-to-Pay for the Royal Theatre in Copenhagen As a Public Good," *Journal of Cultural Economics* 21, no. 1 (1997): 1–28; and regarding the Musée de la Civilisation in Quebec, Fernand Martin, "Determining the Size of Museum Subsidies," *Journal of Cultural Economics* 18 (1994): 255–70. However, submissions of such studies to the *Journal of Cultural Economics* are growing, and two technical papers were presented at the Eleventh Biennial Conference of the Association for Cultural Economics, International, Minneapolis, Minnesota, May 28–31, 2000: Robert Kling et al., "Estimating the Public Good Value of Preserving a Local Historic Landmark: The Role of Non-substitutability and Information in Contingent Valuation," and Tiziana Cuccia and Giovanni Signorello, "A Contingent Valuation Study of Willingness to Pay for Visiting a City of Art: The Case Study of Noto, Italy."

33. For example, see Carl M. Colonna, "The Economic Contributions of Volunteerism toward the Value of Our Cultural Inventory," *Journal of Cultural Economics* 19 (1995): 341–50.

34. From Byung Hee Soh and Yong Joong Yoon, "Economic Development and Public Support for the Arts and Culture in Korea" (paper presented at the Eleventh Biennial Conference of the Association for Cultural Economics, International, Minneapolis, Minnesota, May 28–31, 2000).

III

Trends and the Arts Sector

10

Comparing Cultural Patronage: Traditions and Trends

Kevin V. Mulcahy

The increasing globalization of economic activities and information technologies has had a profound impact on national cultural policies. Most prominent has been the increasing emphasis placed on the "privatization" of culture as a general principle and acceptance of U.S. management practices emphasizing earned income and philanthropy. Overall, there is an increasing deference within the cultural milieu to the market determination of production costs as well as aesthetic values. Certainly, greater sensitivity on the part of cultural institutions to financial costs and audience preferences is an important corrective to any lingering notion that the arts and culture are exempt from the purview of fiscal as well as public accountability. However, an excessive market triumphalism with its primacy of earned income and popularity can induce a "cultural Darwinism" in which there is a supposed survival of the organizationally and artistically fittest. Of course, this extremist version of U.S. exceptionalism belies the tripartite funding structure of the nonprofit—501(c)(3)—cultural institutions in the United States comprising earned income, philanthropy, and public subsidy. While the precise proportions of each component have been highly debated, the general principle of public responsibility for cultural services has not been questioned except by ideological zealots on the extreme right.

Furthermore, other industrialized democracies have commitments to culture that for a variety of historically and socially conditioned considerations preclude an exclusive reliance on market determinations of the public's cultural conditions. These considerations may involve matters of national prestige and identity, concerns for social egalitarianism and cultural equity, and issues of institution building and cultural representativeness that require a policy in support of public culture that transcends market values and tax incentives. For example, the cultural market may successfully allocate what individuals (as consumers) want in entertainment while failing to reflect the needs of the public (as citizens) in a multicultural society. Understandably, ideologies such as privatization and market determination will be mediated by the political and cultural values inherent in different models of civil society.

This discussion is an essay in comparative cultural policy analysis, that is, an effort to systematically explore the varieties of ways in which cultural affairs are supported in France, Norway, Canada, and the United States. What will be attempted here is a broad overview of the patterns of public support for the arts with reference to (1) administrative structures, (2) funding policies, and (3) cultural politics. Each nation will be discussed as it represents a particular mode of cultural policy making. Of course, any such broad, cross-national survey cannot do justice to the complexities and nuances of each nation's cultural policy. The goal is to provide comparisons that will highlight the different models that these nations employ in cultural administration, financing, and policy making. Essentially, these models are designed as "ideal types" that represent the possibilities available in the construction of a national cultural policy. Underlying much of the discussion herein is the theoretical assumption that a nation's political structures and public policies reflect the historical experiences and value systems that have characterized its societal development. The conceptual framework used here treats a nation's political culture, that is, an orientation toward politics involving general attitudes about the system and specific attitudes about the role of self in the system, as a major explanatory variable.[1] With regard to the variety of institutions and policies that have been created to implement public culture, their organization, mode of support, and aesthetic values reflect the cognitions, feelings, and evaluations of the population. Public cultural policies, then, represent particularly sensitive barometers of macrolevel consensus and conflict.

In sum, the variability in cultural patronage is rooted largely in different sociohistorical traditions, of which it is possible to delineate four ideal types:

1. a *nationalist* public culture that began in the latter part of the seventeenth century as part of the centralizing policies of dynastic states like the Bourbons in France;

2. a *social-democratic* public culture that emerged in the twentieth century in the trade union movements and socialist governments of the Nordic countries and the Netherlands;

3. a *liberal* political culture that created public and quasi-public cultural institutions as part of social and educational reforms in nineteenth- and twentieth-century capitalist societies; and

4. a *libertarian* political culture that is skeptical of sociocultural policies in general, particularly those at the national level, preferring nonprofit cultural institutions and market allocations of cultural goods.

Table 10.1
A Typology of Public Cultures and Systems of Cultural Patronage

Mode of Public Culture	Representative Nations	Models of Cultural Administration	Form of Cultural Funding	Types of Cultural Politics
Nationalist	France	Statist	Subsidies	Hegemony
Social-Democratic	Norway	Localist	Benefits	Redistribution
Liberal	Canada	Consociational	Grants	Sovereignty
Libertarian	United States	Pluralist	Tax Exemptions	Privatization

Among contemporary political systems, it is possible to associate each of the nations discussed here with a dominant mode of political culture while recognizing that different cultures can coexist along with the dominant form and ideal types offer essentially idealized descriptions. Table 10.1 presents a typology of public cultures and the system of cultural patronage associated with each mode and its representative nation.[2]

ADMINISTRATIVE STRUCTURES

As a general rule, the industrialized nations of the world have a recognizable and definable commitment to culture as a matter of public policy. On the other hand, the cultural policies and institutions created to implement public culture differ significantly. "This variety reflects not only differing national traditions in the organization of public functions and the delivery of public services, but differing philosophies and objectives regarding the whole area of culture and the arts."[3] Cultural policies are an expression of national identity and public cultural policies are concerned in various ways with maintaining a distinctive cultural identity. Depending on their cultural heritages, governments vary in the ways in which cultural affairs are administered. For example, a country with a tradition of centralized administration and a highly developed cultural patrimony with an accompanying ideology of art and the state is one model. This can be juxtaposed against an equally idealized cultural marketplace in which private institutions and individual values determine the cultural institutions that are needed without government involvement. Of course, these ideal types are tools for analysis rather than a prescription for a realizable, or desirable, outcome.

Table 10.2 summarizes schematically the four major models of arts administration that have been discussed with reference to two variables: (1) whether the role of the national government in the administration of cultural affairs is

Table 10.2
Models of Cultural Administration in Comparative Perspective

		Role of Central Government	
		Direct	*Indirect*
Nature of Public Culture	*Strong*	France Statist	Canada Consociational
	Weak	Norway Localist	United States Pluralist

either largely direct or indirect; and (2) whether the public culture is weak or strong, that is, the degree to which a self-conscious and articulated policy of governmental responsibility for cultural affairs is present.

In the case of France, state responsibility for culture is a national policy commitment of long-standing. Various regimes—royalist, Jacobin, Napoleonic, republican, as well as Vichy—have been substantial patrons of the arts; and not just the high arts but crafts and the decorative arts as well. While the Ministry of Culture has operated in its present form only since 1958, French cultural patronage actually dates from the creation by Louis XIV of the great French institutions devoted to the performing arts: the Comédie Française, the Opéra, and the Opéra Comique.[4]

Norway has only been an independent nation since the beginning of the twentieth century. As a provincial dependent of Sweden and, earlier, of Denmark, national cultural institutions have only recently developed. Norwegian culture survived locally and it is local governments that are the major providers of cultural services. Also, as a "small language" culture, Norway (like the other Nordic countries and the Netherlands) promotes extensive instruction in English while also encouraging Norwegian-language cultural industries and local arts activities.

Canada, as it emerged from colonial status in the British North American Act of 1867, is constitutionally and administratively a strong federal arrangement; indeed, the extent of the policy-making powers possessed by its provincial governments suggest more a Canadian confederation. In a system designed to accommodate disparate societies, as well as Quebec's "distinct society," strong powers on matters concerning identity (including culture and education) are exercised by the subnational governments. Canada is, in effect, a consociational society, that is, one that must accommodate its national cultural policies to recognize the special status of a large and historically recognized region within its political system.[5]

The United States represents a unique model of cultural policy making with its reliance on pluralism in administration and funding. There is no public agency that approximates a ministry of culture. First, responsibility for public culture is spread among a variety of federal agencies; among these the National Endowment for the Arts (NEA) may be *primus inter pares,* but it is not paramount.[6] Second, in support for the arts, the NEA's efforts are dwarfed by those of state and local arts agencies.[7] Third, and most important, U.S. culture is largely composed of commercial enterprises in film, music, design, theater, and publishing as well as nonprofit cultural industries.[8]

FUNDING POLICIES

Nations fund cultural activities by a variety of mechanisms and for different public policy purposes. In particular, there are three modes that will be examined here. First, and most common, is the direct appropriation of subsidies or grants to underwrite the operations of cultural institutions. Second, there are a growing number of alternative sources of revenue other than the direct appropriations that are increasingly popular as sources of support for culture in the United States. Third, outside of the United States, governments have long provided indirect subsidies to a variety of cultural industries that are judged important for the nation's cultural policy objectives.

The preponderant form of support for the arts in Western Europe and Canada is an appropriation by the government to a public cultural agency (national, regional, or municipal) or a grant to an arts organization (museums, orchestras, opera houses, theaters, or dance companies). Arts organizations are usually public institutions subject to the government's cultural policy although their artistic fare tends to be more independent. While tax incentives for philanthropy often exist, their share of funding remains quite small. Similarly insignificant is earned and commercial-type income.[9] However, most European nations provide significant indirect subsidies to their private cultural industries. Table 10.3 is schematically a summary of the dominant modes of public funding of the arts in France, Norway, Canada, and the United States.

France, with its long tradition of centralized government and a strong national cultural identity, provides an extensive system of subsidies for the arts throughout the country and direct management of national cultural institutions in Paris. France may be the preeminent patron state with its placement of culture as a part of the definition of its national identity.

For Norway, also a generous national provider of cultural financing, culture is more a matter of an individual social right than an element of national prestige. In this sense, broad access to cultural activities is as integral a benefit of the social welfare state as is health care or housing. Cultural affairs are delivered largely on the local level with a strong emphasis on popular participation.

Canada, unlike France and Norway, is a strongly federal system that allocates control over domestic affairs to its provincial or territorial governments. The administration of cultural affairs is an important provincial privilege. The Canadian government, however, does subsidize a number of national museums

Table 10.3
Forms of Arts Funding in Comparative Perspective

Role of National Government			
		Direct	*Indirect*
Nature of Public Culture	*Strong*	France Subsidies	Canada Grants
	Weak	Norway Benefits	United States Tax Exemptions

and historical sites and the Canadian Broadcasting Corporation. Moreover, the Canada Council, modeled on the British Arts Council, is a semiautonomous (arms-length) entity within the Department of Canadian Heritage that makes grants to artists and arts organizations on a competitive basis nationwide.

It is the United States that represents the great exception in the funding of public culture with its extensive reliance on tax exemptions for charitable deductions and on nonprofit, 501(c)(3) organizations. "To a degree unparalleled elsewhere, the nonprofit sector in the United States is enshrined in constitutional law, instrumental in the delivery of many social services, and inextricably bound up with broad social processes of change and governance."[10] Cultural activities in the United States may not be directly as well funded as in other nations, but the government's role is hardly negligible given its provision of tax advantages for the cultural organizations and their contributors.[11] Whether a highly privatized system of subsidy best promotes the public interest in cultural development is another issue.

CULTURAL POLITICS

Table 10.4 summarizes the major cultural policy concerns that engage the four nations compared in this study as these relate to the national government's role and the nature of the public culture that is supported.

French cultural policy has been a long-standing high-profile issue of national debate. Both right and left in France accept the principle of *l'etat culturel* whatever the differences in programmatic emphases. The hegemonic status of French culture, that is, the claim of its language, literature, philosophy, and fine arts to represent a model worthy of emulation, is a widely accepted principle of political discourse. Whether a Malraux in a conservative government or a Lang in a socialist government, ministers of culture have often employed aggressive policies to promote these hegemonic claims such as the *maisons de la culture* at home and the *Alliance Française* abroad. Of course, it is Anglophone culture, particularly U.S. popular culture, that has displaced French preeminence as a

Table 10.4
Types of Cultural Politics in Western Europe and North America

Role of National Government			
		Direct	*Indirect*
Nature of Public Culture	*Strong*	France Hegemony	Canada Sovereignty
	Weak	Norway Redistribution	United States Privatization

cultural hegemon. For many French intellectuals, EuroDisney was not just a theme park, but a "cultural Chernobyl."[12]

French intellectuals frequently position themselves as the last exponents of high culture and artistic taste especially as these are under attack by the popular culture, mass entertainment industry. In particular, it is U.S. popular culture, or as Jack Lang liked to put it in the early 1980s, U.S. "cultural imperialism," that is seen as the enemy of aesthetic excellence.[13] The French government sets a quota of 50 percent for films of French origin; and in 1993 the French government successfully lobbied the European Commission to secure an exemption for cultural products from the General Agreement on Tariffs and Trade on free trade.[14] This was widely interpreted as an effort to defend the French film market from increasing competition from Hollywood; for example, the French share of its film market has fallen from 50 percent to 34 percent while the share for U.S. films rose from 29 percent to 55 percent. The French government also sets a quota to give French songs 40 percent of time devoted to popular music on French airwaves.[15]

What is most notable about Canada's cultural policy and, which may account for the seriousness with which it is engaged in the public arena, is the relationship between cultural identity and political identity. For the Royal Commission on National Development in the Arts, Letters, and Sciences, chaired by Vincent Massey from 1949 to 1951, it was an article of faith that there was an identifiable Canadian culture that would serve as a unifying principle of national identity.[16] For the members of the Massey Commission and its disciples, opposition to U.S. mass culture was the basis of a Canadian cultural identity.[17] As Seymour Martin Lipset states, "Canadians are the world's oldest and most continuing un-Americans."[18] Indeed, many English-Canadian intellectuals mobilized to fight the Canada–U.S. Free Trade Pact because they saw it as a threat to their national culture and distinct Canadian values. However, it may be that an unanticipated consequence of the Massey Commission's emphasis on a distinctive Canadian culture, that is, the creation of a national culture distinct from Britain and the United States, was to encourage artists and intellectuals in Quebec to want to become a "distinct society"—namely, to assert the distinctiveness of their Francophone culture.[19]

This cultural "crisis mentality" has persisted in Canada where 70 percent of radio airtime, 80 percent of magazines sold, 75 percent of prime time television, and 96 percent of movie-screen time are dedicated to foreign (mainly U.S.) products. Shelia Copps, the deputy prime minister and heritage minister, has been particularly outspoken on the subject of U.S. cultural domination. She declared Canada was prepared "to use all the tools in our arsenal to fight the decisions that restrict our capacity to build our own culture."[20] The context of Copps's remarks concerned a World Trade Organization (WTO) ruling on a Canadian tax intended to prevent the proliferation of Canadian editions of U.S. magazines. Also, in recent years the United States and Canada have also clashed over Canadian efforts to ban U.S.–owned broadcast networks from Canadian cable systems, to prevent U.S.–controlled bookstores from expanding into Canada, and to levy a tax on blank audio tapes to raise money to support Canadian performers and producers. In 1998, Canada convened a meeting of nineteen ministers of culture (and pointedly not inviting U.S. representatives to participate) to discuss measures that could be taken to protect their national cultures from the escalating threat from Hollywood and the U.S. popular entertainment industry.[21]

In Norway, cultural politics takes a different form than the other nations considered here. With a small, homogenous, affluent population, a common cultural heritage, and a strong social-democratic ideology, debates about public culture concern the scope of state intervention and the best mode of implementation. There are no emotional debates about cultural imperialism nor is there a cultural region with claims to autonomy as a distinct society. Norwegian governments in the post–World War II era have accepted responsibility for public culture as a logical extension of the welfare state. "The welfare ideology implied that 'cultural goods' should be fairly distributed throughout the country, and that the population should have extended influence upon decisions affecting the cultural life of its own community."[22] The welfare principle also applies to the artists' right to economic security and recognizes that cultural activities—the crafts as well as the fine arts—are "a national resource for social and economic development."[23] Having largely decentralized cultural administration to the municipal level, the questions have been how best to realize a socially oriented cultural policy.

In the United States, the political controversy involving the NEA and its support for exhibits of photography by Robert Mapplethorpe and Andres Serrano called into question the fundamental assumptions underlying public support for a national-level commitment to culture. The degree of public scrutiny far surpassed the magnitude of the public expenditure involved and the rarity of controversial grants from among the totality of those that have been awarded. What should have been a political side show that the NEA could have routinely survived developed into a "kulturkampf," that is, a struggle over the legitimacy of public support for the arts and the NEA as a public arts agency.[24] Unfortunately, many members of the cultural community were content to dismiss criticisms of the NEA as simply atavistic. However, the range, intensity, and impact of such criticism has been too great to be dismissed as solely a delusion of the ideological fringes. In the minds of many moderate citizens and their elected representatives, the NEA became labeled as one of the nation's promoters of pornography. In fact, an underlying issue with many controversial grants has been the absence of an accepted public purpose in the NEA's grant-making decisions.[25]

THE STATE OF PUBLIC CULTURE

It is difficult to offer even the most tentative generalizations about comparative public policy making. Cultural policies are peculiarly enmeshed within national histories and political cultures. However, it does seem possible to outline certain broad developments that generally characterize the state of public support for the arts in the four nations of this study and that suggest the structural arrangements, funding policies, and policy debates of the foreseeable future. To begin, there are certain observations that can be made concerning the prospects that increasing privatization and market economics present for public culture and cultural policy making.

First, there is a seemingly inexorable demand that the arts "carry their own weight" rather than rely on a public subsidy to pursue art for art's sake. This "cultural Darwinism" is most pronounced in the United States where public subsidy is limited and publicly supported arts are expected to demonstrate a public benefit. Most cultural institutions outside of the United States are less constrained by the need to maintain diversified revenue streams that include ticket sales and individual and corporate donations as well as government funding. However, all cultural institutions are increasingly market driven in their need for supplementary funds and a source of justification. European and Canadian cultural institutions are actively seeking alternative revenue streams such as corporate sponsorships and increasingly looking to the U.S. model of mixed funding for guidelines.

For example, there is a strong movement throughout Europe to privatize the governing structures of the mostly state-run high-culture institutions and reconstitute state museums, theaters, and orchestras as nonprofit organizations along the U.S. lines. High-cultural institutions are increasingly counseled to put more emphasis on the management and marketing aspects of their operations such as fund-raising, corporate sponsorship, and extended gift shop and restaurant operations. The market-based approach to financing the arts is strengthened as municipalities shift from the traditional practice of deficit subsidization to giving state cultural organizations fixed budgets on which to operate. "This development is both recent and remarkable, as it represents a reversal of the traditional preferential treatment for high culture."[26]

Second, while there is much to recommend the U.S. model of mixed funding and nonprofit cultural institutions, it must be remembered that a predominantly privatized cultural sphere is less disposed to address questions of aesthetic diversity, public accessibility, and cultural representativeness. The corporate sector may be concerned about distributional equity in its investment in cultural products; but it is, at root, market driven and necessarily concerned with profitability.[27] In a system of mixed funding, the public cultural sector can support activities that are important aspects of individual self-worth and community definition even if not competitive in the marketplace. In effect, public cultural agencies can offer the means for achieving greater "cultural equity," that is, the right of every citizen to participate in some form of cultural activity and to experience the diversity of a nation's cultural heritage regardless of socioeconomic condition or geographic location.[28] The real issue is not whether a public cultural agency should exist, but what constitutes the public interest in a funding triad composed of individual and institutional philanthropy, earned income, and government funding. Whatever the role a government chooses to play in cultural patronage, its administrative structures, funding mechanisms, and political values will be conditioned by its historical development and political culture.

Third, there appears to be a clear movement toward the decentralization of government support for cultural affairs. In federal systems, such as Canada, this is a long-standing administrative practice; in the Canadian case, the provinces, led by Quebec, have long asserted virtual autonomy in matters of local government including education and culture. Even France, a model of the centralized state since the seventeenth century, has pursued a strong policy of cultural decentralization over the past fifteen years. It is French municipal governments, not the Ministry of Culture, that administer the largest share of the cultural budget. In the United States, where support for culture has traditionally been a community initiative, state and local governments are assuming even greater responsibility for cultural affairs as the presence of the national government has diminished in both funding and policy direction.

Fourth, the increasing importance of local administration and funding of cultural activities is paralleled by the increasing salience of particularistic cultural concerns. This may be a reflection of the political nationalism of cultural regions or of nation-states facing a challenge to their cultural hegemony. Usually, these particularistic concerns are manifested in policies promoting cultural protectionism. For a cultural leader like France, cultural protectionism often takes the form of a ritualized opposition to U.S. cultural imperialism. For the French, the fear is less of the penetration of their culture by U.S. popular culture (although that is a frequent complaint among some French intellectuals) than of the displacement of *la civilisation française* as a viable alternative to the U.S. model of social and cultural organization. For Canadians, proximity to the United States presents a pervasive reminder of the U.S. omnipresence in television, film, books, magazines, and popular music. Exacerbating the question of how to maintain a cultural identity in the shadow of the United States is the issue of how to construct a Canadian national culture that can accommodate

Francophone Quebec, as well as the First Peoples, within a multicultural framework. Quebec (like Catalonia and Scotland) has made cultural survival through regional autonomy a major issue in national politics.[29]

Fifth, it may be that one of the valuational contradictions of globalization is that the integration of commerce and technologies is not paralleled by political and cultural integration. Political devolution and cultural protectionism (as noted in Scotland, Catalonia, and Quebec) coexist with advanced capitalist economies. Indeed, it appears that issues of national identity and cultural nationalism are a form of compensation for the perceived diminution of political sovereignty and aesthetic distinctiveness associated with cultural globalization. Some of this ambivalence about globalization has been vented with vandalism directed at McDonald's and Starbucks. More significantly, there has been a growing emphasis on language, heritage, and regionalism within the West European nations and Canada.[30] In essence, the hegemonic aspects of globalization are mitigated by the growing importance of the cultural dimension in public policy making. As the globalized economy produces the goods and services of the marketplace, the public cultural sphere shapes the context and contours of a nation's identity.

Last, the hegemony of U.S. popular culture, the Internet, and the English language has created a dualism concerning cultural globalization. Most vocal has been the cry for cultural protectionism against the onslaught of U.S. cultural imperialism and the defense of a certain *terroir de la culture* that maintains the same sacred and site-specific character of culture as with cuisine. Resistance to the "McDomination" of the arts and culture has been highly pronounced in Canada (from proximity) and France (from competitiveness), but the protection of domestic cultural products is a staple policy in many nations (including those with which the United States enjoys free trade). Advocates of cultural laissez-faire denigrate the empirical foundations of protectionism particularizing the advantages gained in broader choice and lower cost from cultural free trade. On the one hand, the implied assumption is that, inevitably, U.S. popular culture is becoming everyone's second culture and should be accommodated. On the other hand, this may be too sanguine an assumption about the ability of local traditions to survive as the main source of everyone's identity in a globalized cultural market. Certainly, the opposition to the WTO (as well as McDonald's and Starbucks) is as much cultural as economic.

With the globalization of communications, most nations have little choice but to accept some of the consequences of being in a sphere of U.S. cultural influence. The alternative to further "cultural colonization" is probably not a futile attempt at "cultural isolationism," but the adoption of a form of "cultural syncretism." This middle way accepts the realities of U.S. sovereignty in popular cultural products while promoting the high-cultural sphere through expanded public subventions and subsidies.[31] It may be that enhanced support by the public sector will help a nation to sustain a cultural milieu reflecting its own history and values while coexisting with the United States' monopoly of entertainment commodities. Cultural syncretism would enable nations to move from a position of cultural complaint, which reacts defensively to the ubiquity of U.S. popular culture, to a more positive and self-assured national culture that is distinctive without being parochial or particularistic. In sum, a policy of cultural syncretism might serve as a means for nations threatened by cultural globalization to retain their heritage and identity without retreating into dependency or autarchy.

NOTES

Thanks to Brad Seal, my student worker, for his unstinting editorial assistance and in the preparation of this chapter.

1. Gabriel A. Almond and Sidney Verba, *The Civic Culture: Political Attitudes and Democracy in Five Nations* (Boston: Little, Brown, 1965), 15.

2. See Kevin V. Mulcahy, "The Government and Cultural Patronage: A Comparative Analysis of Cultural Patronage in Canada, Norway, France and the United States," in *The Public Life of the Arts in America,* ed. Joni M. Cherbo and Margaret J. Wyszomirski (New Brunswick, NJ: Rutgers University Press, 2000), 138–68.

3. Milton C. Cummings Jr. and Richard S. Katz, eds, *The Patron State: Government and Arts in Europe, North American, and Japan* (New York: Oxford University Press, 1987), 4.

4. Frederick Dorian, *Commitment to Culture* (Pittsburgh: University of Pittsburgh Press, 1964), 135.

5. Arend Lijphart, *Democracy in Plural Societies* (New Haven, NJ: Yale University Press, 1977).

6. Joni M. Cherbo, "A Department of Cultural Resources: A Perspective on the Arts," *Journal of Arts Management, Law, and Society* 22 (winter 1992): 44–62.; Margaret J. Wyszomirski and Kevin V. Mulcahy, "The Organization for Public Support for the Arts," in *America's Commitment to Culture: Government and the Arts in the United States,* ed. Kevin V. Mulcahy and Margaret J. Wyszomirski (Boulder, CO: Westview, 1995), 121–43.

7. Kevin V. Mulcahy, "Cultural Patronage in the United States," *International Journal of Arts Management* 2 (fall 1999): 53–58.

8. Dick Netzer, "Arts and Culture," in *Who Benefits from the Private Sector?,* ed. Charles T. Clotfelter (Chicago: University of Chicago Press, 1992), 174–75; see also James Heilbrun and Charles Gray, *The Economics of Art and Culture: An American Perspective* (New York: Cambridge University Press, 1993).

9. Annette Zimmer and Stefan Toepler, "Cultural Policies and the Welfare State: The Cases of Sweden, Germany, and the United States," *Journal of Arts Management, Law, and Society* 26 (fall 1996): 167–93.

10. Charles T. Clotfelter, "The Distributional Consequences of Nonprofit Activities," introduction to *Who Benefits from the Private Sector?,* ed. Charles T. Clotfelter (Chicago: University of Chicago Press, 1992), 1.

11. Kevin V. Mulcahy, "The Abused Patron of Culture: Public Culture and Cultural Patronage in the United States," *Boekmancahier* 44 (June 2000): 169–81.

12. For a contrary argument to the "Chernobyl-sur-Marne" thesis, see Andrew Lainsbury, *Once upon an American Dream: The Story of EuroDisneyland* (Lawrence: University of Kansas Press, 2000).

13. Robert Gildea, *France since 1945* (New York: University of Oxford Press, 1996), 158; see also René Remond, *Nôtre Siecle de 1918 à 1991* (Paris: Fayard, 1991).

14. Gildea, *France since 1945*, 159.

15. Ibid., 163. For a detailed study of French cultural policy making, see David Loosley, *The Politics of Fun: Cultural Policy and Debate in Contemporary France* (Oxford: Berg, 1995); Jacques Perret and Guy Saez, *Institutions et Vie Culturelles* (Paris: La Documentation Francaise, 1996).

16. Paul Litt, *The Muses, the Masses, and the Massey Commission* (Toronto: University of Toronto Press, 1992), 3–7; see also Kevin V. Mulcahy, review of *The Muses, the Masses, and the Massey Commission*, by Paul Litt, *Governance* 7 (winter 1994): 102–3.

17. John Meisel, "Government and the Arts in Canada," in *Who's to Pay for the Arts*, ed. Milton C. Cummings Jr. and J. Mark Davidson Schuster (New York: American Council for the Arts, 1989), 82–83; John Meisel and Jean Van Loon, "Cultivating the Bushgarden: Cultural Policy in Canada," in *The Patron State: Government and Arts in Europe, North American, and Japan*, ed. Milton C. Cummings Jr. and Richard S. Katz (New York: Oxford University Press, 1987), 276–310; see also John Meisel, "Extinction Revisited: Culture and Class in Canada," in *Seeing Ourselves: Media Power and Policy in Canada*, ed. Helen Holmes and David Taras, 2nd ed. (Toronto: Harcourt Brace, 1996), 249–56.

18. Seymour Martin Lipset, *Continental Divide: The Values and Institutions of the United States and Canada* (New York: Routledge, 1990), 53; see also Allan Smith, *Canada—An American Nation? Essays on Continentalism, Identity, and the Canadian Frame of Mind* (Montreal: McGill-Queen's University Press, 1994).

19. Kevin V. Mulcahy, "Public Culture and Political Culture," in *Quebec under Free Trade: Making Public Policy in America*, ed. Guy Lachapelle (Sainte-Foy, Quebec: Presses de l'Université du Quebec, 1995).

20. *Los Angeles Times*, 18 February 1997. For a discussion that opposes the "cultural protectionist" view, see Keith Acheson and Christopher Maule, *Much Ado about Culture: North American Trade Disputes* (Ann Arbor: University of Michigan Press, 1999).

21. *New York Times*, 1 July 1998; see also Emile G. McAnany and Kenton T. Wilkinson, eds., *Mass Media and Free Trade: NAFTA and Cultural Industries* (Austin: University of Texas Press, 1996).

22. Per Mangset, "Risks and Benefits of Decentralisation: The Development of Local Cultural Administration in Norway," *International Journal of Cultural Policy* 2, no. 2 (1995): 67–86.

23. Anita Kangas and Jill Onsér-Franzén, "Is There a Need for a New Cultural Policy Strategy in the Nordic Welfare State?," *International Journal of Cultural Policy* 3, no. 1 (1996): 15–26.

24. Margaret Jane Wyszomirski, "From Accord to Discord: Arts Policy during and after the Culture Wars," in *America's Commitment to Culture: Government and the*

Arts in the United States, ed. Kevin V. Mulcahy and Margaret J. Wyszomirski (Boulder, CO: Westview, 1995), 1–48.

25. Kevin V Mulcahy, "The Public Interest in Public Culture," *Journal of Arts Management and Law* 21 (spring, 1991): 5–27.

26. Zimmer and Toepler, "Cultural Policies and the Welfare State," 189.

27. George Yudice, "Civil Society, Consumption, and Govermentality in an Age of Global Restructuring," *Social Text* 45 (1995): 1–26.

28. Kevin V. Mulcahy, "The Public Interest in Arts Policy," in *America's Commitment to Culture: Government and the Arts in the United States,* ed. Kevin V. Mulcahy and Margaret J. Wyszomirski (Boulder, CO: Westview, 1995), 205–28.

29. Kevin V. Mulcahy, "Public Culture and Political Culture: La Politique Culturelle du Quebec," *Journal of Arts Management, Law, and Society* 25 (fall 1995): 225–49.

30. "Although Europe has largely been moving in the direction of removing national boundaries, local cultures and languages have been reasserting their strength. Historians say that more people appear to be interested in protecting minority languages and asserting local differences than at any other time in the last 100 years." See Dan Barry, "Gaelic Comes Back on Ireland's Byways and Airwaves," *New York Times,* 25 July 2000.

31. For a discussion of cultural syncretism with reference to Canada, see Kevin V. Mulcahy, "Cultural Imperialism and Cultural Sovereignty: US–Canadian Cultural Relations," *American Review of Canadian Studies* 30, no. 2 (2000): 181–206.

11

Pandora's Bottle:
Cultural Content in a Digital World

Andrew Taylor

Something there is that doesn't love a wall, That wants it down.

—Robert Frost

For the past several centuries, formalized culture has been built on the concept of containment. While the drives of creation, composition, inspiration, and insight have always been the *source* of cultural content, it has been the "containers" that convey these drives that we recognize as art. The live theater performance, the printed novel, the sculpture, the painted canvas, the dance, and the audio recording are all such containers—the actions and artifacts that carry the creative impulse into the physical world. The venues where these artifacts and actions exist—theaters, arts centers, museums, community centers, and festivals—are also containers, providing the context for cultural experience.

If there is a central impact of digital communications and computer technology on traditional arts and culture, it is this: Digital information technology doesn't love a wall, it wants it down. The containers we have used to define and distribute cultural content are becoming soft and permeable. For good or ill, that changes everything.

In his insightful 1999 article for *Wired* magazine, John Perry Barlow outlines the implications of this truth for patent and copyright law: "Thus, the rights of invention and authorship adhered to activities in the physical world. One didn't get paid for ideas, but for the ability to deliver them into reality. For all practical purposes, the value was in the conveyance and not in the thought conveyed. In other words, the bottle was protected, not the wine."[1] Barlow goes on to suggest that the framework is being stretched to the limit: "This vessel, the accumulated canon of copyright and patent law, was developed to convey forms and methods of expression entirely different from the vaporous cargo it is now being asked to carry. It is leaking as much from within as from without."[2]

While copyright remains a core issue for arts and culture, this new truth of digital information has broad implications outside the legal arena as well. All other controls secured by the containment of cultural product—on a canvas, in a concert hall, or on a compact disc (CD)—are suddenly challenged. Creative control by the author or artist, the carefully crafted stewardship of great works by arts organizations, the context of a cultural work torn from its intended means of conveyance, the cultural integrity of ritual or celebratory expression, and the financial transactions such containment allow (event tickets, retail book sales, organization- or discipline-specific philanthropy, and so on) are all issues that lose their foothold in the information age.

Of course, these same challenges also provide outstanding opportunities to dissolve the less constructive barriers around arts and culture. Barriers of access—whether geographic, economic, physical, or educational—can be greatly reduced through digital information exchange. Works of art formerly available only to visitors of the Louvre are now available to the entire connected world (at least, digitized representations of the art are available, but more on this later). Educational materials supporting cultural understanding are available on-line to anyone, thereby breaking the limits of physical document distribution.

Access barriers to the artists themselves have also begun to dissolve. What once was a connection twice or thrice removed between creator, commissioner, presenter, and audience is now often short-circuited, as in the direct e-mail interaction between middle school students and professional composers in Vermont's public school Millennium Project.[3]

Access barriers to artists distributing their work have also become much lower. The intense filtering process of the U.S. music industry, for example, involving a gauntlet of record producers, artist representatives, record company executives, marketing directors, and broadcast and retail distributors, can now be completely bypassed by posting a high-quality digital recording directly to any of a number of public Web sites.

Information technology is also bridging the barriers to creative collaboration between artists, revitalizing traditional art forms, and creating entirely new ones. The Gertrude Stein Repertory Theatre, for example, is blending theatrical art forms such as Chinese opera and modern theater with cutting-edge information technology through its "UBU" project. The project was not only developed through long-distance collaborations, but also performed live by an international cast in the United States, Japan, and Russia.[4]

Furthermore, the combination of communications technology and cultural content can be a powerful tool in bridging the "digital divide" between society's technology "haves" and "have nots," as evidenced in a recent on-line forum of the Benton Foundation.[5]

To be sure, the evaporation of traditional barriers to cultural experience brings a wealth of positive opportunities. But on the cusp of this rapidly opening worldview, it is essential for arts creators, presenters, curators, researchers, and archivists to understand both what is gained and lost in the transition.

BARRIERS LOST: AN OVERVIEW

The idea that digital and electronic communications technologies dissolve barriers on many levels has become a common assertion. However, the roots of that power are well worth exploring. In his study of the effect of communications technology on social structure, Ithiel de Sola Pool outlines five aspects of electronic communications that are likely to change society as much as the printing press did five centuries ago:

1. Distance is ceasing to be a barrier to communication. As a result, the spatial organization of human activity will profoundly change.

2. Speech, text, and pictures are being represented and sent by the same kind of electrical impulses, a common digital stream. Separation of these modes is diminishing.

3. In this "information society," a greatly expanded proportion of all work as well as leisure is being spent on communication. Information handling is a growing portion of all human activity.

4. Computing and communication are becoming one, which is to say that communicating and reasoning are being reunited. With messages converted into electronic bits, they may be not only electronically transmitted, but also manipulated by logical devices and transformed.

5. The mass media revolution is being reversed; instead of identical messages being disseminated to millions of people, electronic technology permits the adaptation of electronic messages to the specialized or unique needs of individuals.[6]

For the purposes of this discussion, items one and two in de Sola Pool's list strike closest to the issue. First, electronic communications technology eliminates the impact of distance on interaction—ten yards or ten thousand miles make no difference in the cost or quality of electronic data transfer. And, second, the emergence of a single format for the transfer of information (speech, text, still images, and moving images) has created a new container that consolidates the fractured storage and distribution mechanisms of the past. As Barlow states: "With the advent of digitization, it is now possible to replace all previous information storage forms with one metabottle: complex and highly liquid patterns of ones and zeros."[7] These two points impact our traditional conceptions of arts and culture in many ways. Most importantly, as the opening paragraph of this chapter suggests, they challenge the traditional "containers" of cultural content.

CONTAINMENT AND CONTROL

> At a time like ours, in which mechanical skill has attained unsuspected per-
> fection, the most famous works may be heard as easily as one may drink a
> glass of beer, and it only costs ten centimes, like the automatic weighing
> machines. Should we not fear this domestication of sound, this magic that
> anyone can bring from a disk at his will? Will it not bring to waste the
> mysterious force of an art which one might have thought indestructible?
> —Claude Debussy, 1913[8]

We can view cultural content as being contained in two primary ways: within a physical space and time, and by its means of conveyance. Put more simply, to experience art and culture you traditionally "had to be there" (in the theater, at the museum, or in the jazz club), and you often needed people or decoding devices to bring the experience into being (the orchestra translating and interpreting musical notation into sound, the actors invoking the playwright's script, the dancers enacting the choreographer's instructions, the printing press manufacturing the bound novel, the compact disc player converting a digital bitstream into analog sound waves). Visual art and physical artifacts are notable exceptions to the need for decoders or mediators, but the need to "be there" is arguably stronger.

Over the past century, audio recordings, high-volume color printing technology, broadcast radio, and television have provided alternatives (not direct replacements) to "being there." But fidelity and immediacy limited their impact on live attendance. In addition, most of these new technologies (except for print) added another decoding scheme to the mix. To hear a phonograph, you needed a phonograph player (78 rpm, 45 rpm, or 33 rpm, and so on). To listen to broadcast radio, you needed a different device, or at least a device that contained a radio receiver component. While these reproductions shattered the time and space limitations of cultural content, they replaced that loss with new containers of physical product and information encoding.

Because each advancement in reproduction technology usually carried the requirement of a new and often incompatible decoding device, some level of content and access control was still feasible and, more importantly, still profitable. Phonographs, cassettes, compact discs, video cassettes, printed posters, and books were all fixed, physical products that could be counted and sold. Radio broadcasts of copyrighted materials, because centralized to licensed broadcast stations, could be regulated and charged for use of creative content (not with perfection, to be sure, but with some estimate of actual use). While these technologies were the first baby steps into the electronic age, they still fit fairly neatly into copyright law since they were physical manifestations of creative content. They were the bottle, not the wine. But as Debussy's quote shows, even these first steps challenged the traditional containers of cultural production. The quote suggests that, from Debussy's perspective, recordings of live performances disconnected the music from its intended context of time and place, cheapening it both literally (10 centimes) and philosophically (bringing to waste "the mysterious force"). Quality of reproduction was not a key issue in 1913. The separation of content and context, and the breach of the intended container were perceived as the true enemies of the art.

While recording and distribution technology were taking their first steps, advances in transportation technology and growth in personal income reduced the cost and effort barriers to actually "being there." But again, the container of the physical space allowed for careful control of content and context, as well as the means for a financial transaction. Arts consultant Steven A. Wolff often refers to the collection of live arts, entertainment, cultural, and sports activities as "gated events," recognizing the importance of the gate to the process and product of cultural consumption.[9]

In a world of high-bandwidth, high-fidelity digital information exchange, however, the traditional gates of physical walls, fixed time, physical distance, and multiple decoding technologies become locked doors in an open field. Imagine Debussy's reaction to a digital-quality, disconnected orchestral phrase used as a freely downloaded start-up sound to a desktop computer.

MP3, NAPSTER, AND THE FREEDOM OF IDEAS

> That ideas should freely spread from one to another over the globe, for the moral and mutual instruction of man, and improvement of his condition, seems to have been peculiarly and benevolently designed by nature, when she made them, like fire, expansible over all space, without lessening their density at any point, and like the air in which we breathe, move, and have our physical being, incapable of confinement or exclusive appropriation. Inventions then cannot, in nature, be a subject of property.
>
> —Thomas Jefferson[10]

> Before Napster came about, people thought MP3s in themselves were a problem.... But Napster, it's the most insidious application that I've ever seen.
>
> —Marc Geiger, chairman and chief executive officer, ArtistDirect[11]

Minor breaches of the containers of cultural product have occurred throughout recent history, most notably in the piracy of audio and video recordings. But the world caught its first real glimpse of a containerless environment in late 1999 and early 2000. The litigation storm surrounding Napster and the audio file format MP3 could become known as the first salvo in this war about walls.

MP3 (or more specifically, ISO-MPEG Audio Layer-3) is a protocol for compressing digital audio content to reduce its file size while maintaining its fidelity. The MP3 format strikes a favorable balance between high audio quality and small file size, thereby enabling a new class of audio devices and a growing trend in storing libraries of audio content on personal computers.

Napster, a software program made available for free on the Internet, allowed anyone to share MP3 files with any other Napster user worldwide. If a user ran the program and transferred a favorite compact disc onto his or her computer hard drive, any other Napster user could then search for and access those sound files from anywhere in the world.

To use our earlier terms, MP3 is part of the "metabottle" that can contain all previous storage formats (in this case, circumventing the compact disc), and Napster is the shared community space where distance is irrelevant.

When the combination was used to share materials with the copyright owner's consent, the system achieved the noble and open-community ideals of Jefferson's quote. When unauthorized copyrighted materials found their way onto the system (which they did immediately), copyright holders became concerned.

In December 1999, only months after Napster's first public tests, the Recording Industry Association of America filed suit against the program's developer for contributory copyright infringement.[12] By January 2000, major universities were banning the program from their networks since active use by students was clogging digital traffic.[13] By May 2000, under legal pressure from the rock band Metallica, Napster banned more than 317,000 users accused of trafficking Metallica's copyrighted music.[14] Since the company, by law, could not attach personal information to its members' usernames, most of those banned could have quickly signed on again as new members.

Napster defended its software by saying that it simply provided a means for a community to share with each other. No music files sat on the company's computers, nor did they pass through the company's network when transferring from one user to another. (Music files were stored and retrieved from the individual user's personal computer. Napster simply provided the index.)

Furthermore, since Napster dissolved political boundaries, it was unclear which country had jurisdiction to prosecute which software users. For example, if a user in Sweden downloaded a copyrighted music file from a user in Egypt, without ever passing data over U.S. soil, whose crime was it anyway?

In the case of Napster, an appeals court ruling in February 2001 and a cascade of negative rulings thereafter led to the sudden attrition of the service and the threat. But while Napster—the company—flounders to reinvent itself, Napster—the archetype—continues to raise profound issues for the field. With or without Napster, the challenge of containing digital content will become exponentially greater as more sophisticated and less centralized file sharing programs become available, and as more acts and images of cultural creation find their way into digital format.

In early 2000, for example, a twenty-one-year-old employee of America Online developed a new version of the Napster concept, called Gnutella, that removed all centralized indexing or processing from the mix. As the *Washington Post* described it: "Both the beauty and danger of Gnutella are that it is a more sophisticated version of Napster.... [U]nlike users of Napster, Gnutella aficionados can trade files without going through a storage center, making it impossible to shut down the system without unplugging every computer on the network and difficult to control by laws because there's no central authority."[15] Compounding the issue is the fact that the owners of compact discs or other recorded media have rights, too. Under the doctrine of "fair use," there are legitimate and legal uses of copyrighted materials, including quotes in a book review, musical parody, and copies for personal, noncommercial use (e.g., a tape of a CD you own for use in your car). The new wrinkle of digital technology is that the copy is just as good as the original. In fact, in many ways, it *is* the original.

WHAT ABOUT THE REST OF US?

> I think in a broader cultural sense, the creation of content has become more interesting than the content itself.
> —Michael Hirschorn, cofounder, Inside.com[16]

The case of MP3, Napster, and Gnutella has clear implications for the recorded music industry and other purveyors of "soft content" (computer software vendors, video distributors, filmmakers, authors, and so on). In fact, Gnutella makes no distinction about the format of files it exchanges—it could be an MP3 file, a software program, a movie, or a high-resolution impressionist image. But how does the story relate back to the traditional containers of cultural content mentioned at the opening of this chapter—the live theater performance, the sculpture, the painted canvas, and the dance? How, also, does it challenge the physical venues of cultural presentation?

Part of the answer is that more individuals experience cultural content through broadcast and recorded media than by attending live events. The National Endowment for the Arts' (NEA) *1997 Survey of Public Participation in the Arts* showed participation rates via these media for jazz, classical music, and opera were more than twice the rates for live events.[17] But these statistics were not limited to musical performances. The NEA notes: "Viewing presentations about the visual arts such as programs on museum exhibitions on television or video was the most popular activity among American adults, with 45% reporting they had watched visual arts programs during the previous 12 months. Although dance and visual art were seen primarily via television, the other art forms attracted large numbers of listeners on radio and recordings."[18] To the extent that audience contact with cultural content is already experienced through electronic media, all content providers face the same challenges as the recording industry, especially as the fidelity and clarity of digital reproduction improve.

Beyond that obvious fact, however, there are other direct implications for live attendance at cultural presentations or physical attendance at visual art exhibitions. Most striking is the redefinition of what unique services cultural organizations provide to their audiences.

PRODUCT REDEFINED

In the world of cultural containers, mere access to content was considered the service. To experience a musical performance, for example, you either had to be there or you had to purchase the right to hear how it sounded. In a digital age, this access is available in increasing quality at diminishing or zero cost. The same could be said for visual art, as digital imaging technology and reproduction continue their astounding progress. Debussy's concern about the "domestication of sound" is a thriving reality for many expressions of creative thought (which many would claim as a positive revolution). As a result, many cultural organizations find themselves in search of a service not co-opted by electronic media.

Of course, there is a thousand-pound gorilla in this discussion that has been sidestepped until now: A digitized reproduction of a performance or a tangible cultural product *is not the same* as the product itself. It would be foolish to suggest that watching a theatrical production on a television or computer monitor, even at the highest resolution, would be the same as experiencing it in a theater as part of an audience.[19] Yet, it would also be foolish to suggest that the reproduction does not capture essential elements of its source. A viewer of the digitized theater piece still hears the dialog, sees the actors, and experiences the arc of the dramatic line. But the result is obviously a different experience than a live attendance. Therein lies the point.

The elements of live attendance that are missing from the media experience—immediacy, immersion, fresh invention, physicality, ritual, social interaction, and so on—suggest a refined or redefined mission for arts and culture providers. As high-quality content becomes a decreasing component of the perceived unique value, the *context* of the experience becomes a defining element of consumption. Arts presenters and curators, therefore, move from being straight *content providers* to *context providers*, managing not only the art form itself, but the environment and experience surrounding it.

Experience management is not a new concept for arts and culture providers. The Guthrie Theater in Minneapolis, for example, has a history of attention to environmental detail. From intensive training for ushers and front-of-house staff, to the trumpet fanfare announcing theater seating, to the synchronized closing of the theater's lobby doors at the beginning of a performance, the Guthrie clearly perceives its product as extending beyond the rise of the curtain.[20] More recently, the Minnesota Opera discovered through focus groups that audiences perceived the performance as only a component of their opera experience. Social activity, a night out, the sense of place in the hall and lobby, and even a sense of tradition were also integral to the purchase decision.[21]

Other organizations are more aggressively employing environment as a part of their artistic palette. London's Bubble Theatre Company, for example, is experimenting with "promenade performance" as a means to increase the intimacy between artist and audience. Using outdoor venues like parks, woods, and green spaces, Bubble Theatre presents performances where artists and audiences move through the environment. Early focus groups reinforced the impact of this integration. "[A]udiences value the promenade experience, not only as a theatrical, but also as a communal experience," writes Artistic Director Jonathan Petherbridge. "Focus groups talked enthusiastically and in detail about the audience, and the environment as part of the experience."[22]

The dynamics of the emerging "experience economy" only reinforce these implications. The growing category of experiential retail and restaurants (e.g., Nike Town, American Girl Place, and Rain Forest Cafe) expose a trend in for-profit organizations to rethink the bundle of goods and services they provide consumers and the environment in which they provide them.[23]

B. Joseph Pine II and James H. Gilmore suggest that "you are what you charge for," implying that a true experience provider does not charge for products within an environment, but charges for the right to enter that environment.[24] Couple this suggestion with Barlow's earlier quote about copyright law ("For all practical purposes, the value was in the conveyance and not in the thought conveyed"), and we may be closer to a redefined sense of place for arts and culture providers in the digital age.

In a world where traditionally contained cultural content becomes as fluid as thought, the broader conveyance of this content becomes the means to recapture value and creative control. In other words, the straight content of a performance or artifact may be the defining factor of a cultural arts attendance, but it is the broader experience surrounding that content that provides much of the unique value of the experience.

CONVEYANCE AND ACCESS

For artists and arts organizations, redefining the nature of cultural product can be an exercise filled with apprehension. If we aren't in the business of art, what business are we in? If we seek to serve anything else, do we risk compromising or bringing to waste "the mysterious force of an art which one might have thought indestructible"?

Clearly, the process and product of artistic creation and achievement must remain the core values of any discussion. Without them, there is no distinction between art, culture, and commerce. However, without exploring the boundaries of that process and product, and the places at which individuals and groups connect to it, we would be ignoring the factors that help arts and culture thrive.

A 1998 study sponsored by the Heinz Endowments and the Pew Charitable Trusts sought to explore these issues, specifically focusing on "how members of the community related to the arts generally" and "how and whether they connected with it as a personal enterprise."[25] Using a highly intensive, nonverbal, and image-based process (the Zaltman Metaphor Elicitation Technique [ZMET]), the study explored the mental images and relationships individuals associated with cultural activity. Among other things, the study developed four "thematic metaphors," or underlying themes, that were common among participants.

1. The Arts As Transporter: Participants in the study viewed the arts as a way of acutely experiencing time and space—as the report puts it, "living in the moment and stepping away from daily reality."

2. The Arts As Redeemer: Participants in the study described the arts as providing a means of recapturing—however temporarily—a lost or unrealized potential, such as to be a singer, an artist, or an actor. "The arts are, in large part, about retrieving lost, buried, untapped desires and impulses and indulging them in safe, bounded places for temporary amounts of time."

3. The Arts As Appropriator: Through this theme, participants described the ability of the arts to strip away layers of socialization and thus to carry them back to a more "pure" and "innocent" stage of development, namely childhood, when it was easier to shift from reality to fantasy. "Ironically," the report finds, "while the arts seem to speak to the child within, they also help [participants] evolve themselves toward some higher state of being: becoming more mature, more confident."

4. The Arts As Intermediary: Participants in the study viewed the arts as aggrandizing them by giving them the ability to see the world and themselves somewhat differently—they valued its power as a lens to give them a new perspective. They also appreciated how the arts "humanize and personalize the complexities of the world by putting a face on abstract issues."[26]

Clearly, many of these thematic metaphors derive from the experience of cultural content, rather than solely from the content itself. Also, the results suggest that ticket buyers are purchasing more than merely the access rights to a performance or exhibition. Finally, these thematic metaphors allow a different perspective on the "product" of arts and cultural organizations and suggest how they can differentiate content experienced via information media and content experienced in person.

This chapter suggests two framing statements to help explore further the function and boundaries of arts and cultural organizations in an increasingly digital world:

The product of arts and cultural organizations is not cultural content in itself, but the conveyance of cultural content.

The transactions supporting that product take place at the myriad gates of access (physical and otherwise) created in the process.

The distinction in the first statement may seem overly semantic, but it seeks to define a fundamental difference. "Cultural content" is what's on stage in the theater, what's on the wall of the gallery, what's encoded onto a CD—the traditional containers we have come to call art. "Conveyance" encompasses that content, but also the environment and medium in which it is experienced.

The second statement seeks to clarify the point-of-sale for any transactions supporting the process, from ticket sales to volunteer labor to discounted staff salaries to corporate, foundation, and individual contributions. While the true value of cultural content remains within the actions and artifacts, the transaction value is captured at "the gate." Tickets and memberships provide entry to the venue. Donations provide higher levels of access (early purchase, better seats, contact with the artists, perceived social status, thematic social events, and so on). Corporate sponsorships provide access to association with an organization's brand identity, as well as direct access to a target audience. Even the purely philanthropic donors gain access to a sense of connection to a vision or mission resonant with their own beliefs.

In the information age, as earlier sections of this chapter suggest, an increasing proportion of these "gates" of transaction will be virtual rather than physical. Managers of arts and cultural organizations will increasingly focus on context as part of their strategic activity—not just tacking on events and frills to cultural attendance, but finding ways to magnify and inform the cultural experience. To balance the books, managers may also become more strategic in identifying points of access to their product and assessing the perceived value of each gate they find. This activity will no doubt raise a wealth of aesthetic and ethical issues regarding the privacy of the creative artists and the sanctity of the creative process (e.g., what level of donor access to an artist begins to violate privacy and personal space?). However, in the digital age, identifying, defining, and leveraging these boundaries may become the new role of arts managers, whether they realize it or not.

RESEARCH NEEDS AND FUTURE STREAMS

Given the scope of technology's impact on arts and culture, this chapter intentionally narrows the range of discussion. There is a host of related issues demanding extensive research and analysis. Equity of access to technology—for artists, for underserved or rural communities, and for schools, libraries, and cultural organizations—is a growing stream of study spearheaded by organizations such as the Benton Foundation and the Digital Divide project of the U.S. government. Equity of understanding and ability is a parallel track, often forgotten, suggesting that not just tools are necessary, but the informed ability to use those tools. Preservation is an ongoing area of essential study on many fronts, including the preservation of recorded media archives, the capture of arts and culture of the present, and the reinforcement of our collective cultural memory in a rapidly advancing information age. The role of public or community space in an on-line world is yet another road to follow.

For the purposes of this chapter, it seems clear that the nature of cultural experience could be much more clearly articulated through research. The elements that define cultural consumption through all media—video, text, computer, live interaction, and so on—must be teased apart (respectfully, of course) through audience study, motivation analysis, and other means. More cognitive approaches, such as the ZMET system, may be required to balance the traditional research methods. A fascinating extension of this study could branch from earlier work by John Peters, Gabriel Tarde, Elihu Katz, Daniel Dayan, and Eric Rothenbuhler[27] that explored the "public event" qualities captured through the separate but simultaneous experiences of live broadcasts (such as the televised Olympic Games). Currently, we can make fairly broad and unsupported guesses about how live cultural experience differs from mediated experience in the mind of the viewer. These assumptions must be tested, refined, and revisited in the face of digital communications technology.

It also appears reasonable to suggest that as the walls of cultural containment fall away, so too fall the walls of cultural categorization. The universe of artifacts and actions we have traditionally bundled as "arts and culture" has already expanded beyond the borders of "high art" and "popular culture" to include ritual, consumerism, informal creative expression, and other forms left off the list. Efforts to view the full spectrum of arts and cultural activity will grow in importance as this trend continues.

Ultimately, we must also come to realize that research has traditionally been based on containment. To study something, we must define its limits and measure it over time. In the digital age, as this chapter suggests, limits become increasingly amorphous, and time is becoming a volatile random variable. The challenge, then, becomes not just continually rethinking the findings of past research, but rethinking the research process itself.

NOTES

1. John Perry Barlow, "The Economy of Ideas: A Framework for Rethinking Patents and Copyrights in the Digital Age," *Wired* (March 199): 85.

2. Ibid., 85

3. Donald Druker, "E-Culture" (panel discussion hosted by the Center for Arts and Culture, Washington, DC, April 11, 2000).

4. For more information on the Gertrude Stein Repertory Theatre, visit <http://www.gertstein.org>.

5. Jamal Le Blanc and Victoria Bernal, "The Role of the Arts in Bridging the Digital Divide," Benton Foundation, 28 April 2000, <http://www.benton.org>.

6. Ithiel de Sola Pool, *Technologies without Boundaries: On Telecommunications in a Global Age* (Cambridge, MA: Harvard University Press, 1990), 8.

7. Barlow, "Economy of Ideas," 86.

8 Claude Debussy, *La Revue S.I.M.*, quoted in Raymond Kurzweil, *The Age of Intelligent Machines* (Cambridge: MIT Press, 1990), 351.

9. Steven A. Wolff, AMS Planning and Research Corp., conversations with author.

10. Quoted in Barlow, "Economy of Ideas," 85.

11. "Cross Talk," *Inter@ctive Week*, 24 April 2000, 110

12. "RIAA Sues Napster, Claiming 'Music Piracy,'" SonicNet.com, 7 December 1999, <http://www.sonicnet.com>.

13. Lisa Guernsey, "MP3–Trading Service Can Clog Networks on College Campuses," *New York Times*, 20 January 2000, <http://www.nytimes.com>.

14. Ben Hammersley, "Out to Destroy Copyright Killers," *The Times* (London), 15 May 2000.

15. Ariana Eunjung Cha, "E-Power to the People," *Washington Post*, 18 May 2000.

16. David Rakoff, "The Way We Live Now: Questions for Michael Hirschorn and Kurt Andersen," *New York Times Magazine*, 16 April 2000, 14.

17. National Endowment for the Arts, "Research Division Note #70," in *1997 Survey of Public Participation in the Arts* (Washington, DC: National Endowment for the Arts, 1998), 2.

18. Ibid., 2.

19. For more on this part of the discussion, see E. Andrew Taylor, "Rethinking the Performing Arts for the Media Age," *Journal of Arts Management, Law, and Society* 25, no. 3 (fall 1995): 206–24.

20. Glyn Northington, marketing director of the Minnesota Opera, interview by the author, 20 July 2000.

21. Ibid.

22. Jonathan Petherbridge, "Escape from the Black Box," *artsbusiness*, 24 April 2000, 5–6.

23. For a more detailed exploration of the experience economy and its impact on arts and culture, see E. Andrew Taylor, "The Experience Brokers: The New Role for Arts Administrators in the Information Age," in *Looking Ahead: A Collection of Papers from the International Social Theory, Politics and the Arts Conference*, ed. Cecelia Fitzgibbon (Philadelphia: Drexel University Press, 1999), 66–71.

24. B. Joseph Pine II and James H. Gilmore, "Welcome to the Experience Economy," *Harvard Business Review* 76, no. 4 (July–August 1998): 99.

25. Heinz Endowments, "Bringing the Arts to Life," Pittsburgh, PA (1999): 3.

26. Ibid., 9, summarizing Gerald Zaltman, "Thoughts and Feelings about the Arts," Harvard Business School (1998).

27. For an overview of the issues, see Eric W. Rothenbuhler, "Live Broadcasting, Media Events, Telecommunication, and Social Form," in *Information, Communication and Social Structure*, ed. David R. Maines and Carl Couch (Springfield, IL: Charles C. Thomas, 1988), 231–43.

12

Trends in Private-Sector Support
of the Nonprofit Arts

Erin V. Lehman

Trends in private-sector support of the nonprofit arts reflect the era in which we live. On the one hand, we have vast fortunes created by a booming economy and the media, technology, and a dot.com revolution that have generated what one observer calls "philanthropic gigantism." On the other extreme, we see the enormous pressures facing the nonprofit sector resulting in what Lester M. Salamon calls "America's nonprofit sector at a crossroads."[1] The examples that follow represent the kaleidoscopic nature of private-sector funding of the arts and foreshadow issues to be highlighted in this chapter.

Example #1: Former Senator Alan K. Simpson has said, "We have a strong commitment to the arts in Wyoming because people are interested in our history. It's close to us. Wyoming was only admitted as a state in 1890. That is why it's easier for us. We have the Buffalo Bill Historical Center in Cody, Wyoming, the Wyoming State Museum in Cheyenne, Mountain Man Museum in Pinedale, the Nicholaysen Museum in Casper, and various museums in most communities. Heck, in Cody, we have 270,000 square feet of museum space, and over 250,000 visitors each year. There are new ones being built and old ones being updated—such as the Plains Indian Museum in Cody—and all without a penny from the federal government."[2]

Example #2: Creative Capital was founded in January 1999 as a pilot program—a "national experiment to create a place friendly to and supportive of artists." The idea was to fill a gap in public resources by creating a fund designed to support individual artists in the visual, performing, and media arts. The fund, which is aimed to grow to $40 million over twenty years, is expected to be replenished by a portion of the revenues generated by artists whose work has been supported by Creative Capital.[3] In this way, Creative Capital has not only created a venture capital fund of sorts, but a revolving financial system that will benefit a stream of artists into the future.

Example #3: The Chicago Symphony Orchestra (CSO) made a conscious decision in the early 1990s that it needed to expand to survive. That expansion was funded by two means: heavy borrowing and a massive capital campaign. As Michael Gehret, vice president for marketing and development, said, "We issued $50 million of tax-exempt bonds in 1994 ... and we began a capital campaign for $92 million, which later increased to $110 million as the project costs increased."[4] Of course, the project had a significant head start with a $50 million pledge from a group of the largest corporations in Chicago. By the end of the campaign, the CSO's net worth had grown from $98 million to over $245 million. As Gehret said, "The secret to the orchestra's dramatic growth owes more to Warren Buffet and arbitrage than to either Beethoven or Brahms!"[5]

Example #4: Andrew P. Mellon Foundation recently made a $30 million multiyear commitment to the development of symphony orchestras in the United States. This level of investment in a single art form (and a select subgroup of it) is one of the largest since the Ford Foundation's $80 million initiative to support orchestras back in the 1970s. The Mellon initiative entails operating grants, designed (1) to better match grantees' artistic operations with institutional behavior, and (2) to "institutionalize behavioral, structural, and cultural modifications"[6] over the long term. Also noteworthy are plans to create a kind of think tank around issues in the field of symphony orchestras.

BACKGROUND: NEW DEMANDS
ON THE NONPROFIT ARTS

The nonprofit arts world can finally exhale a long sigh of relief. The 1990s are over and with it the chaos caused by controversy over government subsidy. The good news is that the tumult has passed (save episodes such as the Brooklyn Museum controversy), but the bad news is that the funding challenge remains. As a result, the role of private giving continues to be an extremely important part of the arts funding equation in the twenty-first century.

For arts organizations in Wyoming, perhaps, this is "a given" because the private sector there has played and continues to play a vital role. For artists and arts organizations elsewhere, however, the hunt for individual donors, foundation grants, corporate sponsorship, and any other means of generating contributed and earned income has not abated in this moment of relative calm—it is intensifying.

Other demands are being placed on the nonprofit arts. Many are burdened by the need to fulfill a social and educational agenda (and often their commercial partners' priorities) in addition to their main arts-focused purpose.[7] And most organizations are expected to turn their enterprises into as near net-profit making and high-performance businesses as they can.

The environment for private funding of the nonprofit arts at the advent of a new century gives us cause for both optimism and concern. While the U.S. economy is still red hot and overall individual philanthropy is setting new records, giving to the arts continues to represent a small slice of the overall philanthropic pie. Corporate America's donations continue to grow, but their criteria and objectives for investing in the arts have narrowed. Foundations remain firm in their commitment to the field, but they are wary about the future; and while workplace (and even on-line) giving is becoming a strong element in the funding equation, government subsidy remains a "marginal player." What all this portends is that individual artists and arts organizations must continue to think (and act) "outside the box," just as the founders of Creative Capital have. The landscape of arts funding is shifting from a predictable-yet-controversial-and-not-totally-satisfactory system to one where anything is possible.

Hopefully, in the years ahead, we will move beyond the old debates over what constitutes art, be it "high brow" or "low brow," capital "A" or little "a"; how it should be funded (we have a pluralistic system that, at its best, is actually synergistic, not zero-sum); and what the purpose of art is—"art for art's sake," serving public purposes, or market success (all of these are valid performance measures). Perhaps we will be able to focus instead on the central question: How best to preserve, advance, and sustain our myriad art forms, artists, and creative legacy? Answering this question begins with the private sector.

THE FORMULA FOR FUNDING THE NONPROFIT ARTS AND HOW THAT EQUATION IS CHANGING

The formula for funding the arts in the United States can be captured in a simple financial equation: artists' subsidy + earned income + contributed income (from corporations + foundations + individuals) + endowment income and other = gross income. Trends in these areas are as follows:

Artists' Subsidy

Artists' subsidy is an extremely important aspect of the U.S. arts funding system. John Kreidler argues that "discounted labor" has been pivotal to the growth of the nonprofit arts (and, as a result, to the arts funding equation). "No other occupation has such highly trained people who must earn most of their penurious incomes outside their field."[8] And he also believes it is coming to an end in the near future. Kreidler warns that "[i]nterventions made in absence of a thorough understanding of the new systemic realities of nonprofit arts organizations, including the key issue of waning labor resources, may result in what systems authorities call, 'unintended consequences.'"[9] Joan Jeffri also has an opinion on the subject. In fact, her research details just how (and how much) individual artists have subsidized and continue to subsidize their own profession.[10]

Earned Income

As a rule of thumb, the amount of earned income in the nonprofit arts typically ranges between 30 percent and 50 percent of an organization's annual operating budget.[11] But there is pressure to do even more. According to Salamon, "For arts institutions, the significant slowing of federal support along with increased difficulties in attracting corporation and foundation support have necessitated a wide variety of innovative 'marketing' efforts."[12]

Nonprofit arts organizations have gone to great lengths to expand their earned income, retailing everything possible. This is why, for example, the "blockbuster" exhibit has become so incredibly popular among U.S. museums.[13] It not only generates substantial attendance and ticket sales, but adds significantly to the bottom line through sale of related items. Just look at the Web site of any nonprofit museum and you will find a growing list of items for purchase, at any time of the year, in their expanding retail shops or even on-line.[14]

That said, it is contributed income that plays the pivotal role in the very survival and sustainability of the nonprofit arts. As Henry Hansmann explains, that is precisely why they are incorporated as nonprofits.[15] Although some might suggest that marketing efforts by nonprofits are pushing the line of tax-exempt status or "commerciality," as Salamon calls it,[16] these organizations still remain charitable institutions. As such, it is the private sector (i.e., corporations, foundations, and individuals) that will remain critical to completing the funding equation.

Corporate America

Business support of the arts is on an upward trend, according to the Business Committee on the Arts (BCA). BCA's latest available data show that corporate arts philanthropy reached a record $1.16 billion in 1997, up from $875 million in 1994, and just $22 million in 1967. Sixty-five percent of all business support to the arts in 1997 was attributed to "small businesses"—those with revenues of $1 million to $49 million—which represent 96 percent of the U.S. business community. Their philanthropy was distributed as follows: 92 percent to projects/organizations that were located in the community of the company's headquarters and major operating communities; 7 percent to national projects; and, 1 percent to international projects. Typical of corporate support are such projects as the CSO's upgraded facility and general expansion. Corporate donors, in effect, are investing in the leading arts institutions in their communities. And they are doing so, for the most part, without impinging on recipient organizations' operations.

But not everyone is so sanguine about the nature, intent, and impact of corporate philanthropy in the arts. A February 1998 PBS–sponsored forum "The Art of Corporate Sponsorship" posed such questions as: "Is corporate sponsorship and the arts a problematic partnership? Can corporate sponsorship affect the content of an exhibit? Will corporate sponsorship produce a wealth of 'blockbuster' exhibits and leave smaller, experimental works out in the cold? Or does corporate sponsorship offer benefits federal funding cannot provide?"[17] The subsequent commentary revealed "fears of increasing dependence on business dollars forcing cultural institutions to play by the rules of the corporate world, either by changing the content of a show, or overwhelming the exhibit with marketing and promotional material."[18] Another concern was that "more cause-related funding initiatives rather than pure philanthropic partnerships in which the outcomes are not as easily measurable has led to a real shift in orientation."[19]

Philip Kotler and Joanne Scheff warn that "[c]orporate support is becoming more commercial than philanthropic and is often conditioned on arts organizations becoming leaner, more business-oriented, and able to meet the corpration's own marketing objectives."[20] They see these as negative inducements. But is the call to be leaner, more business-oriented, and in sync with funders necessarily bad? Opinion is growing, among scholars and practitioners alike, that the more nonprofits are encouraged and motivated to become high-performance organizations, the better.[21] Indeed, the growing trend for all nonprofits is that they develop higher standards, more accountability, greater leadership and organizational capacity, and greater overall effectiveness. Allowances can no longer be made for underperforming organizations no matter their terms of incorporation, be it 501(c)(3) or otherwise.

Foundations

Foundations, too, are increasingly expecting high performance and more predictable and measurable outcomes from the arts organizations in which they invest. The Andrew P. Mellon Foundation and other foundations dedicated to supporting the arts are increasingly concerned about the adaptability and sustainability of their grantees as well as their own ability, as grant makers, to have a long-term impact on their preferred areas of focus. With a collective annual investment of nearly $2 billion, foundations continue to command the attention of their grantees, as well as being able to shape the environment in which these organizations operate.

Americans for the Arts reports that foundation support grew by over 20 percent from 1992 to 1996, with the number of grants increasing by almost the same percentage.[22] In addition, the Foundation Center has conducted surveys that show that foundations gave a higher proportion of their funds to the arts than did corporations or individuals, with the fastest growth being in arts education, arts and community development, and arts and youth projects. Their surveys also indicate that although grants to media and communications, multidisciplinary and community arts, as well as historic preservation saw the greatest increases, two-thirds of all grants were made to traditional art forms, that is, the performing arts and museums.

The Foundation Center's 1999 survey, cosponsored by Grantmakers in the Arts, included interviews with thirty-five leading foundations and corporate arts donors. The report identifies key issues and trends shaping future foundation support of the arts, among which are the following:

- Concern for the sustainability of arts organizations
- The shifting landscape of audiences and demand for the arts
- Broadening definitions of the arts and culture
- For-profit and nonprofit arts activities that are indistinguishable
- The impact of technology on how artists and arts organizations work
- Growing interest in the potential impacts of the arts on society
- Grant makers' increasing focus on arts education and youth programs
- Continuing expectations for accountability among grantees
- Funding that mixes types of support and is integrated across programs[23]

In addition, while continued wealth accumulation and new opportunities for philanthropy are predicted, Foundation Center survey respondents also predict that the arts' share of overall funding will remain steady. A negative prediction is that funders may place too much emphasis on asking the arts community to be all things to all constituencies.

Individual Giving

A high level of personal responsibility-taking for supporting arts and culture is the hallmark of the U.S. funding system. Indeed, individual giving, although temporarily overshadowed by the prospects for public funding and other kinds of support, has been the backbone of U.S. culture. And it remains central to the arts funding equation.

Individuals account for 77 percent of giving in the United States. Americans gave a record $190.16 billion to charity in 1999, continuing a strong upward trend according to Giving USA.[24] The "arts, culture, and humanities" received an $11.07 billion slice of that pie, a 5.12 percent increase over 1998. This is encouraging news since this area of philanthropy had experienced a slight decline since 1997 (1997 giving was 2.8 percent less than 1996; and 1998 was just .08 percent less than 1997 giving).[25] Still, we should be concerned.

According to Giving USA, it is the middle-sized organizations that lag behind in contributed income, but no reason is given. We need to know why. And why is it that although giving to the arts has been on a steady upward climb during the 1990s (with the previous exception), the arts never seem to get beyond 10 percent of the overall giving figure in the United States? Ten percent. Giving USA's analysis indicates just how far the arts are trailing behind other areas in the nonprofit sector such as religion, health, human services, and education. This is a trend worth watching closely. But we need more complete and reliable data.[26]

We need to know what is happening in private giving to the arts in much more detail and we need to understand the causal relationships. Tom Riley proposes several explanations for the pattern of individual giving to the arts from a "lack of public confidence in our art institutions and in those who lead them" to the "bloodiness in rhetoric and body count" of the art wars, as well as the lack of "cultivation of policymakers, the public, and the media"[27] and the complicity of arts grantees, such as the Brooklyn Museum of Art. But this is only a small step in the direction we need to head in order to fully appreciate what is going on here, in this most important element of the arts funding equation.

CONCLUSION: TRENDS IN PRIVATE-SECTOR SUPPORT OF THE ARTS

There are three trends that strike me as most likely to have a significant impact on the nonprofit arts in the coming decades.

Philanthropy

Along with the booming economy and the dot.com revolution's "democratization of wealth in America," we are witnessing an overnight explosion in concern for philanthropy. Why the fascination? The answer is obvious. First, we are a nation of phenomenal largesse.[28] Second, we are expecting an imminent intergenerational transfer of wealth. The Council of Economic Advisors reports that baby boomers may inherit $12 trillion over the next twenty years, swelling to $41 trillion by the year 2054.[29] Third, there is an increasing acceptance that government can no longer be looked to as an arbiter for meting out public resources. The private sector, therefore, has increasing opportunity, authority, responsibility, and influence. And yet serious efforts are needed to expand arts philanthropy. Will the private sector continue to support the nonprofit arts to previous levels, let alone ever increase the level of giving? There is ample uncertainty about the answer.

Organizational Development and Performance

The "postcrisis period for the nonprofit arts" (as I call it) is also marked by a new set of challenges and expectations that have been colored by the strong influence of the private sector's value system and way of operating. Heightened standards are being applied to the entire nonprofit sector. Likewise, the nonprofit arts are being called on to develop organizations just as savvy and aggressive in their financial management and operations as their for-profit counterparts. (We are not sure what resources are being made available to help the nonprofit arts make the transition, but the expectation still holds.) Moreover, these organizations continue to have the added burden of filling the gap in our public education and social welfare agendas. How (and how well) arts organizations respond to multifarious demands will tell us a great deal about the future health, vitality, and sustainability of the arts sector in the decades ahead.

Making the Case for the Arts

A final challenge the nonprofit arts face is the need to "make a better case for itself." The nonprofit arts field, with a few exceptions, has failed to make a clear and cogent argument for its need for support. Why else is it that philanthropy toward the arts has never surged despite our collective munificence in an era of great wealth? The comparative example often cited is the case of the environmental movement supporters and the enormous success they have had in terms of advancing their cause, developing a constituency, and garnering philanthropic support. By contrast, how is the public being persuaded and educated to value the arts? Where are the convincing spokespersons? It is not clear who will represent the vanguard in this new millennium and how it will make the case for the arts, but it is sorely needed.

NOTES

1. Lester M. Salamon, *Holding the Center: America's Nonprofit Sector at the Crossroads* (New York: Nathan Cummings Foundation, 1997).

2. Honorable Alan K. Simpson, conversation with author, Harvard University, 20 April 2000.

3. Taken from information found on Creative Capital's Web site, <http://www.creative-capital.org>.

4. Speech made by Gehret at the National Endowment for the Arts (NEA) Department of Planning and Stabilization colloquia held in Washington, DC, June 22, 1999.

5. Ibid.

6. See notes on the Orchestra Forum by Catherine Wichterman, program officer for the performing arts, which led to the decision to invest heavily in building organizational and leadership capacity in symphony orchestras: <http://www.mellon.org/orchmain.html>.

7. To which Robert Brustein of the American Repertory Theater at Harvard University strenuously objects. For example, see his comments entitled "Requiem" on the *New Republic* On-Line, <http://www.tnr.com/032700/brustein032700.html>.

8. John Kriedler, "Leverage Lost: Evolution in the Nonprofit Arts Ecosystem," in *The Politics of Culture: Policy Perspectives for Individuals, Institutions, and Communities*, ed. Gigi Bradford, Michael Gary, and Glenn Wallach (New York: New Press, 2000).

9. Ibid.

10. Columbia University's Joan Jeffri is not alone in her study of the artist. The NEA's Division of Research has sponsored plenty of studies over the years (see research reports under <http://www.arts.endow.gov>). Neil Alper, Gregory Wassall, and Anne Galligan of Northeastern University have also studied the careers of artists. For example, see "The Career Matrix: The Pipeline for Artists in the United States," and "Characteristics of Performing Artists: A Baseline Profile of Sectoral Crossovers."

11. See Louise K. Stevens, "The Earnings Shift: The New Bottom Line Paradigm for the Arts Industry in a Market-Driven Era," *Journal of Arts Management, Law, and Society* 26, no. 2 (summer 1996).

12. Salamon, "Holding the Center."

13. For example, see Helmut K. Anheier and Stefan Toepler, "Commerce and the Muse: Are Art Museums Becoming Commercial?," in *To Profit or Not to Profit: The Commercial Transformation of the Nonprofit Sector,* ed. Burton A. Weisbrod (New York: Cambridge University Press, 1998).

14. It seems the only thing these organizations have yet to do in the corporatization of their marketing is to team up with McDonald's in the kind of cobranding efforts that have become formulaic for Walt Disney.

15. See Henry Hansmann, "Nonprofit Enterprise in the Performing Arts," in *Nonprofit Enterprise in the Arts: Studies in Mission and Constraint,* ed. Paul J. DiMaggio (New York: Oxford University Press, 1986).

16. Salamon, "Holding the Center."

17. For more information on this, see PBS's Web page from which this quote was taken: <http://www.pbs.org/newshou/forum/february98/sponsorsh_2–6.html>.

18. Ibid.

19. Ibid.

20. See Philip Kotler and Joanne Scheff, *Standing Room Only: Strategies for Marketing the Arts* (Boston: Harvard Business School Press, 1997).

21. For example, see Christine Letts, Allen Grossman, and William Ryan, *High Performance Nonprofit Organizations: Managing Upstream for Greater Impact* (New York: Wiley, 1999).

22. See Americans for the Arts, Arts Link 3, no. 6 (July–August 1999).

23. For more information on the 1999 Foundation Center survey, see <http://www.fdncenter.org/grantmaker/trends/arts-2000.html>.

24. Giving USA 2000, <http://www.afrc.org>.

25. Ibid.

26. As Deborah Kaple, Hugh Louch et al. found in their research on arts organizations, there is no single repository or source, as yet, that will provide all the information we might seek or answer all the questions we might have about the matter of nonprofit arts organizations. See Deborah Kaple, Hugh Louch et al., "Comparing Sample Frames for Research on Arts Organizations: Results of a Study in Three Metropolitan Areas," *Journal of Arts Management, Law, and Society* 28 (1998): 41–66. This is also true about data on private funding of the arts in the United States. The variety of sources (not to mention the quality and comparability of their data) seem to mirror our pluralistic system of arts funding—it is a veritable Rubik's cube. There is hope, however. Americans for the Arts and the Ohio State University, for example, have teamed up on a research project that will generate more comprehensive data on the arts (see <http://www.artsusa.org/ProfilesProject>). Also, the Center on Nonprofits and Philanthropy at the Urban Institute has a very interesting cluster of projects underway on the collection and dissemination of data that will ameliorate this situation (see <http://www.nccs.urban.org/proj.htm>). See also, for example, the Web sites of

Americans for the Arts (<http://www.artsusa.org>), Chronicle of Philanthropy (<http://www.philanthropy.com>), the Foundation Center (<http://www.fdncenter. org>), Giving USA (<http://www.afrc.org>), the Business Committee on the Arts (<http://www.bcainc.org>), and Philanthropy Roundtable (<http://www. philanthropyroundtable.org>) to name just a few.

27. See Tom Riley, "Who's Afraid of Giving to the Arts? Are the Arts Missing out on the Giving Boom?," *Philanthropy* (January–February 2000).

28. See Matthew Rees, "The Best of Times, the Best of Times," *Philanthropy* (May–June 1999).

29. See Americans for the Arts, *Arts Link* 3, no. 9 (November–December 1999).

IV

Special Issues in the Nonprofit Arts

13

The Nonprofit and Commercial Arts in America: Research on New Interrelationships

David B. Pankratz

The cultural life of U.S. society is shaped, in no small measure, through activities of the commercial arts (film, television, video, recordings, commercial theater, commercial publishing, and art galleries) and the nonprofit arts (producers and presenters of dance, theater, symphonic music, jazz, opera/musical theater, and the visual arts, as well as nonprofit publishing). Diverse organizations and individuals in the nonprofit and commercial arts produce, present, distribute, market, and preserve offerings and products that offer U.S. and world audiences myriad choices to experience the arts and entertainment. They thus create opportunities for work by creative and performing artists and designers. In turn, the nonprofit and commercial arts interact with social and economic dimensions of society in many ways and impact the identity, creativity, well-being, and sense of purpose of the U.S. citizenry.

Traditional discussions of organizations in the nonprofit and commercial arts have stressed differences between them in mission, accountability, purpose, disciplines of creation and performance, relationships to audiences, marketing and distribution expertise, capacities and methods to generate income, and risk taking. "Not-for-profit efforts are viewed as mission-driven, providing specialized fare for niche audiences, while for-profits are viewed as driven by bottom-line considerations. For some, distinctions ... are not matters of legal definition or organizational and financial structures, but rather matters of attitude toward artistic vision and public purposes."[1]

For others, these differences are not academic distinctions, but are tinged with attitudes of envy and resentment. Historically, nonprofit/commercial distinctions have been accompanied by pejorative use of labels, for instance, high versus low, elite versus popular, and fine versus folk. Furthermore, in more practical terms, nonprofit arts advocates sometimes contend that the commercial arts industry draws away creative talent from the nonprofit arts. Nonprofit leaders have tended to view commercial entertainment organizations primarily as funding sources that have not repaid, in philanthropic support, the essential research and development (R&D) that the nonprofit arts are said to provide the commercial sector.

Heretofore, these attitudes, concepts, and distinctions have largely been the province of cultural criticism, dating back to the work of popular culture critics of the 1950s.[2] Their use persists even among populist critics of "high culture."[3]

This chapter, in contrast, is an attempt to reconsider traditional rhetoric and categories used to account for interrelationships between the nonprofit and commercial arts. The chapter is also an effort to outline how research-based knowledge can expand our understanding of these interrelationships. It is an outline of what is known currently and what should be known in the future, and an account of how new knowledge can yield options for action and policy initiatives regarding interrelationships between the commercial and nonprofit arts.

First, the chapter offers background context on trends that will shape answers to such questions.

SHIFTING CONTEXTS

Borrowing by artists across artistic styles and traditions is not new. It has deep historical roots and accounts for U.S. artistic forms of jazz, musical theater, and tap dance. In the television industry, the careers of many actors, producers, designers, and technicians have spanned both nonprofit and commercial settings. Visual artists, after years of exhibiting in community-based arts centers, have often found success in commercial art galleries or nonprofit museums. At the organizational level, many new plays produced by Broadway's commercial theaters have originated in nonprofit regional theaters, while Hollywood filmmakers, for years, have also drawn on scripts first developed in nonprofit theaters.

Debate is emerging over whether cross-sector interrelationships between the nonprofit and commercial arts are increasing and, if so, how quickly. Or is awareness of existing interrelationships merely increasing? Examples of cross-sector overlap and collaboration in the cultural sector could be cited that support both points of view. Some are new; others have a long history. These examples can be further distinguished into two broad categories: blurring and cross-sector collaborations.

Blurring

The nonprofit and commercial arts worlds have yielded artistic products and styles that seem to bridge traditional categories of art and entertainment. There is no shortage of examples.

Paul McCartney writes oratorios while symphony orchestras present "crossover" performances by popular culture stars such as Bobby McFerrin. In dance, the work of choreographer Lynne Taylor-Corbett spans diverse sectors and includes pieces for the Pennsylvania Ballet and Miami City Ballet, the movie *Footloose*, and the Broadway musical *Titanic*. The "Three Tenors" and "Three Irish Tenors" performances, and those of Stomp, Blue Man Group, and Riverdance combine classical, folk, and popular traditions in reaching broad audiences. They achieve marketplace synergy by augmenting live performances with recordings, videos, and appearances on network and cable television and as the stars of and "premiums" for fund-raising appeals on public television.

Commercial television has used its capacities to promote artistic products that otherwise might have limited audience reach—Oprah Winfrey's Book Club being a notable example.

It can also be said that the production and marketing of types of cultural programming has become blurred. Complaints about ancillary entertainment and commercial enterprises associated with museums' "blockbuster exhibitions" have been common for several decades. More recently, many museums, such as the Getty in Los Angeles and the Guggenheim at Bilbao, have become either showpieces for star architects or consumer destinations. For its part, the Guggenheim is franchising its brand name and achieving economies of scale in its exhibition production and marketing, with franchise outlets in Las Vegas, Manhattan, and Bilbao. Government-sponsored "cultural tourism" ventures, drawing on destination marketing strategies, regularly feature venues from both the nonprofit and commercial arts. A recent RAND study of the performing arts in the United States over the past thirty years concludes that the largest nonprofit arts organizations, as reflected in their programming and marketing strategies, have become almost indistinguishable from their commercial counterparts.[4]

Television has accelerated the blurring of cultural production and marketing. On the one hand, public television outlets increasingly try to broaden their audience and membership bases by featuring crossover artists like Charlotte Church, Sarah Brightman, Michael Crawford, the Beach Boys, and classic Motown performers. On the other hand, commercial cable networks, such as A&E and BRAVO, present niche offerings such as independent films and "Breakfast with the Arts" that historically have been associated with public television. Finally, the Academy of Television Arts and Sciences argues that television as a whole must be recognized as the work of artists—directors, cinematographers, animators, production and costume designers, composers and musicians, and graphic artists and makeup artists. This cross-cutting "television as an art form" viewpoint was on display during a recent interview on PBS in which the producers of HBO's *The Sopranos* were asked by Charlie Rose if *The Sopranos* was "art." Furthermore, a joint publication of the J. Paul Getty Trust and Academy of Television Arts and Sciences Foundation—*A Framework for Teaching and Learning through the Arts and Technologies of Television*—was designed to help educators understand how television is created and to appreciate the artistry and technology involved.[5]

Finally, blurring between the nonprofit and commercial arts also extends to the policy issues each is facing. These include "changing audience/market demographics, the effects and opportunities of globalization, the need and ability to customize (as distinct from mass or guild produce), and policy concerns such as copyright and intellectual property, cultural trade, and content concerns leading to labeling, rating, and screening systems."[6] Interactions between nonprofit and commercial arts service organizations have yielded some common ground. Examples include presentations by television and film actors at Arts Advocacy Day ceremonies in Washington, DC, and recognition of the National Endowment for the Arts (NEA) during Academy Awards and Tony Awards ceremonies. The entertainment industry-based Creative Coalition supported the growth in the California Arts Council budget at a June 2001 "Arts Summit." Also, the nonprofit Music Educators National Conference and Mr. Holland's Opus Foundation and commercial entities such as VH1 (the music video cable-television network) and the National Academy of Recording Arts and Sciences, Inc., have jointly advocated for K–12 music education.

Cross-Sector Collaborations

Collaborations between nonprofit arts and commercial arts organizations can take many forms—artist pipelines, incubators, joint ventures, redevelopment and community-building projects, technology and audience development, and cultural preservation.

Artist Pipelines

Both the nonprofit and commercial arts have a great need to identify artistic talent that can satisfy the growing demand for content. Cross-sector artist pipeline models, in higher education, include degree-granting programs at the California Institute of the Arts in character animation, experimental animation, and integrated media, which address current and emerging needs in the commercial arts, nonprofit arts, and new technologies industries. A program of note outside higher education is the Sundance Institute, a nonprofit, whose summer producers' workshop brings young filmmakers together with experienced film industry professionals. As an extension of this pipeline, the Sundance Film Channel, a partnership with the cable-television network Showtime Networks, Inc., presents features, documentaries, short films, and foreign cinema by young and emerging filmmakers.

Incubators

The American Film Institute's 2001 California Digital Arts Workshop, entitled the Arts and Streaming Media, connected practicing, midcareer, and emerging artists from the commercial and nonprofit arts with new media and technologies associated with streaming video. In higher education, the School of Cinema-Television at the University of Southern California (USC) offers internships with film and television companies and First Look, a festival of USC student film projects attended by industry representatives and independent film producers searching for new talent.

Joint Ventures

Joint ventures serve a range of purposes, such as broadening product lines, increasing market share, and the creation of new artistic work. In the theater, especially, there is considerable experience with crossovers between the for-profit and nonprofit arts.[7] For example, Radio City Entertainment (RCE), a commercial company owned by Cablevision, makes deals with nonprofit theater companies producing new work, where the nonprofits get royalties and where RCE can reach broader segments of the entertainment market. Funding from Showtime to the nonprofit Center Theater Group/Mark Taper Forum in Los Angeles for a series of commissions, readings, and workshops is intended to generate new products for Showtime.

Redevelopment and Community-Building Projects

In many U.S. communities, urban revitalization and community-building initiatives involve close partnerships between the for-profit and nonprofit arts. Of special note are formalized, contractual alliances between nonprofit and for-profit partners, in collaboration with local governments and developers, which generate benefits to the general public. For example, the New 42nd Street in New York City is a nonprofit corporation that was created to find a future for six all-but-abandoned historic theaters donated by the city of New York. Over time, the New 42nd Street has created a children's theater, a new office, and a rehearsal building for the arts, leased theaters to two corporations, and negotiated the siting of a multiplex movie theater.

Technology and Audience Development

Artists in diverse media are presenting and marketing their works directly over the Internet, bypassing traditional venues of live presentation in order to develop a niche market. New technologies are a key focus of vertically integrated entertainment megacompanies, which constantly seek content, especially products that can be central to theme-related product lines. Among nonprofit producers, public television has embraced the convergence strategy most fully. Programs have tie-ins with music products, gifts and toys, computer software, and videocassettes, many of which are supplied by for-profit companies. The nonprofit provides basic content; the for-profits bring merchandising expertise to achieve a broad reach for the product line. Commercial–nonprofit relationships appear to provide new possibilities for creating and disseminating diverse content and related products.

Cultural Preservation

Cultural artifacts come from all parts of the arts sector. Both for-profits and nonprofits utilize these cultural materials in projects, productions, and exhibits and to build revenues over time. Cooperation between nonprofit and commercial entities is growing. Nonprofits can identify what needs to be preserved and help find niche audiences for preserved products, thus providing revenue streams to copyright holders. For-profits, for their part, can help make products available at reasonable prices and open up avenues for publicity, marketing, and, in some cases, global distribution.[8] As an example, the American Film Institute's (AFI) identification of the one hundred best U.S. films brought new attention to the nation's legacy in feature films. The project resulted in a prime-time CBS special, Turner Network reruns on cable, increased Blockbuster videocassette sales, and enhanced revenues, donations, and brand recognition for the AFI.

PRIVATE AND PUBLIC DIMENSIONS OF CROSS-SECTOR BLURRING AND COLLABORATION

The many examples of crossover activities cited earlier, both blurring and collaborations, are noteworthy and, in some cases, represent a significant contribution from one arts segment to another and to the general public. Yet, the majority of these examples have occurred as a result of the pursuit of private interests, and often by accident.

The private interests pursued through cross-sector collaborations, who pursued them, and why, are as follows:

1. Nonprofit arts organizations, facing financial challenges and, in some instances, "artistic deficit," are seeking partnerships to enhance their mission, to disseminate their work through new distribution networks, to generate visibility, and to increase earned revenues and donations.

2. Commercial arts organizations, in the face of an explosion of new distribution networks that has outpaced the production of new content and the growth of interactive, "pull" technologies of the Internet, are seeking ways to produce new content for niche and mass markets.

3. New technologies companies, in a highly competitive market where distinctions between entertainment, communications, and information industries are blurring in the face of mergers, acquisitions, and consolidations, seek partnerships that promote corporate visibility and the increased use of software and Internet services and the hardware, microprocessors, and operating systems that support them.

4. Colleges and universities, in light of economic pressures and a mission to prepare students for meaningful careers while maintaining traditional values of general edu-

cation and service, are seeking partnerships in the creation of majors and programs that attract students seeking leadership roles in the growing industries of entertainment, new media, and new technologies.

The pursuit of these private interests through institution-to-institution partnership arrangements, for some, is a cultural step forward and the proper mechanism to help ensure "high-quality culture."[9]

Calls for new and expanded forms of collaboration between the arts and entertainment are not unusual and, in recent years, have come from diverse sources. The President's Committee on the Arts and Humanities, in *Creative America*, urges a greater dialogue among nonprofit and commercial creative sectors to explore their common interests and perhaps form new partnerships to present the arts to a wider public.[10]

The American Assembly report *The Arts and the Public Purpose* recommends that partnerships among the commercial and nonprofit parts of the arts sector should be developed and expanded.[11] The assembly acknowledges, first, that cross-sector collaborations, in general, can be and often are of benefit to the institutions, companies, artists, producers, educators, designers, and technicians involved. At the same time, it offers a cautionary note arguing that collaborations between for-profits and nonprofits do not address all the challenges facing arts sector organizations; neither should they displace what nonprofits do as mission-driven institutions, nor attempt to change the objectives of for-profit companies.[12]

But, further, in answering the question "Why should new and expanded partnerships be pursued?," the American Assembly introduces "public interest" into the discussion. It presents the argument that such collaborations should be built on and extended toward the achievement of public purposes of the arts.

Public purposes that cross-sector collaborations might serve are:

1. helping to define what it is to be an American by building a sense of the nation's identity and the reality of U.S. pluralism by advancing democratic values and peace at home and abroad.
2. contributing to quality of life and economic growth by making U.S. communities more livable and prosperous and increasing the nation's prosperity domestically and globally.
3. helping to form an educated and aware citizenry by promoting understanding in a diverse society, developing competencies in school and at work, and increasing freedom of inquiry and an open exchange of ideas and values.
4. enhancing individual life by encouraging individual creativity, spirit, and potential through release, relaxation, and entertainment.

The introduction of the concept of public purposes raises a broad range of questions that can be pursued through formal research. It also adds another context to the pursuit of research on interrelationships between the commercial and nonprofit arts. Research cannot focus only on the characteristics and private consequences of blurring between the commercial and nonprofit arts. It must also address ways in which cross-sector relationships can and do serve public purposes.

RESEARCH ISSUES AND POLICY OPTIONS

To say that research should address ways in which the commercial and nonprofit arts interact to serve public purposes by no means forecloses other types of inquiry serving a range of functions. For example, individual companies within the commercial arts will continue to sponsor or conduct market research that serves their proprietary interests, such as test marketing and product development. Professional associations within the entertainment industry regularly sponsor research on wide range of issues—copyright protection, consumer trends, the impact of new technologies, and the use of discretionary income, among others. For their part, institutions within the nonprofit arts—symphonies, theaters, and museums—continue to conduct proprietary marketing studies on audience composition and behavior, while their professional associations track trends in administrator compensation and repertoire trends.

At the same time, trends in proprietary research are shifting. Research on product crossovers, market synergy, and reaching multiniche market segments are common. This trend is but one consequence of new environment blurring and increased interaction between the commercial and nonprofit arts. In this new environment, for example, "a current challenge is to use research and analysis to devise coalition-building strategies, to influence agenda setting, and to establish policy linkage between arts issues and other types of issues such as education or trade.... Entire new areas of research and analysis are opened up as the two subsectors seek more opportunities to work together effectively."[13] Opportunities for working together also extend to public agencies outside of the arts, higher education, the technology, and support sectors.

In this new environment, research can serve many of the same general, traditional functions—understanding the past, anticipating the future, guiding practice, and informing policy. But while the new environment may yet spawn new forms of inquiry, as well as new opportunities for collaboration, the focus here is on the kinds of questions that need to be asked.

What are those questions and how can they be characterized? First, questions can be framed within three areas: trends in cross-sector blurring and crossovers, collaborations between the commercial and nonprofit arts, and normative and policy issues. These areas are, needless to say, interrelated. In some ways, the first two areas provide baseline information for the consideration and weighing of normative issues and policy options. This is not to undervalue the description and analysis of trends in cross-sector blurring and interactions.

Indeed, the weighing of normative issues and policy options would be far too abstract for consideration in most policy contexts without a strong foundation in the realities of practice. That point certainly applies to interactions between the commercial and nonprofit arts. Each area will be discussed in turn.

Trends in Cross-Sector Blurring and Crossovers

Before there were formal collaborations between nonprofit and commercial entities, whether they serve public purposes or not, blurring and crossover activity has been common. As noted earlier, borrowing by artists across artistic styles and traditions has deep historical roots, while the careers of many artists span both nonprofit and commercial settings. The production and marketing of different kinds of cultural programming has become blurred and accelerated by television crossovers. Furthermore, blurring between the nonprofit and commercial arts also extends to the policy issues each is facing.

But these statements yield many research questions. Some are status questions: How common is blurring between the commercial and nonprofit arts? Is it found more commonly in the sharing and borrowing of artistic styles, in the cross-sector careers of artists,[14] or in the marketing and programming practices of organizations and institutions in the different sectors? Following these distinctions, is crossover activity more common in some disciplines, for example, the performing, visual, literary, and media arts, than others?

Moving beyond status issues, there are many questions that can be posed regarding the environment for crossover activity. Some questions can focus on assumptions about similarities and differences between organizations in the commercial and nonprofit arts. Traditional distinctions tend to revolve around the premise that the nonprofit arts are mission-driven and provide specialized fare for niche audiences, while for-profits are driven by bottom-line considerations and meeting the interests of mass audiences. Others, however, stress similarities between the commercial and nonprofit arts along many lines. They argue that both (1) depend on identifying and employing artistic talent, (2) face financial challenges, both in the work of individual artists and organizations, (3) use ancillary products and services to expand audience reach, and (4) utilize new technologies in production and audience development. Still others see distinctions between the for-profit and nonprofit arts primarily as a matter of degree. For example, William J. Ivey proposes to enumerate commonalities and differences between the sectors and offers a typology of characteristics for analyzing nonprofit and commercial arts organizations. These characteristics are stability, community expectations, vision, financial flexibility, risk taking, community commitment, corporate self-image, sources of revenue, and the external environment, including the regulatory environment.[15]

Another area of inquiry is the oft-stated claim, according to the NEA, that "the nonprofit arts have long served as sources for nurturing much of the talent, creativity, and content for our America's internationally successful commercial arts and entertainment industries."[16] What evidence exists for the claim that the nonprofit arts provide essential R&D for the commercial entertainment industry? Data and detailed case studies on the topic are not available.[17] But some research has offered guideposts to how such inquiry could proceed, arguing that R&D in the arts is characterized by three key functions:

1. Talent preparation—acquisition of the basic knowledge and skills required to create, interpret, and/or perform works of art, both individually and in artistic groups, at a professional level

2. Artistic development—professional growth over time through the exploration of and experimentation with new techniques, methods, styles, media, settings, personnel, and subject matter, by both individuals and institutions, which yields a body of work reflecting identifiable styles of creation and interpretation

3. Product development and dissemination—the preparation and marketing of works of art and entertainment for public presentation, either individually, in a series of live performances or in a public exhibition, or via the media of television, radio, film, video, recordings, and the Internet, to either targeted or mass audiences

It appears that these components involve both individuals and organizations, require resources to commence and sustain them, and involve sectors beyond the commercial and nonprofit arts, most notably, colleges and universities and new technologies industries. But considerable research is required before the claim that the nonprofit arts provide essential R&D for the commercial arts can be sustained.

The R&D issue leads to a final set of research questions—those that address the impacts of blurring distinctions between the nonprofit and commercial arts. Such questions might center on the effects of blurring and crossovers on individual organizations or the nonprofit and commercial arts sectors as a whole. Do effects tend toward homogenization or greater diversity in cultural products? How is access affected? Within the sectors, is crossover activity prompting innovative cross-fertilization or is it diverting resources from core activities and missions?

A research issue with practical implications is whether nonprofit art entities, as they coproduce with commercial firms and generate income from ancillary products and services, might be jeopardizing their tax-exempt status, especially if those enterprises cannot be tied to their cultural or educational missions. Another R&D "impact" issue regards the notion that the nonprofit arts, by encouraging and subsidizing risky, cutting-edge work, provides incubators for the commercial arts. The career of Julie Taymor, producer of *The Lion King*, is frequently cited as an example. Some fear that if distinctions between the nonprofit and commercial arts become more blurred, appreciation and support for the R&D function of the nonprofit arts will diminish. Yet, some fear that stress on the R&D function of the nonprofit arts relegates them to "farm team" status and to serving a merely instrumental function for the commercial arts. Such status, it is argued, can serve to minimize the unique features of nonprofits, for example, artistic risk taking. This view can, in turn, send the message to young artists that the preferred career track is one of movement, over time, from nonprofit venues to for-profit organizations, without portraying lifelong work in the nonprofit arts as a viable option.

Consideration of these normative and policy issues will be enhanced, immeasurably, by a baseline of information yielded by detailed inquiry into the current state of and trends in R&D relationships between the nonprofit and commercial arts. Before considering related policy and normative issues, the need for research on current cross-sector collaborations will be examined.

Collaborations between the Commercial and Nonprofit Arts

Another type of baseline research needed is inquiry into current collaborations and partnerships between organizations and institutions in the commercial and nonprofit arts. Types of collaborations, as cited earlier, can include artist pipelines, incubators, joint ventures, redevelopment and community-building projects, technology and audience development, and cultural preservation. Some serve the private interests of those collaborating, while others impact the public in significant ways.

Key research questions for all these collaborations include the following: What is the nature of these relationships? Are they formal or informal in nature? What kinds of organizations are involved? To what extent are they the province of individual nonprofits and commercial organizations? Or are universities, technology companies, and public agencies involved? If so, how? Of the commercial and nonprofit arts organizations involved, do rates differ by artistic discipline? Do rates vary by the size and location of the partners?

Beyond these "status" questions, there are issues to explore concerning the benefits sought and the barriers encountered. Anecdotal evidence, as noted earlier, suggests:

1. Nonprofits seek partnerships to enhance their missions, to disseminate their work through new distribution networks, to generate visibility, and to increase earned revenues and donations

2. Commercial arts organizations seek ways to produce new content for niche and mass markets

3. New technologies companies seek partnerships that promote corporate visibility and the increased use of software and Internet services and the hardware, microprocessors, and operating systems that support them

4. Colleges and universities seek partnerships in the creation of programs that attract students seeking leadership roles in the growing industries of entertainment, new media, and new technologies

Is this anecdotal evidence on motives for cross-sector partnerships borne out by formal research?

Formal research can also serve to test anecdotes suggesting that the design and implementation of cross-sector partnerships face numerous barriers:

1. Lack of widespread, ongoing communications across the full arts sector

2. A shortage of cultural translators to convene and broker such communications

3. A dearth of research documenting the design and implementation of cross-sector collaborations, and the legal, administrative, and economic underpinnings of deals

4. Skepticism about past deals that have yielded minimal pay-offs for nonprofit partners

5. A funding community for which collaborative action, on behalf of cross-sector connections, may prove challenging

6. Concern that cross-sector partnerships built on existing equities may lead to a stratified system among nonprofits of those that benefit from commercial partners and those that do not[18]

Finally, formal research can explore claims about "keys" to effective cross-sector partnerships:

1. Mutual understanding of the different cultures, styles, interests, and objectives that representatives from nonprofits, entertainment and new technologies companies, and colleges/universities bring to potential partnerships

2. Targeted market research on the potential audiences for cross-over products

3. Sound business and legal plans that protect the rights and interests of artists and designers and the arts and entertainment organizations with which they work

4. Realistic expectations of income and visibility that new product partnerships can yield

5. Mutual appreciation for the intellectual capital resources each partner brings, plus respect for the financial vulnerability of nonprofits and the market volatility commercial enterprises face

6. Awareness that a nonprofit leader's focus on partnerships with commercial businesses may create a conflict of commitment regarding the nonprofit's mission and priorities[19]

Research can also explore the broad societal factors that shape prospects for the development of cross-sector arts partnerships. For example, a study could analyze the impacts of new corporate structures and new technologies in the arts and entertainment industries, the changing character of arts disciplines, and the economics underlying the arts sector, including cross-sector partnerships. An accompanying study could examine Internal Revenue Service, legal, and regulatory constraints and opportunities that for-profits and nonprofits face as they consider joint ventures.

Finally, case studies could explore the great diversity of collaborations that have occurred historically, large and small, in diverse settings and across the full spectrum of arts disciplines. Attention to collaborations that were successful and those that were not could be included. Furthermore, these case studies could address several key issues, including the benefits received by collaborating partners; criteria that successful collaborations seem to exhibit; balancing success in collaborations with staying true to artistic visions; and the role of leadership in developing and implementing cross-sector partnerships.

Normative and Policy Issues

Baseline research on trends in cross-sector blurring and crossovers and collaborations between the commercial and nonprofit arts can pave the way for detailed consideration of normative issues that should be addressed in considering policy support for the development of cross-sector partnerships.

Key questions might include:

1. Do partnerships that nonprofits undertake have the potential to limit, in effect, both the risk taking and artistic freedom of creative artists?
2. Do such partnerships threaten the 501(c)(3) legal status of nonprofit arts organizations?
3. Will larger nonprofits, with their financial and personnel resources and publicly recognizable brand identities, disproportionately benefit from new cross-sector collaborations?
4. Will nonprofit collaborations with technology and entertainment companies, in an era of consolidation into fewer megacompanies, contribute to an exacerbation of the digital divide?

Another very important focus of inquiry is the degree to which collaborations between the nonprofit and commercial arts serve public purposes. Review of existing collaborations might take researchers only so far, especially since many such relationships seem geared to benefiting, primarily, the partners involved directly in the partnership. But it certainly seems possible to identify some collaborations that serve public purposes, such as building a sense of the nation's identity, advancing democratic values, contributing to the nation's quality of life and economic growth, helping to form an educated and aware citizenry, and enhancing individual life. In other cases, it may be possible to gauge the potential public benefit of collaborations between the commercial and nonprofit arts.

Such research can help a range of agencies to decide whether support of cross-sector partnerships is consistent with their mission and serves the public interest. The question then becomes whether particular means of intervention are more likely to maximize the range of public benefits from cross-sector collaborations. Agencies making these decisions can be public arts agencies (federal, state, and local), public agencies (economic development, neighborhood improvement, public housing, parks and recreation, public safety, and convention and visitors' bureaus), foundations, and corporations. Professional associations can also support cross-sector connections, either singly or in partnership with other entities.

The types of interventions each can choose ranges widely. Their effectiveness in meeting objectives, in turn, can be the subject of evaluation research and outcomes analysis. Options include:

1. Forums for leaders in the arts, entertainment, higher education, technology, philanthropy, and the public sector to communicate and weigh pros and cons and normative dimensions of pursuing or supporting cross-sector partnerships
2. Training opportunities and technical assistance for practitioners in the legal and administrative dimensions of designing cross-sector arts partnerships, including interactive, on-line peer and mentoring networks
3. Funding opportunities, such as

   a. Grants and fellowships[20]

   b. Venture capital funds

   c. Program-related investments and returnable grants[21]

CONCLUSION

Collaborations between the nonprofit and commercial arts are likely to continue far into the future. A key question is whether these relationships will be examples of blurring and crossover between styles and genres, and partnerships that benefit the private interests of participating partners, or, in some sense, the public interest. The kinds of research outlined in this chapter—trends in cross-sector blurring and crossovers, collaborations between the commercial and nonprofit arts, and normative and policy issues—were proposed as means to generate policy options by which a range of agencies might serve public purposes.

But a fitting conclusion to this chapter might be a return to a normative policy question raised earlier, namely, the fear that if distinctions between the nonprofit and commercial arts become more blurred, appreciation and support for the R&D function of the nonprofit arts will diminish. If public and private support is increasingly directed to the nurturing of cross-sector partnerships, then initial support for the artistic risk taking characteristic of many nonprofit arts organizations could decline. A "homogenized" middle ground could be created, whereby the R&D risk taking of the nonprofit sector would be diminished as a resource for many commercial firms and the public at large.

As an alternative policy future, Steven Lavine, president of the California Institute of the Arts, calls for stimulating creativity and innovation through fellowship and residency support for emerging artists. He argues that

[i]nvesting in emerging artists and the organizations that support them has a high probability of one of three outcomes, all productive. Either the artist and/or organization de-

velops a not-for-profit niche from which to produce ongoing work that exerts pressure on or offers an alternative to more immediately "popular" art and entertainment; or the artists supported move into the more general culture whether from the for-profit or not-for-profit side of the sector; or for reasons of economics or choice the artists move early on into for-profit arts careers but with their own visions and skills more developed, thereby preparing them to make a more productive contribution.[22]

Research, again, has a role in assisting the development of cross-sector partnerships that serve public purposes. Research, as the previous example illustrates, can also help us envision and generate debate about alternative futures and the potential means to realize those visions.

NOTES

1. American Assembly, *Deals and Ideals: For-Profit and Not-for-Profit Arts Connections* (New York: American Assembly, 1999), 13.

2. For example, see David Manning White, ed., *Popular Culture (The Great Contemporary Issues)* (North Stratford, NH: Ayer, 1975).

3. For example, see Herbert J. Gans, *Popular Culture and High Culture: An Analysis and Evaluation of Taste* (New York: Basic, 1999).

4. Kevin F. McCarthy et al., *The Performing Arts in a New Era* (Santa Monica, CA: RAND, 2001).

5. Academy of Television Arts and Sciences Foundation, *A Framework for Teaching and Learning through the Arts and Technologies of Television* (North Hollywood, CA: Academy of Television Arts and Sciences Foundation, 2001).

6. Margaret Jane Wyszomirski, "Creative Assets and Cultural Development: How Can Research Inform Nonprofit–Commercial Partnerships?," *Journal of Arts Management, Law, and Society* 29, no. 2 (summer 1999): 136.

7. See Joni Maya Cherbo, "Creative Synergy: Commercial and Not-for-Profit Live Theater in America," *Journal of Arts Management, Law, and Society* 28, no. 2 (summer 1998): 129–43.

8. For a discussion of cultural preservation issues, see Alberta Arthurs, Frank Hodsoll, and Steven Lavine, "For-Profit and Not-for-Profit Arts Connections: Existing and Potential," *Journal of Arts Management, Law, and Society* 29, no. 2 (summer 1999): 80–96.

9. See Tyler Cowen, *In Praise of Commercial Culture* (Cambridge, MA: Harvard University Press, 1998).

10. President's Committee on the Arts and Humanities, *Creative America: A Report to the President* (Washington, DC: President's Committee on the Arts and Humanities, 1997).

11. American Assembly, *The Arts and the Public Purpose* (New York: American Assembly, 1997).

12. This point is made in the American Assembly, *Deals and Ideals.*

13. Wyszomirski, "Creative Assets and Cultural Development," 133.

14. For discussion of cross-over activity in the careers of artists, see Ann M. Galligan and Neil O. Alper, "Characteristics of Performing Artists: A Baseline Profile of Sectoral Crossovers," *Journal of Arts Management, Law, and Society* 28, no. 2 (summer 1998): 155–77.

15. William J. Ivey, "Bridging the For-Profit and Not-for-Profit Arts," *Journal of Arts Management, Law, and Society* 29, no. 2 (summer 1999): 97–100.

16. National Endowment for the Arts, "Non-profit Gateway," <http://www.arts.endow.gov/gateway>.

17. For a detailed discussion of this issue, see David B. Pankratz, "R&D and the Arts Sector: Components and Criteria for Development," in *Building Creative Assets: New Ways for the Entertainment and Not-for-Profit Arts Industries to Work Together,* Americans for the Arts, White papers for a November 12, 1998, forum, Los Angeles, CA.

18. These points were originally made in the American Assembly, *Deals and Ideals.*

19. These points were originally made in Pankratz, "R&D and the Arts Sector."

20. For a detailed discussion of funding opportunities for artists, such as the creative capital initiative, see Cora Mirikitani, "The Role of Philanthropy in the Intersection between Culture and Commerce," *Journal of Arts Management, Law, and Society* 29, no. 2 (summer 1999): 128–31.

21. For a discussion of program-related investments, see Loren Renz and Cynthia W. Massarsky, *Program-Related Investments: A Guide to Funders and Trends* (New York: Foundation Center, 1995); Christie I. Baxter, *Program-Related Investments: A Technical Manual for Foundations* (New York: Wiley, 1997).

22. Steven Lavine, *The Artist at the Beginning of the 21st Century* (unpublished manuscript, 2000).

14

The Arts in the Market Economy

Louise K. Stevens

In the relatively short but intense history of policy writing on the arts in the United States, little space—and certainly little positive commentary—has been given to the concept of the arts in the market economy. When addressed either implicitly or explicitly, it has traditionally been with regret and concern from the supposition that art—meaning "high" art—should not have to or, perhaps, could not succeed in a market economy. The support systems for high or elite art were, as noted by Paul J. DiMaggio, set up by "men and women who designed the high culture system in both structure and ideology to buffer a high culture from market forces. The virtue of the high culture systems is that it succeeded in cordoning off a sector of cultural production from the demands of the marketplace."[1]

The questionable fate of the arts in the market economy was for many years—and from various perspectives—a part of the rationale of government support and its leveraging of other philanthropic support for the nonprofit arts. In panel discussions, media coverage, and as commonly addressed by arts organizations or artists, "the market" has long invoked perceptions of selling out to the masses or suggested a commercialization with the potential to corrupt or at least challenge the artistic intent of nonprofit arts.[2]

Much public- and private-sector grant funding was designed to offer a balance, to provide enough revenue separate from the box office through general operating support, in review processes where success was not judged on gate admissions and public attendance. Indicative of the sentiments of many, it was only in fiscal year 1997 that the National Endowment for the Arts (NEA), whose grant guidelines and criteria serve as the model for most state and many private-sector funders, inserted the idea of "broadening public access to the arts" into its mission. However, even today, the closest the NEA comes to asking organizations to engage the public is stated as an organization's "potential to enhance public knowledge, understanding and appreciation of the art form, the art work, and/or the artist."

Despite attempts to ignore the market economy, the arts have crept into the market over the past decade and are beginning to live solidly within it. (Or, perhaps, the market has crept into the arts.) The debate over whether or not it should happen is moot. The questions now are why and how to make this reality workable.

THE EROSION OF THE HIGH CULTURE SYSTEM

Several factors led to the joining of arts and market into a new relationship. First, the funding upheavals that took place during the early to mid-1990s shifted and tilted the dynamic of grant funds as a counterbalance to earned income—the market.[3] The draconian cuts in NEA funding hit organizations large and small, mainstream and cutting-edge arts alike, and in many regions across the country were mirrored by similar drops in state and philanthropic funds.

A 58 percent drop in grant dollars from 1992 to 1996 had been just slightly preceded by an 18 percent drop in grant funds through state arts agencies. Local arts agencies, channeling funds from local governments and often from the private sector through the form of united arts funds, dropped in funding by 8.5 percent during the same time period. Public funding for individual artists virtually evaporated. In essence, the market intervention of significant grants based on peer panel review was diminished long enough to force arts institutions and artists to consider new realities. And while at the end of the decade the overall funding for art improved from the mid-decade lows, the symbolic and real reduction in the importance of NEA grants as market intervention remained. "Even among organizations and in communities largely untouched by the NEA cuts, such as San Francisco, where combinations of municipal and philanthropic dollars increased to offset state and federal cuts, arts leaders shifted their thinking, and looked to growing their audiences—and related earned income—more than ever before."[4]

Second (although it may be an accident of timing), the building of audiences for the arts became an issue of growing importance during the same years that brought reduced grant funds for artistic purposes. Arts institutions and their funders alike began turning their eyes to issues of audience early in the 1990s, and continued to do so throughout the decade. (In 1999, audience development remained one of the primary topics at national gatherings such as the annual Grantmakers in the Arts conference.)

Early in the decade, audience aging, attrition, narrow demographics, and changed consumption patterns had already come to the attention of many within the field and were addressed in reports such as the American Symphony

Orchestra League 1992 Financial Condition of Symphony Orchestra report. Public- and private-sector funders, concerned about the narrow demographics of the audience for the "high" arts, also began major funding initiatives such as the massive grant programs targeted to audience development by the Lila Wallace Reader's Digest Fund.

Simultaneously, as the successive Study of Public Participation in the Arts (SPPA; 1982, 1987, 1992, 1997) became well known, the evaluation of participation and consumption—and strategies to increase both—grew increasingly interesting to researchers and practitioners alike. Clearly, throughout the "culture wars" making the case for public funds for the arts required that the field demonstrate its ability to serve the broad public, not only the elite few. As baseline and benchmark national studies gave individual organizations a point of comparison, boards of directors and local funders began demanding that their institutions work increasingly harder to invite, involve, and retain broad public participation, and to equal or better the national SPPA statistics. This came first from the perspective of social responsibility, put forth in funding programs and guidelines from the NEA, state arts agencies, and private funders. Then, more gradually, it came from the economic perspective: When many institutions were presented with the need to increase earned income, they were ill equipped to respond to trends within the multiyear SPPA studies showing that increasing market share would be harder than anticipated.[5] It also came through the realization, uncomfortable to this day for many to admit, that with rare exception the arts were no longer playing to full houses, and that what had filled those halls in earlier decades were audiences who came as much out of civic pride as interest in the art form. In a recent examination of seats sold, it was unusual to find a performing arts organization with more than 68 percent of house sold per year.[6] With a downturn in civic pride as a motivator to arts participation, audience attribution was palpable.

The third factor contributing to the field's evolution into the market economy—which also played out during the 1990s—was the change in the expense of doing business within the nonprofit arts. In the economy of professional sports, the arrival of multimillion-dollar player salaries could be countered with lucrative revenue opportunities. But when Luciano Pavarotti broke through the $100,000 glass ceiling recital fee for a classical artist, and the ripple effect changed all performing arts fees, only the largest organizations or those with the deepest underwriting could afford the change. Parallel expense increases hit museums, with major jumps in the cost of touring and presenting exhibitions. At the same time, a generation of people doing the business of the arts that had come of age in the Comprehensive Employment and Training Act–inspired world of the 1970s reached a point where they needed living wages to remain in the field.[7] Basic operational costs needed to increase in response. Expenses, always out of balance with revenue in the arts field, jumped dramatically. The 1965 prophesies of William J. Baumol and William G. Bowmen became uncannily more real than ever: "Because of the economic structure of the performing arts, these financial pressures are here to stay, and there are fundamental reasons for expecting the income gap to widen steadily with the passage of time."[8]

ART VERSUS THE EXPERIENCE

Simultaneously, throughout the 1990s the entertainment world (i.e., the "experience" world) grew in every way. Satellite television made the former plethora of cable channels look miniscule, while the dot.com world of the Internet offered thousands of arts and entertainment options. The experience world began transforming restaurants, shopping, and leisure events to the point where the performing arts were noted to be among the most passive and therefore among the least interesting of experience options within the new experience economy. "At one end of the spectrum lies passive participation, where customers do not directly affect or influence the performance. Such participants include symphonygoers, who experience the event as pure observers or listeners."[9]

And finally, by the end of the 1990s the lines between nonprofit and commercial, always thinly drawn in some sectors of the arts field, all but disappeared in the eyes and perceptions of the consumer. Only thirty years earlier, in the growth years of government funding for "high" art, the distinctions had been easily made. As Russel B. Nye drew the line in his 1970 book *The Unembarrassed Muse:*

[P]opular art is an art more aware of the need for selling the product. It is an art trying to perfect itself, not yet complete, not yet mature. Elite art is produced by known artists within a consciously aesthetic context and by an accepted set of rules, its attainment (or failure) judged by reference to a normative body of recognized classics. Elite art is exclusive, particular, individualistic; its aim is the discovery of new ways of recording and interpreting experience. Popular art confirms the experience of the majority, in contrast to elite art, which tends to explore the new. Popular art assumes its own particular kind of audience, huge, heterogeneous, bewilderingly diverse in its combination of lifestyles, manners, interests, tastes, and economic and educational levels. This audience is much less self-conscious than an elite art audience; its standards are less clearly defined, its expectations less consistent and integrated. The audience for elite art possesses commonly held aesthetic and intellectual standards and has its own specialized idiom of appreciation and criticism. The popular audience expects entertainment, instruction, or both, rather than an aesthetic experience.[10]

Do those distinctions hold up today? "During the last thirty years, the high-culture system has been eroding, and with it the strong classification between a sacred high culture and its profane popular counterpart."[11] The 92nd American Assembly's 1997 report *The Arts and the Public Purpose* directly defined the arts as inclusive of "the nonprofit arts and the commercial arts, as well as the range of citizen arts that is referred to as 'unincorporated.'"[12]

Consumer research among experienced performing artsgoers, conducted through repeated focus groups, tells us that even if arts participants do understand differences between nonprofit art and commercial art they care less about classifications, and more about the quality of the experience each offers. "Casual attendees, in particular, don't understand that nonprofits, by nature, might be expected to have less capital to invest in product than commercial enterprises. What's more, they don't care. It's what they see on stage that matters, and no level of discussion about the merits of nonprofits will change their perceptions."[13]

Artists, as well as audiences, know that old distinctions no longer have meaning. Conservatory-trained artists work in popular idioms. Popular artists move fluidly to high art idioms. More and more schools of the arts are training their students to move comfortably and creatively between new and traditional. The high-tech dot.com world is as alluring to highly talented artists today as the then exotic worlds of movies and television once were to their grandparents and parents. And as the arts field evolves, more schools of the arts are consciously playing out this transformation through changed practices and priorities.

The evidence of blurred lines is everywhere, even beyond the training grounds. Cirque du Soleil evolves out of the anticommercial New Pickle Circus, moves to dual homes in Las Vegas and Disneyland Orlando, and receives serious coverage in the *New York Times,* coverage to which any nonprofit cutting-edge artist would aspire. In theater, work moves regularly from the nonprofit stage to commercial productions. Cutting-edge performance artists, such as California's Highways, find that their competition for audiences isn't other performance art nonprofits, but MTV and stylized commercial club venues. Clear Channel buys SFX and offers the ability to present touring productions that it can simultaneously cross-promote through its ownership of virtually every type of entertainment and advertising media. Presenters that would once have used a "performing arts festival" to showcase symphonies and ballet, now consciously and routinely attach the performing arts' tag line to popular acts.

The forces have been so numerous as to demand change in the way the field sees itself and operates. And yet adapting to operate comfortably within a market economy continues to be viewed with suspicion, largely because the old economic and social models were so ingrained. Change is "sticky" and "enterprises hang on to existing ways of doing things far beyond the time these have ceased being the most efficient way of operating. Change is irrational, in the sense that enterprises typically do not change as a result of economic calculations of cost and benefit but because their current mode of operation loses its legitimacy."[14]

SUCCEEDING IN THE MARKETPLACE

Just what does it mean for the arts to exist in the market economy? I would propose there are several requirements: (1) to compete in the marketplace for audiences (market share); (2) to compete in the market for funding and finance; (3) to compete for practitioners; and (4) to compete as a societal value or force. By succeeding in all of these, at whatever scale, large or small, an arts organization or individual artist succeeds in working within the market economy. In fact, can the arts be successful in these ways? Many organizations and artists clearly are, and are working quickly to gain the sophistication needed to become more competitive, more capable of winning and gaining a larger share of the market. They are doing so with an eye to consistently high artistic quality as well—long feared as the fallout to market success. Quality, in fact, may be more important than ever in the market economy. As B. Joseph Pine II and James H. Gilmore note, "Just as people have cut back on goods to spend more money on services, now they also scrutinize the time and money they spend on services to make way for more memorable—and more highly valued—experiences."[15]

As consumers have become more and more aware of their power, the pressure for quality on the arts sector has increased. A consumer in a recent focus group of regular arts attendees said, "I think the subject is always the quality, right? Because time is limited, you want quality whether it's a big or a small organization." One performing arts marketer recently noted in analysis of the impact of artistic excellence on market share, "there are times when it isn't bad work, but lack of a strong artistic voice, and that makes a difference (in market success)."[16]

A key difference between succeeding within the market economy or trying to live outside of its forces is the role of the consumer: for most arts makers and arts institutions, the consumer is a necessary partner. The consumer marketplace, though, is so complex and consumers are so well conditioned that it is impossible to enter the game unless prepared with the skills to compete and win, balanced by a philosophical through-line that grounds every market decision and keeps mission-integrity solidly in mind. This isn't necessarily bad if in fact the strategy can make the arts competitive enough to win, gain, and regain a passionate audience (consumer) market share. But it is a new way of thinking.

In fact, sophistication to maneuver in the consumer-driven marketplace requires new thinking about virtually every aspect of artistic production and presentation, as well as new thinking about the traditional lack of emphasis given to true marketing. The consumer no longer views the nonprofit arts as a separate sector, but sees that the sector of the market economy into which the arts fall as product—separate from the arts as facets of education, community development, or social services—and is part of the entertainment sector, which "is fast becoming the driving wheel of the new world economy."[17]

Entertainment has outpaced fundamentals such as clothing and health care as a share of U.S. household spending, and "has seeped into every part of the consumer economy in much the same way that computerization made its presence felt in previous decades."[18] This arts as a segment of the entertainment economy is a hard concept for many to accept, much less to use as a means to build a larger and newly vigorous following. "Commodified culture is emerging as the world's foremost economic industry. The worlds of scholarship and commerce, education and entertainment, previously separated, are becoming increasingly conjoined.... [C]ultural institutions can no longer be the preserve of the elite or the refuge of the scholar or curator."[19]

THE NEW ARTS AUDIENCE

However uncomfortable commodified culture may be, it is succeeding in reaching and involving larger and more diverse audiences for the arts. The arts have gone beyond playing to a narrow sociodemographic band of the population. Based on the Simmons Survey of the American Household from 1992 to 1996, spending on movie, theater, opera, and ballet tickets in households in the third economic quintile rose nearly 20 percent. It increased 14 percent for members of the fourth quintile. This means that the arts are no longer the province of the sociodemographic elite, but that more moderate- to lower-income households are going to the arts—the broadly defined arts. The arts are reaching the broad audience they've sought. But in the process they, and their consumers, have both changed.

Now, going the next step is the challenge, artistically, financially, and operationally. Competing in the marketplace for audiences—consumers—is a constantly fluid and massive undertaking, as it means staying current with market behavior. Audiences no longer check their consumerism at the door when they come to the nonprofit arts. They are demanding and empowered by their larger control in the consumer economy. The shift from "audience" to "consumer" shifts power. For the arts, this means adjustments. It places enormous new power in the hands of the consumer and suggests that all customers be treated specially, something most arts organizations are not set up to do. How does a performing arts organization that has typically reserved privileges for subscribers and donors make the occasional attendee feel noticed? How does a museum build a rapport with the unnamed visitor? Knowing how to do this now must become standard, if nonprofit arts institutions are to compete for market share. "Choice decisions for experience products (such as performing arts) are influenced by emotional expectations, not by cognitive assessments of product attributes. This adds to the critical role of emotions in certain realms of consumer behavior. We also find that informational inputs from critic reviews, word of mouth, and latent product interest are important determinants of consumer choice."[20]

The new skill set for competing in a market economy cannot be underestimated, nor can the need for outside sparks to fire consumer interest. These sparks have unfortunately been too few and too seldom to further the arts' need for larger market positioning, and they need to be rekindled. Critical attention to the arts, within mass media, continued to diminish during the 1990s despite the best efforts of ventures such as the Pew Charitable Fund's investment in arts criticism at the Columbia School of Journalism. Without the benchmark of the critical review, many consumers don't know how to gauge their own potential interest in the artistic product. This leads to less knowledge, less participation—a classic consumer pattern. Must it then be the task of arts institutions to, in effect, create their own media—their own electronic or traditional networks for critical commentary—to provide the grounding consumers need? Perhaps this, too, is part of the task.

Changed consumption patterns also require attention for the arts to achieve success in the market economy. Cultural tourism, and its arts tourism subset, are replacing (and may soon outpace) hometown participation as consumption patterns shift toward "going while on vacation" rather than going locally, a trend that is already beginning to drive new alliances between the arts and the tourism industries. Will satellite museums continue to grow using the Guggenheim Bilbao model as creative opportunities for new consumption patterns? Will performing arts organizations find the formula they need for extended residencies not only at summer festivals, but also throughout the year? Will the ubiquitous subscription season give way to packaged spurts of programming that are no longer the ho-hum, but instead serve as engines to drive new excitement and participation? Thinking about the potential change quickly brings to mind the risks, the financial resources required for experimentation, and the scale of changes necessary.

MARKETING, MARKETING, MARKETING

Simply surviving in such a fast-forward environment is a tall order for an industry in which many major performing arts and museum institutions only evolved from public relations to "marketing" staff positions or departments within the last ten years, where program packaging and sales are done much as they have been for decades, and where consumer research—when available—is used more to quantify the known than to explore the possible.[21] Part of the problem is lack of understanding about marketing.

Many (nonprofit) institutions misunderstand marketing. They confuse marketing with either hard-selling or advertising, and, therefore, don't show an aptitude for it. The important tasks in marketing have to do with studying the market, segmenting it, targeting the groups you want to service, positioning yourself in the market and creating a service that meets needs out there. Advertising and selling are afterthoughts. The contrast between marketing and selling is whether you start with customers or consumers or groups you want to serve well—that's marketing. If you start with a set of products you have and want to push them out into any market you can find—that's selling.[22]

The complexity of the marketing task alone—not even extending to the larger issues of organizational responsiveness—is difficult for many organizations to address. Marketing requires savvy in analysis and segmentation, and the explicit notion that narrow and well-studied target groups rather than the broad public are the likely audience for particular events and exhibitions. This suggests tremendous investment in systems and infrastructure to become truly competitive in the marketplace, an investment that typically requires capitalization rather than incremental adjustments to budgets. And market segmentation and target marketing—that is, tools and methods that are the stock in trade of the market economy—appear to some to fly in the face of reaching and appealing to the broadest possible audience.

The discomfort is philosophical and financial. It is cultural and historical. It might suggest overhauling long-held systems of series, subscription mechanisms, and memberships. The discomfort is so significant that many arts organizations—especially if the size of their endowments allows them to do so—may happily distance themselves from the issues and try to function as they traditionally have, even with dwindling numbers of seats sold.

Responding to the market economy, then, takes a new kind of financial underpinning and risk taking—it requires thinking differently about product lines, brands, targeting, packaging, and dissemination. It takes investment and venture capital. It takes working cash reserves, elasticity in venues, and flexibility in contracts. Market responsiveness of this scale is not simply a matter of adding a staff person or two or tweaking a marketing budget. It implies—demands—total organizational transformation, beginning with mission and extending through every aspect of the nonprofit institution.

As Derrick Cook notes:

The lack of response to rapid change by managers, artists, presenters, and funders should concern us, because as any Darwinian will tell you, when challenged by change, the fatal response is denial. At this very time, when we should be innovating and experimenting broadly (not just in some narrow, avant-garde manner), we have become uptight, hesitant to take risks. Let's hope this soon changes. Each of us should immediately consider strategies to prompt experimentation, rational innovation, and cumulative learning in all aspects of the arts in our lives. Word of mouth and word on the Net will replace our flagging marketing strategies. No problem to download, at home, a brief performance scene of the current production, an interview with its leading actor, or the comments of last night's audience members as we decide whether or not to key in our online reservation.[23]

THE FUNDING PUZZLE

Readiness to function in the market economy thus may come slowly and only with a support network of funding to make it possible. Decades of economic analysis have reinforced the concept that revenue needs to come from several sources, not just admissions at the museum door or the performing arts box office. In the market economy, art organizations will need to continue to make the case—more competitively than ever—for grants. Those grants will likely continue to span a wide range of funder interests. Much will go to building endowments, a trend well established as a market antidote even among smaller nonprofits, to provide safety from the yin and yang of consumer trends. In addition, grants should ideally build on the past decade of funder interest in public access, though more narrowly and deeply focused on addressing the practical need of creating new means of product distribution and points of consumption within the marketplace. Within the context of funding as venture capital, much can be done. It is, perhaps, venture funding—with an acknowledgment of the need for taking risk in finding the new market economy model of success—that is most appropriate at this juncture.

Much is already being done to develop not only new venture funding but also financing by entrepreneurial arts organizations that see advantages both to the dissemination of their art and the broadening of their audience by developing new joint ventures with for-profit partners. These differ from the "unrelated business" revenue sources ranging from gift stores to condominium towers, as mechanisms to advance the artistic product in the marketplace. As an extreme example, the California-based Cornerstone Theater Company—known since the mid-1980s as a touring company with a strongly held philosophy against paid admissions and earned income—has recently used its creativity to both meet its mission and generate revenue. Today, it develops products that bring its theater to more audiences across the country through commissioned collaborations with for-profit partners and HBO joint ventures.

They are hardly alone. Limited liability corporations and partnerships between commercial and nonprofit corporations have already become widely used means to both increase revenue options and build market share for artistic product that crosses the commercial–nonprofit lines. New thinking for many is opening the door to new opportunities for revenue, market share, and institutional reinvention.

This, in turn, will likely win practitioners who now may question the current viability of the nonprofit arts to connect to the public. As audiences and consumers find new ways to connect to the arts and artistic work, artists may gain a newly vital, if different, role in the marketplace. Artists may see a larger opportunity to connect to the public and to maneuver between sectors. Their work may be packaged differently, disseminated differently, and more carefully targeted. Their stage may be more public and larger, and their impact greater.

Such new structures and new hybrids as they and their institutions create may be what is needed to bring the public back to square one—to valuing the contribution the arts make societally, as a shared experience that creates and maintains cultural meaning. This, in the end, is precisely why it is worth arguing for the arts to become skilled and competitive at functioning within the market economy.

NOTES

1. Paul J. DiMaggio, "Social Structure, Institutions, and Cultural Goods: The Case of the United States," in *Social Theory for a Changing Society*, ed. Pierre Bourdieu and James S. Coleman (Boulder, CO: Westview, 1991).

2. Marc Raboy et al., "Cultural Development and the Open Economy: A Democratic Issue and a Challenge to Public Policy," *Canadian Journal of Communications* 19, no. 3–4 (summer–autumn 1994).

3. John Kriedler, "Leverage Lost: Evolution in the Nonprofit Arts Ecosystem," in *The Politics of Culture: Policy Perspectives for Individuals, Institutions, and Communities*, ed. Gigi Bradford, Michael Gary, and Glenn Wallach (New York: New Press, 2000).

4. Louise K. Stevens, *California Arts Audience Research Project*, vol. 1 (November 1999).

5. Richard A. Peterson and Darren E. Sherkat, "Effects of Age on Arts Participation," in *Age and Arts Participation, with a Focus on the Baby Boom Cohort*, National Endowment for the Arts, Research Division Report no. 34 (Santa Ana, CA: Seven Locks, 1996).

6. Stevens, California Arts Audience Research Project.

7. Kriedler, "Leverage Lost."

8. William J. Baumol and William G. Bowmen, "The Performing Arts: The Economic Dilemma," *Twentieth Century Fund Report* (1965).

9. B. Joseph Pine II and James H. Gilmore, *The Experience Economy: Work Is Theatre and Every Business a Stage* (Cambridge, MA: Harvard Business School Press, 1999).

10. Russel B. Nye, *The Unembarrassed Muse: The Popular Arts in America* (New York: Dial, 1970).

11. DiMaggio, "Social Structure, Institutions, and Cultural Goods."

12. From American Assembly, *The Arts and the Public Purpose* (New York: American Assembly, Columbia University, 1997).

13. Stevens, California Arts Audience Project.

14. Robert MacIntosh and Arthur Francis, *The Market, Technological and Industry Contexts of Business Process Re-engineering in UK Business* (Glasgow: Business Processes Resource Center, 1997).

15. Pine and Gilmore, *The Experience Economy: Work Is Theatre and Every Business a Stage.*

16. Stevens, California Arts Audience Research Project.

17. Michael J. Wolf, *The Entertainment Economy: How Mega-media Forces Are Transforming Our Lives* (New York: Times Books/Random House, 1999).

18. Ibid.

19. Richard Kurin, "The New Study and Curation of Culture," in *Reflections of Culture Broker: A View from the Smithsonian*, by Richard Kurin (Washington, DC: Smithsonian Institution Press, 1997).

20. Ramya Neelamegham and Dipak Jain, "Consumer Choice Process for Experience Goods: An Econometric Model and Analysis," *Journal of Marketing Research* (August 1999).

21. Stevens, California Arts Audience Research Project.

22. Philip Kotler, interview by Peter Drucker, in *Managing the Nonprofit Organization* (New York: HarperCollins, 1990).

23. Derrick Cook, *Theater News* (January 2000).

15

Government Support for the Arts:
A New Forecast

John K. Urice

In 1988, the editors of the precursor to this book asked me to submit a chapter about the long-term future of government arts funding. The chapter—"Government Support for the Arts in the United States, 1990–2015: A Forecast"[1]—was submitted in late 1988 and published unchanged in 1990. With fingers crossed and a great deal of presumption, I had consolidated my research, the studies of other scholars, and added to the mix my "gut feelings." The chapter that was published was in press a year *before* either Andres Serrano or Robert Mapplethorpe had become practically household words linked to obscenity and sacrilege.[2] I wrote:

My premise is not that government support of the arts in the United States is inherently good and that the biggest problem is inadequate funding. This [chapter] is neither positive nor optimistic. I foresee serious and fundamental changes....Whether these changes, if they occur, are for the better will, of course, depend on how one perceives the past and current state of government's role in the arts in the United States. I foresee [that] ... the structure of support ... will be markedly different from the status quo.[3]

A REVIEW OF THE PREDICTIONS OF 1990

At this point, it only fair to review key forecasts I made more than a decade ago.

Rising Costs

Rising costs are a reality for programs, administration, and even capital expenditures; the last may be the biggest financial time bomb. In the halcyon days of 1960s and 1970s, American cultural institutions had an "edifice complex" and erected or rehabilitated structures around the country.... Now these buildings are aging ... and the need for improvement or replacement of ... "major systems" will require millions if not billions of dollars in improvements in the next decade and beyond. Most organizations do not have adequate reserves or endowments to cover the costs of such improvements.[4]

This forecast was generally correct. Costs for operations and capital improvements *have* been and remain a major concern for arts organizations. What I had not foreseen—nor do I think anyone did in 1988 when the country was entering a major recession—was that less than four years later we would begin the longest period of economic prosperity in the nation's history. Undoubtedly, the economic buoyancy of the past eight years has affected virtually all government programs, as most states and the federal government were amassing budget surpluses. However, the basic issue—that the arts are labor-, space-, and equipment-intensive—has not changed. The majority of arts organizations have not been able to build adequate reserves, with notable exceptions, especially among those that conducted capital campaigns.

The National Endowment for the Arts' Budget Prospects

[T]here is little [probability] that the Arts Endowment will ... receive any major budget increases, and certainly not on a scale needed to make up for the losses due to the inflation of the past decade [1980s]. Probably the National Endowment for the Arts will continue to be reauthorized until at least the end of the century, and by then its budget will be in the realm of current level funding or lower.[5]

This forecast was quite accurate. The National Endowment for the Arts' (NEA) program budget from fiscal year (FY) 1990 through 1999 declined from $124.255 million to $66.022 million, a decrease of more than $58 million— about 47 percent in unadjusted dollars. The underlying reasons for this trend are worthy of brief consideration, as they will influence predictions about future funding.

First, the well-documented controversies surrounding issues of "obscenity" and "sacrilege" were partially responsible for increasing the negative perceptions of the NEA. Another significant factor was the poor state of the national economy at the time, which sharpened the focus on what was "appropriate" use of taxpayers' money.

Second, conservatives, the religious right, and others detected arrogance by the NEA and its supporters—basically, "we know what we are doing, and we do not need further accountability nor restrictions on free expression." On the other hand, the arts constituency and artists became concerned that the NEA would *not* support continued free expression with the use of public funds. The issues boiled down to *accountability*. While Congress rejected the broad Helms Amendment that would have severely restricted NEA grants, it did pass a ban on works that might be "considered obscene, and that do not have serious literary, artistic, political or scientific value."[6]

Third, due to huge budget cuts in the NEA's appropriation the agency was forced to make major structural changes in 1996, essentially eliminating the discipline-based program offices.[7] Staff was reduced by 47 percent.[8] With the reduction of budgets and the elimination of discipline "homes" within the NEA, many constituents and long-standing grant recipients came to the conclusion that the NEA was becoming irrelevant. For many, the NEA became a *symbol*, more than a functioning agency. The mid-1990s reorganization was a means of *surviving*, not necessarily the means of achieving the original and subsequently modified *purposes* of the NEA.[9]

Private Giving

Individual gifts and donations will likely decline.[10]

Again, this prediction was accurate. The 1998 *Giving USA*[11] annual report revealed: "Giving to arts, culture, humanities reached an estimated $10.53 billion in 1998. Between 1990 and 1998, there has been a total decline in giving of 6.56%."[12] These patterns of giving to the arts are not positive, especially considering the overall growth in personal wealth. Furthermore, "giving to the arts is concentrated in a small number of large institutions. When these organizations raise large amounts, that increase propels statistics on arts giving."[13]

In 1996, and continuing today, many large arts organizations are involved in major capital campaigns including, for example, the Museum of Modern Art ($300–$450 million), Metropolitan Museum of Art ($300 million +), Carnegie Hall ($75 million), and Brooklyn Academy of Music ($70 million).[14]

With regard to grant-making private foundations, a 1998 report from the Foundation Center[15] states: "Arts giving as a share of all giving in the 1996 *Grants Index* sample fell to the lowest level reported in the 1980s and 1990s, despite solid increases in arts grant dollars awarded.... Adjusted for inflation, arts giving gained nearly one-tenth (9.8 percent). Nonetheless, *overall* grants dollars in the sample grew ... by 33.4 percent."[16]

In sum, giving to the arts by two major sources—individuals (more critical to the arts than any other part of the profit segment) and foundations—fell behind growth in other areas during the 1990s for a variety of reasons, one especially relevant. With the NEA being reduced to a negligible factor in overall arts funding, the "imprimatur" that NEA grants used to bestow on recipients is now gone. Appropriately or not, in the past many private donors saw an NEA grant as a stamp of artistic/peer/government approval.

Giving USA also notes that "[i]n 1998, small and large arts organizations ... reported increased giving. Mid-size organizations, however, report contribution revenue had declined."[17] This statement was no surprise to me. Indeed, in my original chapter I wrote, "Many current middle-size organizations ... will no longer exist."[18]

My explanation for the current funding trends is fairly simplistic, but probably valid. The contributions to "large organizations" are long-established centerpieces of culture. As noted, many are in the midst of major fund-raising campaigns and can attract money from a national donor constituency. Furthermore, works of art rapidly appreciated during the 1990s. Donors had new tax incentives to contribute paintings and sculpture at market value, especially if a donor—as many did—needed to offset significant capital gains on investments.

Small organizations tend to rely mostly on local individual contributors, family foundations, and community foundations. As "local" arts organizations, donors are able to simultaneously help the arts, enhance their communities, and make their gifts to institutions unlikely to support offensive or challenging art that might be unwelcome within the context of a particular community.[19]

A NEW LOOK TO THE FUTURE OF PUBLIC FUNDING

Now it is time again for me to look to the future. As I did before, I will make some forecasts and predictions based on evidence and trends analysis. I also hope that these projections encourage the arts community to continue to forge plans for new arts-funding mechanisms, as we are obviously in a radically different political, cultural, economic, and arts environment than we were just a decade ago.

The Presidency

George W. Bush is now the president of the United States. In the context of this chapter, does it really matter? Only to a limited degree. Presidents have the power of appointment, the veto, and—most important—the best bully pulpit in the world. Historically, presidents have played two major roles with regard to the arts. First, they have set a "tone" for the arts and culture by the symbolic and actual emphasis they place on art or performance in the White House and elsewhere. They can indicate or not that the arts are given deference and relevance. Does culture receive, for lack of a better phrase, "executive respect"? Presidential rhetoric regarding—and explicit support for—the arts, not just at reauthorization time, can further set a tone and establish the priority for the arts among many competing needs. Presidents can indeed help or hurt the arts. Ironically, for example, it seems obvious that when former president Ronald Reagan called for the elimination of the NEA in 1981, he did so not to attack the *arts*, but to attack the *bureaucracy*. He was firm in his belief that there were better and less cumbersome ways of helping and funding the arts.

Of course, the president also has the responsibility to nominate the chairperson of the NEA, a job that history has shown is often ambiguous and difficult. As it should be, individuals with very different personalities and backgrounds have held the position in different times and circumstances. The selection of the "right" chairperson can be a critical decision for the NEA. A mismatch of style, political skill, or administrative/leadership ability could end in disaster.[20]

Unless there is a major scandal—and many are getting tired of these, even as legislatures try to stop public funding for plays like *Corpus Christi*—I believe President Bush will face great contention and conflicts about priorities as the United States enters its next phase in the post–Cold War world. There will be critical matters such as Social Security and Medicare preservation, crime, drugs, education, new weapons—especially the so-called Star Wars program—trade treaties, and so on. It seems doubtful that—unless forced by special political circumstances—Bush is going to do more than appoint a chairperson, express the usual support for the arts and the "highest values of civilization that they represent," and move on to more pressing matters.

National Endowment for the Arts

As I wrote in 1990, "I see no 'white knight' (in either the executive or legislative branches of government) who has the will and power to help the arts significantly. Historically, those sincere and committed congressional advocates (such as Pell) will have many battles to fight and other agendas to address (e.g., defending major social programs)."[21] Nothing has substantively changed in the last dozen years. Realistically, the severe budget reductions and program restructuring of the NEA have led to the loss of constituents and supporters, not only in the arts community, but also within a battle-weary Congress.

The NEA will become even more irrelevant and be at the periphery of the arts unless it can achieve two goals. First, it must demonstrate that the new structure—a structure that could be changed, of course, by an incoming chairperson—truly serves the field and is not just a group of "innocuous" themes— education and access, or heritage and preservation. Second, it also must find ways to increase its budget so that it has funds to exert leadership and influence outcomes. I believe that neither is likely to happen.

Many organizational and political theorists believe that organizations have a fixed life span; it is likely that the NEA is one of these.

Do the NEA's supporters want to keep going to *prove they have beaten the forces of darkness and doom from the Right?* If so, they must now recognize that they have already lost. The FY2000 program budget, in adjusted dollars, is about equal to the budget of 1971—that is, thirty years ago!

Does the NEA hang on because of its *symbolic role,* as some have suggested? All the conflict and turbulence surrounding the NEA has had a negative effect on the general support for the arts from other sources—private funding has not risen in the arts at the rates of other areas of the nonprofit sector during the 1990s.

Or does the NEA fight to stay alive in the *hopes of better times ahead?* If so, what constitutes "better times"? Increased budgets and the ability to rebuild constituencies seem unlikely, as most constituents have already looked elsewhere for support and often found it. Others are dealing with their own Darwinist demises.

New models for the distribution of federal arts funds must be found. I predicted one such model in my earlier chapter:

The National Council for the Arts will serve as a panel and will review on five-year cycles the plans submitted by the state arts agencies and national cultural treasures. But, as is now the case with the review of state plans, the review will be tempered with the knowledge that, except in blatant cases of abuse, the grants are a virtual certainty. Additionally, the National Council on the Arts will serve an expanded ceremonial role and encourage more awards for artistic excellence. This will be necessary to maintain a "federal arts presence" in the media and on Capitol Hill.[22]

The NEA was a noble experiment, conceived with good intentions, but always tenuous due to constitutional issues, subject matter, and politics. It has endured so many attacks for so long that it is now virtually irrelevant and ineffective—in terms of budget, constituency, and influence. I cannot predict that the NEA will close up shop in the next ten years; bureaucracies rarely close themselves, and it is unlikely that anyone else will expend the time and effort to shutter the doors and zero-out the appropriation. Sadly, I believe the arts will continue to be burdened by an agency that has outlived its usefulness.

State Arts Agencies

In my 1990 chapter I wrote, "Aggregate state appropriations likely will continue to maintain at least [inflation adjusted] current levels through the 1990s.... The state agency missions will be to support, through regranting, the statewide and regional organizations.... State agencies will, in many cases, also have increased responsibility for fellowships and individual artists support."[23]

It appears that I was quite accurate in most aspects of these forecasts. Nonetheless, it is important to look at what has happened and how it helps presage the future. During the period FY90 to FY99, aggregate state agency appropriations increased from $292+ million to almost $370 million, an increase of 25 percent.[24]

State arts agencies (SAAs) continue to provide "statewide" regranting programs. Significantly, as the NEA virtually eliminated grants to individuals as part of its 1996 reorganization,[25] many states continued or expanded their support of individual artists through grant or fellowship programs.

But what of the future? If one looks at the aggregate state agencies' legislative appropriations over the past three decades, one is struck by three observations. First, in adjusted dollars, the state agencies have seen on average about a 3.3 percent increase each year. Second, of the total appropriations by state legislatures, line-item appropriations have grown dramatically. In 1979, line items totaled $3.6 million or 4.6 percent of appropriations; they grew to $49.5 million or 13.4 percent in 1999. This is the highest percentage ever, and virtually doubles the percentage of the previous year. Thus, state councils and their panels have virtually no control over a large segment of their appropriations.[26] The concern for the future is that when legislatures earmark funds for designated organizations and include this amount in the agencies' budget, they distort the meaning of the appropriation. Furthermore, line items undermine long-standing principles of peer review, competitiveness based on quality, and accountability.

Third, while the overall state appropriations to the arts have remained on a fairly predictable upward curve, as we speculate about the future it is important to note that *there have been major reductions in state arts appropriations during times of economic stress*. When the country entered a major recession in the early 1990s, aggregate appropriations dropped successively in FY91 through FY93; the three-year reduction totaled almost 28 percent.[27] The implications are that it is a virtual certainty (except for those who believe in the "new economy" philosophy that says the past is so different from the present and future that former predicative models no longer apply) that the country *will* go into a recession. When, how long, and how deep are unknowns,[28] but clearly we are teetering on the edge of a mild to moderate recession now. If so, the key question is whether state legislatures will continue to increase support for the arts, or will competing and other pressing needs (e.g., social services, prisons, and education) reduce the funds available for the arts in a time of scarcity?[29] Furthermore, an overall reduction in state funding for the arts will likely *accelerate* the trend toward line items, as legislators scramble to protect certain constituent organizations.

Local Arts Agencies

In my earlier chapter, I understated the role of local arts agencies (LAAs):[30] "Local arts agencies will thrive in middle-size cities. Smaller cities will find they lack the critical mass ... to sustain funding for facilities and programs. [Those with] well-endowed community foundations may be exceptions."[31]

Beginning in 1984 with the NEA's Locals Test Program,[32] many local arts agencies gained access to government support at the local, county, state, and federal level. "Local arts agencies" vary widely in name, size, mission, and source of funds.[33] Some are private, some are units of government. Americans for the Arts, the primary national service organization for local agencies, says there are four thousand LAAs, but other sources cite lower figures—which is natural, as definitions vary. As noted earlier, I had predicted good times for LAAs in midsized cities. According to Americans for the Arts, between 1993 and 1997 LAAs' budgets for communities with populations between 30,000 and 499,000 saw dramatic increases.[34] Critically, during this period there was notable growth in funds received from government sources. Indeed, for LAAs located in communities of 100,000 to 499,000, local and other governmental support accounted for just over half of their collective budgets, most of which came from local governments.[35] The NEA accounted for only 1.3 percent.[36]

I believe the overall trend of support for LAAs during the 1990s bodes well for the future. While local agencies are not immune to effects of poor economic conditions or competing priorities, among the three levels of governmental agencies considered, they appear to be the most durable, with the greatest likelihood of increased funding into the indefinite future. It also seems probable that LAAs will grow in influence within the larger arts community as others experience declines.

Conclusions and Additional Forecasts

"The arts—which do not exist in a vacuum but are, rather interactive with myriad aesthetic, social, cultural economic and political forces—will change."[37] When I wrote that sentence twelve years ago, it was stating an obvious but often unspoken truth. The arts are not isolated from other forces, including political whim. As we have seen—especially at the federal and state levels—the arts have been highly politicized whether through controversy over content, by increased expectations of "accountability," or through line items. Over the next decade, especially when the country goes into its next recession, there will be a further Darwinian decline in the number of arts organizations, perhaps leaving more funds for the organizations that survive. There does remain a concern that "survival of the fittest" will mean that large and long-established organizations may prosper at the expense of smaller ones that for many have led the way in providing access to the arts. As yet, no one really knows what the implications of changing technologies might be. Even though for two decades[38] we have heard about the potentially profound implications of various technologies and the arts, there is scant evidence that technology is affecting how audiences experience the arts. There is a decreasing federal influence that probably will not change regardless of future presidents. The SAAs will continue to grow in influence, but they likely will be more vulnerable to macroeconomic conditions than will LAAs. On the positive side, I believe that the future of the arts—the creation and dissemination of expressive works—looks bright. What we will see is what I had predicted: major changes in the way the arts are funded and the changing role that governments at all levels might play.

I have no doubt that some of the as-yet-unfulfilled predictions (e.g., the increasing role of colleges and universities) I made twelve years ago will, in fact, occur in the next decade. I also believe that the arts community has already made major adjustments to the changing environment, albeit sometimes painfully. Artists and arts organizations, no longer able to depend on NEA funding, have adjusted or are doing so. They are finding new sources of funding, or—more critically—adjusting their missions and programs to fit within available resources. This has been beneficial to some organizations that are finding they now do less, but they do it better. The ongoing growth of local arts funding, increasingly critical in the past six years, is leading to new opportunities to collaborate, improve access, and meet the needs of both artists and audiences.

My final prediction is this: There will be major realignments of government funding sources. Roles will change or be eliminated. *But arts organizations will adjust.* The organizations' artistic imperative will be manifest not by trying to recreate the funding mechanisms and models of the 1960s and 1970s, but rather through a recognition of, and adapting to, new realities about the appropriate and inevitable roles of government and the arts.

NOTES

1. John K. Urice, "Government Support for the Arts in the United States, 1990–2015: A Forecast," in *The Future of the Arts: Public Policy and Arts Research,* ed. David B. Pankratz and Valerie B. Morris (New York: Praeger, 1990), 243–62.

2. The two artists became the focus of attention and a means of attacking the NEA when each was associated with NEA–funded projects. Andres Serrano placed a plastic crucifix in his own urine, photographed it, and called it "Piss Christ." Selections of the homoerotic and graphic photographs by the late Robert Mapplethorpe, a respected photographer, were assembled into a touring exhibition. For further details, there are many sources. See especially John Frohnmayer, *Leaving Town Alive: Confessions of an Arts Warrior* (Boston: Houghton Mifflin, 1993); also see Margaret Jane Wyszomirski, "From Accord to Discord: Arts Policy during and after the Culture Wars," in *America's Commitment to Culture: Government and the Arts,* ed. Kevin V. Mulcahy and Margaret Jane Wyszomirski (Boulder, CO.: Westview, 1995).

3. Urice, "Government Support," 243.

4. Ibid., 247.

5. Ibid., 248.

6. Wyszomirski, "From Accord to Discord,"4.

7. The NEA program budget peaked at $124 million in FY1991. There were steady declines in subsequent years. In one year, between FY1994 and FY1995, the program budget declined by 40 percent. See National Assembly of State Arts Agencies, *State Arts Agency Funding Sourcebook* (Washington, DC: National Assembly of State Arts Agencies, 2000), Tab III, Table 3a.

8. National Endowment for the Arts, *The National Endowment for the Arts 1965–2000: A Brief Chronology of Federal Support for the Arts* (Washington, DC: National Endowment for the Arts, 2000), 54.

9. As I have noted in various publications and presentations, the apologetic nature of the original Preamble of the 1965 enabling legislation was a predictor of future problems.

10. Urice, "Government Support," 250.

11. Ann E. Kaplan, ed. *Giving USA: The Annual Report on Philanthropy for the Year 1998* (New York: AAFRC Trust for Philanthropy, 1999), 88.

12. Ibid., 135

13. Ibid., 137. The word "propels" may not be the best choice of words. I believe that "distorts" is more accurate.

14. Ibid.

15. Loren Renz and Steven Lawrence, *Arts Funding: An Update on Foundation Trends* (New York: Foundation Center, 1998).

16. Ibid., 4.

17. Kaplan, *Giving USA*, 89.

18. Urice, "Government Support," 255. In truth, the section that contained that prescient observation about coming problems for midsized arts organizations also made some predictions that, so far, have not happened. I was far afield in predicting that the NEA would be funding primarily large, "national treasure" institutions. However, I still have over ten years for that to come true, as it well may when the "four-themes" structure fails for lack of cohesiveness and constituency.

19. A July 2001 report by RAND and the Pew Charitable Trusts notes: "The biggest challenge suggested by these trends relates to the middle-tier of non-profit arts organizations ... located outside of major metropolitan areas. Likely reductions in demand, rising costs, and static or even declining funding streams will force many of these institutions either to become larger and more prestigious—which many will lack the resources to do—or to become smaller and more community-oriented, using local talents to keep costs down.... Still others will simply close their doors." See Kevin F. McCarthy et al., *The Performing Arts in a New Era* (Santa Monica, CA: RAND, 2001), xxiii.

20. A worst-case example occurred when President Bush appointed John Frohnmayer as chairman of the NEA in 1989. He was fired two and a half years later after many crises and a lack of leadership. For a personal perspective, see Frohnmayer, *Leaving Town Alive*.

21. Urice, "Government Support," 248.

22. Ibid., 255.

23. Ibid., 255–56.

24. These figures include only funds appropriated to the agencies by state legislatures. They do not include grants from the NEA or any other sources. The figures do include, however, pass-through line-item appropriations over which the state agencies have little or no discretion.

25. The exceptions are Literature Fellowships, National Heritage Fellowships, and American Jazz Masters. See *National Endowment for the Arts 1965–2000*, 54.

26. The range is quite remarkable. In FY99, 58.5 percent of the California Arts Council's budget was designated by the state legislature as a pass-through grant. More than half of the fifty-six states and special jurisdictions have no line items. See National Assembly of State Arts Agencies, *State Arts Agency Funding Sourcebook*, Tab II, Table 2a.

27. Ibid.

28. As I write this in the spring of 2000, the stock markets have seen major reductions (a "bear market" or "corrections"?) in the last two months. Inflationary indicators are rising and the Federal Reserve has raised interest rates six times in less than a year.

While presidential election year recessions are rare, they still happen. After the election, the uncertainty rises.

29. See Sarah Hebel, "Public Colleges Feel Impact of the Economic Downturn," *Chronicle of Higher Education,* 20 July 2001, A 21. As state surpluses disappear, it is likely that there will be increased pressures to fund only "essential services." The arts have rarely been placed in this category by legislators during times of economic stress.

30. I did predict growing alliances between local arts agencies and higher education institutions. It is still too early to assess the accuracy of this forecast. However, significant anecdotal information indicates that the prediction is coming to fruition. See Urice, "Government Support," 256.

31. Ibid.

32. National Endowment for the Arts, *National Endowment for the Arts 1965–2000,* 36.

33. Americans for the Arts, *Monographs: Local Arts Agencies Facts 1998* (Washington, DC: Americans for the Arts, 1998). The cover flap has a lengthy description of how the organization defines a LAA and notes, "each LAA in America is unique to the community that it serves." See also pages 2–3.

34. Ibid., 4.

35. Ibid., 5.

36. Ibid., 7. Also important are the NEA's congressionally mandated efforts to reach "underserved" areas.

37. Urice, "Government Support," 256.

38. In 1984, I had the pleasure of being the guest editor for a special issue of the *Journal of Arts Management, Law, and Society* on the topic of "Information Systems and the Arts," 14, no. 1 (spring 1984). The issue now seems so quaint!

V

Administration of the Arts Sector

16

Administering the Culture of Everyday Life: Imagining the Future of Arts Sector Administration

Kristin G. Congdon and Doug Blandy[1]

Everyday life includes myriad ways in which people assemble, work, and act together for a variety of political, aesthetic, economic, familial, religious, and/or educational purposes. Often referred to as "folklife," this culture of everyday life is expressive of the way individuals and groups "share a common body of traditional knowledge, skills, and behaviors."[2] In coming together to share celebratory experiences of everyday events, people generate creative and symbolic forms such as "custom, belief, technical skill, language, literature, art, architecture, music, dance, drama, ritual, pageantry, [and] handicraft."[3] Broadly conceived of in this way, participating in the culture of everyday life through art is something that virtually all of us do.

The arts and cultural life go hand in hand. Understood by cultural anthropologist Ellen Dissanayake as "making special" the arts is the human predisposition to engage in processes and products that encourage a sense of belonging. They also equip us with the ability to communicate what is important, grant refuge, allow us to respond to the problems and challenges associated with everyday life, provide amusement and pleasure, livelihood, and "exemplify ingenuity."[4] The inclination to make and appreciate art is so ordinary that it is often overlooked for the extraordinary contribution it makes to such commonplace activities as cooking, fishing, keeping house, gardening, computing, and the multitude of other endeavors required in daily life. The culture of everyday life can be understood and appreciated as "community life and values, artfully expressed in myriad interactions. It is universal, diverse, and enduring. It enriches the nation and makes us a commonwealth of cultures."[5]

Art and the culture of everyday life, because of its necessity and pervasiveness, should be of utmost importance to those engaged in the management of the arts locally, regionally, or nationally in a variety of settings. These spaces may include, but are not limited to, museums, schools, colleges and universities, arts councils, festivals, hobby associations, places of worship, recreation programs, and social service agencies. People managing the arts in settings such as these should carefully and mindfully consider the ways in which they facilitate, document, preserve, celebrate, curate, and educate about the arts in the context of everyday life. The development of policy to encourage this mindfulness needs to be considered at all levels and in all settings in which arts policy is conceptualized and implemented.

Cornel West reminds us that the "roots of democracy are fundamentally grounded in mutual respect, personal responsibility, and social accountability."[6] Any discussion of administering the culture of everyday life within the United States must consider West's admonition. Special attention should be given to the fact that the United States is demographically diverse in most all ways including race, ethnicity, political persuasion, sexual orientation, age, socioeconomic status, and religion. Any discussion of the culture of everyday life that takes place in this democracy should occur in a way that encourages the public discourse that democracy requires.

For these reasons, our purpose in this chapter is to examine issues, perspectives, and methods associated with the administration of programs designed to facilitate, explore, discern, debate, and celebrate the culture of everyday life. Folklore and cultural studies perspectives that link culture with the ways in which people experience, understand, and communicate everyday experience informs our orientation to culture in regard to policy making.

We specifically consider art and art making as one way in which culture is expressed. Toward this end, we discuss research, issues, methods, and perspectives associated with the field of folklore that model responsible, critical, and respectful approaches to cultural expression. We conclude with a discussion of approaches that can be useful in administrating arts programs associated with the culture of everyday life and the preparation of future arts administrators. We anticipate that our discussion will also assist in policy-making decisions regarding art and everyday life.

CONCEPTIONS OF CULTURE, ART, AND EVERYDAY LIFE

There is currently no consensus around a definition of "art" among the general public or those who administer the arts or conceptualize and implement arts policy. This lack of consensus reflects the multiplicity of opinions about the arts that one would expect in a democratic and demographically diverse society like that found within the United States. On this issue, we agree with J. A. Hobbs, who claims that there is little to no difference between what we have come to call fine art and other forms of cultural expression other than matters of classification.[7] In other words, the decision-making process used to classify objects as art is a process that is relative, fluid, elastic, and tenuous. Much of what we will discuss in this chapter as art associated with the everyday is often aligned with "low" culture or class, while "fine" art is attached to "high" culture or class. These associations are, in part, due to the taken-for-granted nature of the arts embedded in everyday life in the United States. For example, public infatuation with some forms classified as popular art emerged in the nineteenth century as knickknacks, comic books, film, and pulp fiction thought to be attractive and accessible to the so-called lower and middle classes as opposed to the theater, painting, and literature associated with the upper-class. However, others see the socioeconomic class boundaries associated with the consumption of art as permeable and cyclical. Researchers have discovered common ground for popular and elite culture and periods of time where cultural forms are shared across socioeconomic groups.[8] In addition, the notion of popular culture being market driven and elite culture as not being influenced by the market, but being reflective of a perennial notion of quality, has been dispelled.[9] That such distinctions continue to endure is surprising given that Andy Warhol and other "pop" artists are among those who collapsed definitions of art in the early 1960s and rendered such class distinctions related to art forms as obsolete and transparently classist.

The contentiousness around what constitutes art in the United States is also influenced by the "cult of the artist." Historically, this cult is founded on a select group of people who called themselves "artists" and increasingly began to concentrate their creative efforts on making art for the museum or gallery space. Simultaneously, theory emerged that supported an isolated and decontexulized view of their creations. Continuing to this day, numerous arts administrators focus their energy on developing programs and policies for supporting and exhibiting art created within this philosophical orientation. Within the United States, this orientation is exemplified by many of the programs and exhibits routinely encountered within such cultural icons as the Metropolitan Museum of Art, the Museum of Modern Art, and the National Gallery. These institutions bring public attention to art as a category in and of itself. However, it is important to remember that it was not until the Enlightenment in seventeenth- and eighteenth-century Europe that any society had ever separated art as an individual category apart from its context of use.[10] Once art was viewed in this manner and became removed from everyday life by being placed in art institutions, it was exhibited and seen as objects apart from function. Landon E. Beyer claims that this reductionist view, "while central to the aesthetic attitude," often obliterates "an essential element of the aesthetic experience" that is the social context.[11] In fact, the twentieth-century modernist movement accepted Greenberg's idea that art should withdraw completely from the world of social and political life.[12] One can make judgments about this movement in hindsight, but it is hard to dismiss the power these ideas had on culture and the way we view art today.

Concurrently, folklorists have been building public-sector programs that emphasize art in everyday life. Folklorists, along with individuals from sister disciplines like art education, cultural studies, popular culture, and anthropology are bringing to the public's attention the mutual relationship that exists between aesthetics and function. As a result, serious study has been brought to wrapped fishing rods placed on living room walls, collections of snow domes, salt and pepper shakers, piñatas, altars, and shrines inside and outside homes and religious spaces, quilts used for comfort, saddles, game boards, tattoos, Junkanoo and Carnival costumes, and pysanky (Ukrainian decorated Easter eggs).[13]

The power of everyday arts, such as these, is becoming more recognized by people in administrative positions. It is significant that the American Assembly includes the "unincorporated citizen arts" as an important component of the arts sector in the Unites States.[14] Contemporary artists such as Ahearn, Amalia Mesa-Baines, David Hammons, Pepón Osorio, Saar, and numerous others are incorporating materials, issues, and aesthetic dimensions from everyday life into their work, thereby deconstructing the boundaries that have been drawn between art that is removed and art that is connected to day-to-day living.[15] As a consequence, museums devoted to art are increasingly attempting to provide context, history, ritualistic use, and political orientation through exhibit labels or overall exhibit design. For example, the director of the National Museum of African Art describes a March 1998 family day event on an exhibition by Yoruba artist Olowe of Ise (c. 1875–1938): "We offered storytelling, dance performances, Yoruba and other African board games, as well as art workshops."[16]

Supporting a culturally oriented perspective is the fact that most artwork is best understood in its cultural context. Decontextualizing it often changes, distorts, and/or devalues its importance. In addition, how people respond to art has much to do with cultural upbringing. For example, Dave Hickey explains that for him, during the 1950s and 1960s cars were art: "For me, cars were not just art, they were everything.... Wherever I found myself, kids bought them, talked them, drew them, and dreamed them—hopped them up and dropped them down—cruised them on the drag and dragged them on the highway, and I did too."[17]

Broadly conceiving of art in relationship to everyday life is only part of the challenge for arts administrators in the twenty-first century. The other, perhaps more difficult challenge is creating and implementing policy and programs that reflect this orientation.

FOLKLIFE PROGRAMS

Folklorists in the United States have been, and continue to be, engaged with the culture of everyday life. From 1977 to 1992, the National Endowment for the Arts (NEA) set up programs to place folklorists in more than forty states. The NEA designed guidelines for programs that focus specifically on artistic methods with "unbroken lines of tradition."[18] In 1995, when the NEA's budget was cut by 50 percent, Jane Alexander, the new NEA chair, reorganized folklife programs into a larger umbrella organization called Heritage and Preservation. While this has resulted in folklore being interpreted as more broad-based than simply focusing on artists with "unbroken lines of tradition," it has given folklorists more funding opportunities to present programs that focus on the artistic activities of everyday life.[19]

Folklore programs that celebrate and educate the public about everyday arts can generally be understood by looking at the state of Florida, which has had one of the longest-running folklife programs in the country. Other states have similar programs, although they may not be as well funded or continuously supported.[20] Florida folklorists engage in folklife fieldwork whenever possible, as do folklorists in other states. This is crucial to programming because artists who create in their homes and communities often do so solely for the pleasure of small-group activities.

Established in 1953, Florida has the oldest state folk festival in the country. Most states also have an annual folk festival where traditional artists are highlighted. New fieldwork often feeds into this festival and many others that take place around the state.

Florida collects folk art in its Museum of Florida History. Most states have, or have had, a folklife program related to museum collections. Florida also has two annual programs that most states also make efforts to fund and organize for themselves. The Folklife Apprenticeship Program pairs master artists with apprentices in an effort to maintain a vital part of a culture's heritage. The Folk Heritage Awards, which in Florida are granted by the secretary of state, recognize outstanding folk artists who have made substantial contributions to their cultural communities.

Florida is currently developing radio shows for music presentations and has begun to investigate the use of CD–ROMs for organizing and educating the public about folk architecture. Museum exhibitions have been funded, teacher workshops regularly take place, and folklife institutes are regularly developed to teach the general public to identify, document, and present folklife in their communities. Florida also has a Florida Heritage Education Program, which provides educators with curriculum and resources for teaching. In the past, films, slide packages, and videotapes have also played a role in Florida's folklife programming activities.

Because folklorists have been designing and implementing programs for decades based on everyday art, it is important for arts administrators to study their methodologies. If there is one major problem with folklife programs (besides lack of funding of course), it is that so often, in order to present the artistic traditions, the art and artists are removed from their contexts. Although folklorists work hard to present the context with the artwork as much as possible, many folklorists comment on how difficult this can be. This is especially true with folk festivals, which often "are not effective means for the accurate presentation of folk culture."[21]

Perhaps the most successful folklife programs around the country are the apprenticeship programs, which are inexpensive. They encourage everyday arts to continue in a cultural community. The downside is that this program usually only affects a small group in an age where large numbers are more often utilized as an indication of a program's success.

It is clear that arts administrators interested in the culture of everyday life can look to folklife programs as models for creating and implementing initiatives, policy, and programs. This would include an emphasis on the context in which the culture of everyday life emerges, occurs, is experienced, and appreciated. In this regard, folklorists would have us remember that the culture of everyday life is a type of communication associated with very specific social situations.[22]

Arts administrators can also learn from folklorists that the art occurring within the culture of everyday life is not just material to be conserved and preserved, but is associated with events that are the motivation for its production. Again, the emphasis should be placed on the event or context in which material (art) is produced.

Finally, the culture of everyday life should be associated with all constituencies whether they are rural, suburban, or urban; homogeneous or nonhomogeneous; traditional or innovative; static or evolving. All people, as a "basis for shared identity, shared expressive resources, and culture-based communication," create the culture of everyday life.[23]

RECOMMENDATIONS FOR CULTURAL POLICY DEVELOPMENT

Few people question the power that art can have in the everyday lives of individuals and groups. However, given the pervasiveness of art in everyday life, relatively little time or effort has gone into the development of policy and programs that support and facilitate the culture of everyday life and the kinds of artistic activities and events associated with it. The following discussion of successful programs offers recommendations that we can take into the new millennium toward the development and implementation of cultural policy at all levels.

Cultural policy should recognize that arts and cultural programs can be considered successful when they recognize and reflect the everyday context of art in out-of-context events for the community members who are the original source for the art. Furthermore, interpretive strategies should incorporate not only the way the musical performance, visual work, or other expression is viewed by the artist, but should also tend to the views of those other community members who use and enjoy the art form.[24] Telling stories is one way to engage the audience in understanding interpretive information.[25] While the audience may enjoy the performances, and even learn something about how to understand it from a folklorist's interpretation, what happens to the artists and community members who are recognized outside their own community may be of greater or equal importance. In the case of Bowling Green State University's Fishing Show, fishers reevaluated their activities and their relationship to their occupational and recreational passion as art through the display of wrapped rods, fly ties, and carved lures in an art gallery.[26] When fishers begin to consider themselves artists because they fish and make fishing paraphernalia, new possibilities and relationships to both the art world and the act of fishing open up.

Cultural policy should recognize that folklife apprenticeships, which are in-context programs, are valuable models for celebrating and sustaining the culture and art of everyday life. However, the success of the partnering of a highly skilled artist with one or more apprentices is not easily quantifiable. In a given year, apprenticeship programs may not directly affect large numbers of people. Rather, the value of apprenticeship programs is realized over time. In Orlando, the hymn lining taught by Deacon Troy Demps to several apprentices means that his congregation can continue to hold services that are tied to the worshiping practices of its African American ancestors. These hymns, learned and sung in the days when it was unlawful for slaves to learn to read, continue today in Orlando because of the Florida Folklife Apprenticeship Program.

Cultural policy should encourage programmatic efforts that work across cultural boundaries and borders. For example, Pepón Osorio is an artist from the South Bronx who uses an excess of everyday objects in his artworks. Although he has an international reputation, he still considers himself a local artist. In fact, as he ages, he moves closer to the streets. Speaking about the garish aesthetic of his Puerto Rican neighborhood, he says, "What I do is to embrace this style that I know I am programmed to reject."[27] Some of Osorio's works rotate from house to house in his neighborhood because he believes that his neighbors and not just people who frequent museums and galleries should also be able to enjoy his art.[28] Art products and processes should not only extend out from communities, but should also have ties to the communities from which they originated.

Cultural policy should promote cultural and art programs incorporating new kinds of partnerships. One example that is currently in process in central Florida is an installation project by Natalie Lovejoy. A survivor of years of sexual abuse, her work describes her experiences as a child. First displayed at Project Row Houses, her installation attracted an extraordinary amount of attention. Lovejoy's installation is currently being recreated in a local art center that is partnering with a child advocacy center. It is anticipated that lectures, counseling, and educational information will be part of the event. When art touches people's lives, sometimes it needs to be grounded in ways that artists, galleries, and museums cannot service. When strong partnerships are made, the success of a program may extend beyond the boundaries of what some people call art, and its strength in the community can become more visible, effective, and viable.[29]

Cultural policy should attempt to address the need for more "cultures of desire."[30] Hickey, remembering how his father would bring different groups of people into his kitchen in the 1950s to play jazz, asks that we go back to more natural gathering spaces. The focus should be on the passion that moves across age, gender, race, or ability/disability. We can work toward this goal if we model behavior, knowledge, and skills necessary to work respectfully and effectively with others in a culturally diverse work environment. Hickey describes his father's jazz group coming together informally and his neighborhood friends fostering his love of cars. These diverse "cultures of desire" happened rather naturally, motivated by a passion for an everyday art form. Arts administrators need to recognize, encourage, and give visibility to these kinds of groups. When it doesn't happen in an informal way, a comprehensive management strategy is necessary to plan and implement this goal. Community involvement can, of course, be very instrumental in giving insight into such a plan. Care should be taken not to simply bring in these groups to "rubber stamp" decisions that have already been made.[31] Members of these kinds of cultural gatherings can often provide more insight to policy making and program implementation than the labeled "administrator."

When appropriate, cultural policy should link the culture of everyday life with other social values such as civic participation. Belonging to a cultural group is not necessarily voluntary nor are all everyday activities expressive of the characteristics we associate with civil society. However, the history of the United States includes numerous examples of cultural groups who maintain cultural integrity while simultaneously responding to the political structure within the United States and the civil society that exists here. For this reason, it is possible to discover activities associated with the culture of everyday life that demonstrate civic solidarity, political engagement, social accountability, and the mutual respect that characterize civil society. For example, Castellanoz, a member of the Mexican American community in Nyssa, Oregon, makes flowers from recycled paper and wax. She has been a flower maker her entire life, having learned her trade from her parents. Castellanoz contributes flowers to ceremonies associated with baptism, communion, quincineras (coming-out ceremony for fifteen-year-old girls), weddings, and funerals. Castellanoz's stated purpose is to return ritual and heritage to the lives of the members of the Mexican American community in eastern Oregon and Idaho. In doing this work, she has become a cultural activist, providing flowers for rites of passage and insisting that members of her community should not forget their Mexican heritage. Castellanoz believes in the power of cultural traditions to promote self-identity and community.

ARTS ADMINISTRATION PREPARATION

The pursuit of democracy within the United States is a project that requires a lifelong commitment exercised within multiple and diverse venues. The arts are often a catalyst for dialogue about individual and group identity; local, national, and international concerns; and ultimately the common good.

Arts administration is a multidisciplinary field, focused on promoting the arts and culture for individuals and societies. Knowledge and expertise from the arts is combined with aesthetic, social, cultural, managerial, and educational perspectives for the purpose of creating, implementing, and administering arts and cultural programs in nonprofit, for-profit, and unincorporated organizations and institutions.

Learning to administer the culture of everyday life, as we have described it through programs and cultural policy recommendations, requires arts administration preparation programs that are infused with an appreciation and understanding of the richness, diversity, and complexity associated with the culture of everyday life. This is no easy task given that the United States is a pluralistic and multicultural society in which there are multiple and sometimes conflicting conceptions of quality and desirability in art and culture. Understanding and appreciating this characteristic of the United States can be encouraged within an educational context emphasizing critical pedagogy, culturally democratic perspectives, mutual respect, personal/professional responsibility, environmental awareness, and social justice.[32] Arts administration preparation programs should also demonstrate a commitment to orienting future and current arts administrators to a multicultural and sociopolitical orientation to art and culture; a strong belief in electronic communication and opportunities afforded by the Internet and the World Wide Web; a focus on contemporary and future social, cultural, economic, aesthetic, political, and generational trends; and a belief in the importance of research to the profession. This can be accomplished by providing professional experience, through a combination of theory and practice, that is designed to enhance the ability of graduates to move into professional positions. Also, the development of individual research projects that contribute to the body of knowledge regarding the theory and practice of arts and cultural policy, education, and management in this era of dynamic sociocultural change is desirable.

Administering cultural policy and programs associated with the culture of everyday life requires that preservice and in-service arts administrators demonstrate cultural competence.[33] We believe that, at the very least, arts administrators should be prepared to:

1. promote and support the attitudes, behaviors, knowledge, and skills necessary to work respectfully and effectively with culturally and socioeconomically diverse communities and constituencies in a culturally diverse work environment;

2. utilize formal and informal strategies for community involvement in the creation and implementation of arts and cultural policy and public programs;

3. recruit, prepare, and retain staffs who are socioculturally diverse and who understand the needs, desires, and aspirations of communities and constituencies being served;

4. understand and appreciate the importance of communicating with communities and constituencies in their primary language and cultural context;

5. understand and appreciate the importance of collecting demographic, cultural, economic, aesthetic, and educational information about the communities and constituencies being served; and

6. understand and appreciate the importance of systematic and ongoing organizational, programmatic, and community-based evaluations for the purpose of assessing organizational and programmatic access, participant satisfaction, and future directions.

CONCLUSION

In this chapter, we have examined issues, perspectives, methods, policies, and competencies associated with administrating the culture of everyday life within a democratic society. Toward this end, we used orientations to culture and art from folklore and cultural studies. These orientations guided our choice of exemplary programs and practices. These orientations also influenced our recommendations for policy development. Lastly, we saw arts administrators as crucial players in the facilitation, preservation, and cultivation of the culture of everyday life. For this reason, we identified key areas of competency that graduates of arts administration programs should demonstrate in their future work in the culture of everyday life.

NOTES

1. The order of authors is arbitrary. Both Congdon and Blandy should be considered first authors.

2. Peter Bartis and Paddy A. Bowman, *Teacher's Guide to Folklife Resources for K–12 Classrooms* (Washington, DC: American Folklife Center, Library of Congress, 1994), <http://lcweb.loc.gov/folklife/teachers.html>.

3. Ibid.

4. Ellen Dissanayake, *Homo Aestheticus: Where Art Comes from and Why* (New York: The Free Press, 1992); G. Mathews-DeNatale, "Folk Arts: Art in Everyday Life," <http://www.carts.org/folkarts.html>.

5. Mary Hufford, *American Folklife: A Commonwealth of Cultures* (Washington, DC: American Folklife Center, Library of Congress, 1991 [December 4, 1998]), <http://lcweb.loc.gov/folklife/cwc.html>.

6. Cornel West, "The Moral Obligations of Living in a Democratic Society," in *The Good Citizen*, ed. David Batstone and Eduardo Mendieta (New York: Routledge, 1999), 10.

7. J. A. Hobbs, "Popular Art versus Fine Art," *Art Education* 37, no. 3 (1984): 11–14.

8. For a discussion of cultural forms that are shared, see Doug Blandy and Kristin G. Congdon, "Viewers Sound Off: A Feminist Analysis of Vernacular Art Criticism of 'All My Children' and 'Another World' on Electronic 'Boards,'" *Journal of Gender Issues in Art and Education* (forthcoming).

9. Michael Kammen, *American Culture American Tastes: Social Change in the 20th Century* (New York: Knopf, 1999).

10. Dissanayake, *Homo Aestheticus*.

11. Landon E. Beyer, "Schools, Aesthetic Meanings, and Social Change," *Educational Theory* 4 (1977): 274–82.

12. Victor Burgin, *The End of Art Theory: Criticism and Postmodernity* (Atlantic Highlands, NJ: Humanities Press International, 1986), 24–25.

13. For example, see Doug Blandy and Kristin G. Congdon, "Community-Based Aesthetics As an Exhibition Catalyst and a Foundation for Community Involvement in Art Education," *Studies in Art Education* 29, no. 4 (1988): 243–49; Robert Faris Thomson, *Face of the Gods: Art and Altars of Africa and the African Americans* (New York: Museum for African Art, 1993); Erika Doss, *Elvis Culture: Fans, Faith, and Image* (Lawrence: University Press of Kansas, 1999); Roland L. Freeman, *A Communion of the Spirits: African American Quilters, Preservers, and Their Stories* (Nashville: Rutledge, 1996); O. Loomis, "Buckaroos," in *Webfoots and Bunchgrassers: Folk Art of the Oregon Country*, ed. Suzie Jones (Eugene: Oregon Arts Commission, 1980), 86–103; John Beardsley, *Gardens of Revelation: Environments by Visionary Artists* (New York: Abbeville, 1995); J. Wilton, "Toward an Understanding of Skin Art," in *Pluralistic Approaches to Art Criticism*, ed. Doug Blandy and Kristin G. Congdon (Bowling Green, OH: Popular, 1987); John W. Nunley, and Judith Bettelheim, eds, *Caribbean Festival Arts: Each and Every Bit of Difference* (Seattle: University of Washington Press, 1998); Steve Siporin, *American Folk Masters: The National Heritage Fellows* (New York: Harry N. Abrams, 1992).

14. American Assembly, *The Arts and the Public Purpose* (New York: American Assembly, Columbia University, 1997), <http://www.columbia.edu/cu/amassembly/programs/recent/arts/arts.html>.

15. Ahearn is discussed in Jane Kramer, *Whose Art Is it Anyway?* (Durham, NC: Duke University, 1994). Mesa-Baines is discussed in Lucy Lippard, *Mixed Blessings: New Art in a Multicultural America* (New York: Pantheon, 1990). Hammons is discussed in Kellie Jones, "The Structure of Myth and the Potency of Magic," in *David Hammons: Rousing the Rubble*, by Steve Cannon, Kellie Jones, and Tom Finkelpearl (Cambridge: MIT Press, 1991), 15–37. Osorio is discussed in Nancy Haas, "The Secret of His Excess," *Art News* 98, no. 6 (1999): 96–99. Saar is discussed in Jean Willette, "Stitching Lives: Fabric in the Art of Betye Saar," *Fiberarts* (March–April 1997): 44–48.

16. Michael Kernan, "Making Art Accessible," *Smithsonian* 29, no. 12 (1999): 24–28.

17. Dave Hickey, *Air Guitar: Essays on Art and Democracy* (Los Angeles: Art Issues, 1997), 61.

18. Steve J. Zeitlin, "I'm a Folklorist and You're Not: Expansive versus Delimited Strategies in the Practice of Folklore," *Journal of American Folklore* 113, no. 447 (2000): 3–19.

19. Ibid.

20. Congdon has been on the Florida Folklife Council for six years and was president of the Florida Folklore Society for two years. She therefore speaks as a knowledgeable person on Florida folklife programs. Other information on Florida folklife programs comes from a 1999 brochure on the topic written by State Folklorist Tina Bucuvalas.

21. Camp and Loyd.

22. Virginia Folklife Program, <http://www.virginia.edu/vfh/vfp/histidea.html# commperf>.

23. Ibid.

24. C. K. Dewhurst, and Marsha MacDowell, "Gathering and Interpreting Tradition," *Journal of Museum Education* 24, no. 3 (1999): 7–10.

25. Ruth Olson and Anne Pryor, "Talk Stage: Using Stories in Living Cultural Exhibits," *Journal of Museum Education* 24, no. 3 (1999): 17–20.

26. Blandy and Congdon, "Viewers Sound Off."

27. Haas, "Secret of His Excess."

28. Dina Mitrani, from the Bernice Steinbaum Gallery in Miami, told Congdon in February 2000 that Osorio is increasingly becoming concerned about the ownership of his works. He is therefore taking some smaller pieces and moving them throughout the homes of his Bronx neighbors.

29. William Cleveland, *Art in Other Places: Artists at Work in America's Community and Social Institutions* (Amherst: University of Massachusetts Arts Extension Service, 2000), brings attention to the ways in which artists are responding to community needs and contributing to changes within human service institutions. Blandy and Congdon advocate decentralizing the role of the artist in community and institutional work in favor of a partnership model in which artists and constituents have an equal say in what takes place through their mutual efforts. See Doug Blandy and Kristin G. Congdon, "Arts in Other Places: A Conference Critique," *The Bulletin of the Caucus on Social Theory and Art Education* 7 (1987): 75–79.

30. Hickey, *Air Guitar.*

31. K. E. Wilson, "Crafting Community-Based Museum Experiences: Process, Pedagogy, and Performance," *Journal of Museum Education* 24, no. 3 (1999): 3–6.

32. Some professional associations to which arts administrators belong have developed codes of ethics. For example, see "A Statement of Ethics for the American Folklore Society," <http://www.afsnet.org/ethics.htm>.

33. Other professional groups are identifying such competencies. For example, see U.S. Department of Health and Human Services Office of Minority Health and Resources for Cross Cultural Health Care, <http://www.omhrc.gov/clas/ds.htm>.

VI

Service Organizations and the Arts Sector

17

Understanding the Associational Infrastructure of the Arts and Culture

Margaret J. Wyszomirski and Joni M. Cherbo

Associational activities and organizations have played a significant role throughout U.S. history. In the arts and culture, they have played significant roles in the development and implementation of public policies as well as in the evolution and self-governance of artistic professions. Arts service organizations (ASOs) come in many varieties. Some represent similar groups within a particular art form (e.g., symphony orchestras in the American Symphony Orchestra League, opera companies in Opera America, or noncommercial publishers in the Council of Literary Magazines and Presses). Others represent a particular type of organization across a number of fields or disciplines (e.g., museums of all sorts—art, science, and history—in the American Association of Museums or presenting organizations in the Association of Performing Arts Presenters). Still others represent the corporations within a particular entertainment industry (such as the Motion Picture Association of America) or types of governmental agencies (e.g., National Assembly of State Arts Agencies). Unions (e.g., Actors Equity), guilds (e.g., Screen Actors Guild), and certain professional associations (e.g., American Society of Composers, Authors, and Publishers) focus on individual members rather than organizations. Ethnic and linguistic cultural groups as well as cultural hobbyists and avocational artists have come together in a plethora of service organizations that are as numerous and diverse as U.S. pluralism.

A conservative estimate would count at least eight hundred national arts service organizations (ASOs) with at least an equal number of state, regional, and/or local membership organizations that serve arts and cultural interests.[1] For example, many states have statewide advocacy groups for the arts as well as advocacy groups for arts education and statewide associations of museums. In addition, many U.S. groups support foreign cultural institutions (e.g., the Friends of Covent Garden). Similarly, there are many groups of "friends" or guilds that support specific U.S. cultural institutions.

Out of this multitude of arts and cultural service organizations, only a few are reasonably well known within the cultural community at large and only a handful are active in public policy-making processes at any level of government. There are no cultural interest groups that rise to a general level of public awareness such as the Sierra Club in the realm of environmental policy or the American Council on Education in higher education policy. Only the Motion Picture Association of America and the Recording Industry Association of America are generally regarded as being highly effective lobbying groups in Washington.

In terms of influencing, monitoring, and implementing public policy, service organizations are a crucial part of any policy community.[2] In terms of professional self-governance and development, service organizations perform key functions. And in terms of furthering avocational interests, fostering diverse community and cultural heritages, and building social capital, service organizations are important components of civil society. Despite the range, multitude, recent growth, and importance of service organizations in the arts and cultural sector, we have relatively little systematic knowledge about them.[3] Other than anecdote, we know little about when and why such associations are formed; nor do we understand why some groups become politically active while others do not. We lack organized information about how organizations maintain themselves, what kinds of benefits they provide their members, or the organizational resources with which they have to work. We don't know how service organizations differ across the components of the arts and cultural sector—nonprofit, commercial, and informal. Similarly, we know relatively little about how the services and resources of ASOs vary by discipline, organizational age, or type of members, nor do we have explanations for these variations.

There is little information about the political activities and advocacy strategies that ASOs employ or about the policy issues that concern them. We don't have a clear understanding of when or why ASOs become politically active and if this is an ongoing or an episodic activity. We do not fully understand the variety of ways in which ASOs channel the interaction between government and professions (or interests), between public policy and private policy, or how these associations generate social capital and how that capital is then applied in the various segments of civil society.

Our factual and descriptive understanding of this associational infrastructure is incomplete and fragmented, which, in turn, impairs our ability to explain both the cause and consequences of current conditions. We have relatively few case studies of ASOs in action—whether as organizational histories, attempts to influence policy decisions, or project and service assessment. While some ASOs collect extensive information on their members, this information is seldom comparable among ASOs and is often unavailable in a complete and raw form. In short, when it comes to understanding the roles, functions, activities, variations, life cycles, and effectiveness of arts and cultural service organizations, we confront a substantial but fragmented and spotty body of data that is analytically incoherent representing a field of interests that lacks mutual awareness and established networks of interaction.

While significant in themselves, such gaps in our knowledge and understanding are even more important—and troublesome—at a time when the cultural community faces numerous and new policy issues; environmental forces such as globalization, demographic, and technological change that produce new challenges; and shifts in the roles of government and the private sector in the support, protection, and promotion of cultural activities in U.S. society.

THE IMPORTANCE OF ASSOCIATIONS
AND INTEREST GROUPS

In general, service organizations or interest groups were a notable feature of the American scene when Alexis de Tocqueville was writing in the 1830s. Today, service associations are attracting new interest as generators of social capital, engines of civil society, and promoters of special interests. Such associations come in a variety of forms: from membership associations at the national, state, regional, or local levels to operating organizations that deliver service for fees. National membership organizations themselves exist under a variety of names, including ASOs, professional and trade associations, unions, ethnically specific social groups, interest-based affinity groups, and cause-motivated associations.

If membership associations become politically active, they are commonly called interest groups. These politically active ASOs then become arts interest groups (or AIGs). As political scientists, Frank R. Baumgartner and Beth L. Leech observe interest groups in general:

Groups are at the heart of the political process; they are central to the process of representation.... . They motivate people in elections; they channel participation through neighborhoods, schools, ethnic groups, and in professions; they disseminate information from political elites to the mass public; they are active at every level of government in providing information, in speaking for affected constituencies, and in debating the merits of proposed policy changes; they work in almost every conceivable way to affect the government.... Groups are basic to the practice of politics.[4]

Groups that are inactive politically are sometimes referred to as nascent interest groups. While it is generally the case that AIGs are ASOs, many ASOs do not engage in political activity and hence are not AIGs. AIGs are integral elements of the cultural policy community and crucial participants in the process of cultural policy making. Nascent AIGs are also important because, as the political situation and the character of public issues change, they may become politically involved. In addition, all ASOs play an important role in the self-governance and internal communications of professional and avocational groups. Hence, they have an important role in group self-governance and private policy making.

The last half of the twentieth century saw a dramatic expansion of interest group organization and political activity. During these decades, virtually every interest—whether economically, socially, or ideologically motivated—organized itself into a membership organization. Many of these associations became engaged in advocacy and lobbying activities and thus evolved into interest groups. Likewise, the number of lobbyists-for-hire working independently or out of the Washington offices of law firms, public relations firms, and political consulting firms has grown tremendously. At the same time, the repertoire of political action tactics and targets proliferated to include direct and indirect lobbying; election and media campaigns; inside, outside, and coalition strategies; grassroots and elite foci; legislative, presidential, bureaucratic, and judicial targets; research, monitoring, and policy development activities, as well as advocacy and lobbying. These developments are also reflected in the associations of the arts and culture sector.

ARTS SERVICE ORGANIZATIONS: PRELIMINARY DIMENSIONS

The associational infrastructure includes membership associations and other kinds of organizations that provide support services for the arts and cultural sector. Our focus here is on national membership organizations, which will be discussed in more detail shortly. While we recognize that these are only one part of the associational infrastructure for the arts and culture, this initial focus seems justified because national membership organizations are perhaps the most politically active components of this infrastructure. As such, national membership organizations are an important part of the public policy discussion in ways that seem unlikely for other infrastructure components.

The Components of the Associational Infrastructure

Generally, the associational infrastructure for the arts and culture consists of organizations that provide services and supports for individuals, groups, and institutions engaged in the arts and culture. Sometimes these organizations serve a membership, other times they serve customers or clients—whether on a fee-paying or a volunteer basis. All of these organizations provide some sort of service. Membership organizations clearly serve their members through the provision of a variety of services. Arts and cultural membership organizations exist across the geographical horizon—national, state, regional, and local. Other elements of the associational infrastructure may provide services but lack members or have members who are organized for the explicit purpose of providing services to the arts and culture. Some organizations specialize in specific, professional services—such as consulting firms, conservation services, research institutes, educational and training institutions, and volunteer lawyers for the arts. Hence, these organizations provide services but are frequently not membership organizations. Similarly, other organizations—which may or may not involve members—provide financial support services, such as fund-raising guilds, community art funds, trustee groups, and booster clubs. Here again, the purpose of the organizations is not to represent the interests of its members but rather to coordinate the provision of services by its members to artists and cultural institutions and businesses. Still other associations are made up of members who provide equipment or other support services essential to cultural producers such as associations of musical instrument manufacturers or of craft suppliers.

Membership Services

Membership associations provide a variety of services to their members. Common services include job postings and professional credentialing services; professional development and technical assistance programs; conferences and forums; publications; calendar information on programs and projects of members; legal and insurance services; political/policy representation; information gathering and research; public education efforts; and contacts with other service, funding, and representational organizations. The political activities of associations include advocacy and lobbying, professional self-governance, coalition building, issue identification, and political monitoring, to name some of the most common. Some groups are politically active in many ways and on many issues. Others are politically inactive; and yet others are only narrowly or reluctantly engaged in political activities

Locating the Universe of Service Organizations

Consonant with the expansive meaning of the arts and cultural sector, we do not restrict ourselves to associations that represent interests of the nonprofit art world, but rather consider the entire arts sector: commercial and informal as well as nonprofit. Generically, these groups will be referred to as ASOs, which are generally incorporated as nonprofit organizations. Many are 501(c)(3) organizations (charitable), but others may formally be 501(c)(4) (advocacy groups), 501(c)(5) (labor unions), 501(c)(6) (business leagues), or 501(c)(7) (social and recreational clubs). A preliminary estimate finds that 42 percent of the national membership organizations in the arts and culture represent members located in the nonprofit sector, 38 percent in the commercial sector, 17 percent in the informal or avocational sector, with the remaining 3 percent drawing members from both the nonprofit and commercial sectors or representing public cultural organizations. From an artistic perspective, these associations cluster in the following manner:

Live performing arts	37 percent
Electronic performing arts	20 percent
Visual arts and museums	15 percent
Arts and crafts	7 percent
Cultural heritage	5 percent
Design and graphic arts	5 percent
All others combined	11 percent

In its 1986–1990 planning document, the National Endowment for the Arts (NEA) defined services organizations for the nonprofit arts world as those that "exist not to produce, present, or preserve art, but to help others do so ... [by providing] information, opportunities to communicate, advocacy, public education, professional and volunteer training, and various forms of technical, managerial, and support services." It went on to explain that "the term service organizations covers a heterogeneous assortment of enterprises, some field-specific, some function-specific, and some interdisciplinary."[5] Unions were also identified as another set of service groups that were primarily concerned with collective bargaining activities concerning "bread and butter issues" such as compensation, benefits and retirement, and working conditions.[6]

Historical Development

Today, organizations and individuals across the arts sector are better organized, have secured more resources, and have become more adept at political action than they were fifty years ago. However, different segments of the arts and cultural sector became organized and politically active at different times. For example, one of the most historic of artistic professions, architecture, formed a professional association—the American Institute of Architects—in 1857. In the early twentieth century, companies and workers in commercial arts industries such as movies, Broadway theater, recordings, and publishing formed professional and trade associations to promote and protect their economic interests. These associations grew and evolved with the industries themselves and seem to have become more politically active in the postwar period, both in efforts to influence public policy and to protect (perhaps even expand) the scope of their self-governance.

On the whole, the nonprofit arts sector came later to organizing and engaging in political action. Although a few associations formed in the first half of the century (notably the American Association of Museums in 1906 and the American Symphony Orchestra League in 1942), the period of significant expansion occurred in the 1970s and 1980s.[7] A number of factors would seem to go into explaining this timing. Before the late 1960s, the potential membership in particular fields and occupations may have been too small to elicit organizational efforts or to exert much political influence, particularly at the national level. Until the arts boom of the 1960s and 1970s increased the scale and magnitude of the potential financial, professional, and political stakes of these interests and linked them to the fate of the NEA, the direct effects of public policy decisions were relatively small and infrequent. In addition, organizations and individuals in the nonprofit arts were notoriously independent-minded, difficult to organize, and historically wary of engagement with government and politics.

Historically, the linkage between the NEA and the development and political activity of ASOs and AIGs representing the nonprofit art world has been integral and multifaceted. The NEA acted as a "patron of political action,"[8] providing financial support and enhancing professional status for existing and developing ASOs. It was even instrumental in the creation of a number of associations. In some cases, ASOs became "third-party" agents of the federal agency to administer programs in professional development, technical assistance, and/or field-wide innovation. Alternatively, the periodic authorization hearings and the annual appropriations hearings for the NEA became a catalyst and focal point for the political activity of many ASOs. In contrast, there is little evidence of such close linkages between service and trade organizations representing the interests of the commercial or avocational arts and federal agencies or policies. Furthermore, the patterns of interaction between government and service organizations outside the nonprofit subsector appears to be more distant, and may also be more conflictual and more episodic.

Avocational, informal, and other types of "unincorporated" arts interests formed groups throughout the twentieth century. Economic interests were frequently not the incentive to organize. Instead, the desire was for social solidarity prompted by

- ethnic heritage (e.g., Chinese Music Society of North America, the Slovak Writers and Artists Association, or the Irish American Cultural Society)
- craft skill (e.g., Colonial Coverlet Guild of America, Woodworking Association of North America, or the Embroiders' Guild of America)
- interest in the work of a particular artist (e.g., American Beethoven Society or James Joyce Society); or
- avocational interests (e.g., American Bonsai Society, Sweet Adelines International, or United Square Dancers of America).

More recently, cause-related groups have formed to pursue or prevent public action on specific cultural issues such as freedom of expression, repatriation of cultural property, violence in the media, and diversity/multiculturalism.

Membership

The members of these associations may be individuals, organizations, or (in the case of peak associations) other associations. *Individual members* may be members of a professional or occupational group (e.g., the American Association of Museum Directors or Actors Equity). They may be individuals with a shared personal interest or a common heritage (e.g., Association of Museum Volunteers, the Wagner Society, or the Ethnic Cultural Preservation Council). They may be citizens with a commitment to a common cause (e.g., National Council on Television Violence, the Deaf Artists of America, or the American Booksellers for Free Expression).

Organizational members may be nonprofit arts and cultural organizations such as museums (American Association of Museums), orchestras (American Symphony Orchestra League), or public television stations. They may be corporations in the cultural industries such as motion picture production studios (Motion Picture Academy of America), commercial art galleries, or for-profit publishing houses. Organizational members might be embedded groups, clubs (e.g., National Federation of Music Clubs), or informal groups with similar concerns or activities (e.g., SPEBSQSA—Society for the Preservation and Encouragement of Barber Shop Quartet Singing in America). Or they may be public agencies (e.g., National Assembly of State Arts Agencies).

Individual as well as organizational members of national service organizations may be located anywhere in the arts and cultural sector: nonprofit, for-profit, informal, or public. The members of some associations are located in just one subsector (e.g., the Association of Talent Agents represents for-profit professionals, while the American Needlework Guild includes individual hobbyists and craftspeople). Alternatively, a given association may draw members from any combination of these locations. For example, Americans for the Arts includes both individual and organizational members; its organizational members include both nonprofit and public organizations, as does the American Association of Museums.

Collectively, these different organizing trajectories and membership groupings provide a representational, informational, and policy-making support system for the arts and cultural sector. However, accurate and comprehensive information about the range and variety of this associational infrastructure is not readily available. Without such baseline information, our knowledge of and ability to project about the uses, effectiveness, and potential of these associations and the interests that they represent is severely limited. Although we know that ASOs can play an important role in the evolution of a profession and in professional self-governance, we don't fully understand how this occurs or why certain organizations develop certain programs, self-governance mechanisms, and services rather than others. We can observe that not all ASOs are structured in the same way (e.g., some have local or regional chapters and others only operate at the national level), but we don't understand very much about the ramifications of these differences). In recent years, many ASOs have experienced changes in leadership, such that one can almost discern a generational turnover. Yet, we understand little about the character and effects of differences in leadership style, authority, or context. Nor do we have a clear idea how service organizations can effect leadership succession in their member organizations—influence that might range from providing professional networks and recruitment pipelines to technical assistance in succession planning.

Potentially, these are all important subjects not only because these associations have and continue to play a significant role in the operation of U.S. society but because they may be of special importance in an era that both seeks to reinvigorate civil society and seems inclined toward privatization and private action mechanisms. Furthermore, the growing importance of informational resources and communication channels for the information society would seem to make ASOs potentially more strategic organizations than ever before.

MUSIC: A FIELD EXAMPLE

The foregoing discussion of the various dimensions and varieties of national membership organizations in the arts and culture is both complex and relatively conceptual. Therefore, we have provided an illustrative grouping—or map—of the associational terrain in the area of music. This "music map" is only illustrative not comprehensive at this point. Nevertheless, we think it begins to demonstrate the rich network of kinds of groups that comprise the associational infrastructure of just one artistic discipline: music. These examples draw from the worlds of commercial music, popular music, nonprofit professional music, and community as well as avocational music activities.

1. Musical Groups and Organizations
   American Symphony Orchestra League
   Chorus America
   Chamber Music America
   Association of American Male Choruses
   Association of Concert Bands
   American Music Festival Association
   The Sweet Adelines

2. Individual Music Professionals and Performers
   American Bandmasters Association
   American Composers Alliance
   American Guild of Organists
   International Guild of Symphony, Opera, and Ballet Musicians
   American Federation of Musicians of U.S. and Canada

National Forum of Greek Orthodox Church Musicians
National Association of Negro Musicians
National Flute Association
Music Women International
Conductors Guild
Nashville Songwriters Association International
Amateur Chamber Music Players

3. Allied Music Professionals and Business Groups
Music Critics Association of North America
American Music Therapy Association
Music Publishers Association of the United States
National Association of Band Instrument Manufacturers
National Sheet Music Society
Piano Manufacturers Association International
Society of Professional Audio Recording Services
American Federation of Violin and Bow Makers
American Society of Music Copyists
Independent Music Retailers Association
National Association of Accompanists and Coaches
Recording Industry of America
National Council of Music Importers and Exporters

4. Music Education and Training Groups
Music Educators National Conference
National Association of Schools of Music
Organization of American Kodaly Educators
National Guild of Piano Teachers
American String Teachers Association
International Association of Jazz Educators

5. Groups Concerned with Certain Types of Music
American Society for Jewish Music
Gospel Music Association
Rhythm and Blues Rock and Roll Society
Society for Asian Music
National Academy for Popular Music
International Computer Music Association
Bohemian Ragtime Society

6. Musical Interests Associations
   American Beethoven Society
   American Guild of English Handbell Ringers
   Bruckner Society of America
   International Association of Jazz Record Collectors
   National Federation of Music Clubs
   Society for the Preservation and Encouragement of Barber Shop Quartet Singing in America
   Catgut Acoustical Society

7. Identity-Based Music Groups (e.g., race, gender, religious denomination, or ethnicity)
   National Black Music Caucus
   National Association of Negro Musicians
   Women Band Directors International
   International Alliance of Women in Music
   American Women Composers
   Associated Male Choruses of America
   Christian Instrumentalists and Directors Association
   Fellowship of American Baptist Musicians
   Presbyterian Association of Musicians
   Chinese Music Society of North America
   Norwegian Singers Association

8. Music Research Groups
   Council for Research in Music Education
   International Association for Research in Vietnamese Music

9. University and Collegiate Musical Associations
   College Music Society
   Intercollegiate Men's Chorus
   National Association of Music Executives in State Universities

As this preliminary associational map for music indicates, there are many kinds of national membership groups in the music field—nearly seventy in this illustrative listing alone. Various kinds of musical performing groups—from orchestras and choruses to concert bands and chamber music groups—have specific national associations. Similarly, individual musicians have formed a set of national associations that may focus on the players of a particular instrument (e.g., flute, organ, trombone, violin, and so on), or on directors of musical ensembles (e.g., bandmasters or conductors), or that limit membership on the bases of gender, religious affiliation, or race.

Another cluster of associations represent business and/or occupational groups that support, sustain, and supply the performance and presentation of music, such as equipment and supply manufacturers, copyists, coaches, and critics. Relatedly, various associations represent facets of music education and training. And a handful of associations involve those who provide research services for the music field.

Finally, we see three clusters of music associations that coalesce around what the interest group literature calls "solidarity" benefits—an affinity for a particular type of music, an interest in the work of a particular composer, or identity-based social support or collegiality.

Of course, this is only a preliminary and incomplete "music map." A more comprehensive survey would categorize all the relevant national membership associations as to type of members as well as by motivation for establishment. Further study might examine the relative size, activities, and resources of these groups; explore interconnections between groups; and analyze how their issue concerns overlap and diverge.

Clearly, the location and identification of this set of national music associations reveals a richer, deeper, and more diverse associational infrastructure than we have heretofore recognized. Subsequently, this first step leads to the possibility of more detailed examination and analysis. Furthermore, developing such associational maps for each art discipline and cultural industry is likely to reveal that different disciplines exhibit different contours. Certainly different associations exhibit different patterns of organizational activity. Exploring these discoveries will, in turn, accord us a much better basis for understanding the role that associations play in the professional, political, cultural, and civil life of their members as well as the nation as a whole.

THE POLICY-MAKING ROLE OF ASOs AND AIGs

The cohesiveness, coordination, and effectiveness of these associations as members of a policy community has been weakened by deep and numerous fracture lines that have established niche interests according to discipline, function, and subsector.[9] Even a cursory survey reveals few peak associations across the subsectors, disconnects between the advocacy activities of groups at different levels of the political system, and relatively few explicitly shared issue concerns.

Furthermore, our basic information about the political activities of ASOs is characterized by significant gaps. Let us briefly discuss four of the major dimensions of this inadequacy.[10]

Possible Political Activities across the Entire Policy-Making Process

Historically, AIGs in the nonprofit art world have focused on the middle phases of the public policy-making process, that is, budgeting and program administration. Although much of this effort has been pursued separately by each AIG, in recent years the government affairs directors of many of these associations have banded together into a loose advocacy coalition called the Congressional Arts Group. Many of these arts groups also collaborate in organizing an annual Arts Advocacy Day focused on members of Congress.

As the arts policy paradigm shifts into a cultural policy paradigm, AIGs (as well as other ASOs) are likely to be called on by their members to further develop a capacity to participate effectively in the beginning and end phases of the public policy-making process. That is, to engage in (1) issue and option development as well as agenda setting at the beginning, and (2) policy assessment and program evaluation both as a demonstration of accountability and as a prompt to subsequent program revision and policy innovation.

In order to rise to this challenge, the cultural policy community must expand and deepen its informational resources and intellectual infrastructure. AIGs and ASOs, together with policy scholars and analysts as well as interested foundations, have an important part to play in constructing the intellectual infrastructure necessary to generate the ideas, mechanisms, and information that will shape and legitimate cultural policies for the twenty-first century. Furthermore, as the full spectrum of cultural policy issues becomes more apparent, ASOs will also need to expand their governmental monitoring activities. They may seek to do this through staff expansion individually or find ways to combine their efforts in ad hoc or enduring advocacy coalitions. Furthermore, any such advocacy coalition may also seek allies outside the arts, in other cultural areas such as historic preservation, tourism, the humanities, archives and libraries, and educational and cultural exchanges.

The Variety of Possible Government–ASO Interactions

It is commonplace to equate the political activities of interest groups with lobbying. In reality, however, lobbying is only one of a number of government–ASO interactions that occur or that can be developed—as can be seen from the following list:

1. ASOs act as third-party implementers of public policies designed and/or funded by government agencies

2. ASOs act as a source of expertise and information for government policy and decision making

3. Government policies, decisions, application requirements, judicial decisions, and regulations set parameters and conditions that influence how ASOs function

4. ASOs can act to avoid government action—seeking either to prevent government action by engaging in self-regulation or to present a nonpublic means of implementing public programs

5. ASOs can monitor and evaluate the performance of government actors and organizations

6. ASOs may be advocates for and constituency supporters of government agencies and programs

7. Government can provide financial support for ASOs

8. ASOs can monitor conditions and concerns of their members, identify potential public policy issues, and bring these conditions, concerns, and issues to the attention of government actors

9. ASOs may challenge government actions, policies, and decisions in the courts or organize protests against them in the streets

10. Some interest groups may engage in campaign activities to influence the election of particular public officials

11. ASOs may engage in public education and media campaigns to stimulate citizen efforts to influence government officials and decisions

All of these are possible government–ASO interactions. But we know very little about the range of these interactions. Although we may be able to identify instances of these types of interactions, we lack detailed case studies. Hence, we don't know why some relationships develop rather than others or under what circumstances. For example, ASOs representing the commercial arts (e.g., film, television, and recordings) seem to have been quite effective at preventing government action through the initiation of voluntary rating and labelling systems.[11] Are there comparable instances concerning the nonprofit arts? How prevalent are such avoidance tactics and when don't they work? Alternatively, we know that in the past decade ASOs representing the nonprofit arts have engaged in a number of media campaigns using public service announcements. How effective have these been? When are they used and when not? In short, exploring each of the government–ASO interactions listed earlier—as well as making comparisons across types of interactions and circumstances of their use and effectiveness—is a veritable research agenda in itself.

Types of Political Action Strategies

Political scientists have at least three primary strategies that interest groups may pursue politically:[12]

1. Inside strategy—working within government to effect public policy through such activities as testifying to Congress, contacting agency personnel, serving on public advisory boards, participating in litigation over policy, presenting research and information to government officials, or contacting members of Congress individually

2. Outside strategy—engaging in activities outside government in an effort to influence public officials through such activities as talking with the press, organizing letter-writing campaigns, holding press conferences, protesting, engaging in media campaigns, and publicizing the votes of candidates

3. Advocacy coalition strategy—banding together with other interest groups to pursue shared policy interests and concerns through combining organizational resources and capabilities in coordinated political action activities

What we know about concentrates on legislative lobbying—mostly as it concerns the appropriations and reauthorization for the NEA. However, this leaves us with little information on the political activities and advocacy efforts of ASOs concerning other federal cultural agencies. It also limits our knowledge about the involvement of ASOs in other decision-making and policy-making forums such as the courts, the presidency, state and local government institutions, and international bodies. Although the cultural community has employed media campaigns, we have little research on the content or effectiveness of these efforts. Similarly, our understanding of the utilities and uses of ASO information gathering and research activities is rudimentary, as is our assessment of the political effectiveness of such information.

Nor does this focus on lobbying for the NEA tell us much about relatively recent shifts in political strategy and tactics. During the last decade of the "culture wars," ASOs (which traditionally relied on an inside political strategy) have also sometimes engaged in both an outside strategy and an advocacy coalition strategy. What prompted this change in strategy and how effective was each strategy? What political action strategies are used for other kinds of cultural policy issues: cultural property and trade issues, art education policy, broadcast regulations, alleged censorship, and intellectual property concerns?

Political Action Tactics

Comparative studies of interest group activities in different policy arenas have discerned a broad repertoire of political action tactics that can be used. Baumgartner and Leech identify nearly a dozen commonly used political tactics.[13] Elizabeth J. Reid enumerates seven advocacy tactics that employ a combined total of twenty-five types of political action.[14] It appears that different types of interest groups tend to use different political action tactics and that interest groups also vary their tactics according to the type of policy issue under discussion. In other areas of interest group study, such information is accumulated through case studies and mail surveys of interest groups. Neither source of information is currently available with regard to arts and cultural policy issues or service organizations. However, it is hoped that both case studies and a survey will be part of the future research plan of the Mapping the Association Infrastructure for the Arts and Culture Project.

CONCLUSION

Taken together, ASOs and AIGs across the arts sector constitute an informational, representational, and private policy-making support system for the arts and culture sector. Yet, despite its importance, its potential, and its rapid growth in the past two to three decades, we know relatively little about it holistically or about various components and activities. Certainly, as a key component of the cultural policy system and community, our sketchy knowledge and understanding of ASOs and AIGs diminishes our ability to analyze cultural policy issues and processes. Our lack of knowledge also impairs the ability of policy makers to make well-informed policy decisions and of arts practitioners to influence public policy. Clearly, the research and analysis opportunities concerning the associational infrastructure for the arts and culture are rich with potential. Furthermore, applying the knowledge gained through such research efforts is likely to be a valuable asset in the development and effectiveness of a cultural policy community.

NOTES

1. Unless otherwise referenced, the information about arts and cultural service organizations in this chapter is drawn from the ongoing research project Mapping the Associational Infrastructure for the Arts and Culture. The initial stage of this project is codirected by Margaret J. Wyszomirski and Joni M. Cherbo at the Arts Policy and Administration Program at Ohio State University and has been partially funded by a grant from the Ford Foundation. For more information, see the APA Program, <http://www.osu.edu/arted/apa>.

2. Margaret J. Wyszomirski, "Policy Communities and Policy Influence: Securing a Government Role in Cultural Policy for the 21st Century," *Journal of Arts management, Law, and Society* 25, no. 3 (fall 1995): 192–205; reprinted in Gigi Bradford, Michael Gary, and Glenn Wallach, eds., *The Politics of Culture: Policy Perspectives for Individuals, Institutions, and Communities* (New York: New Press, 2000), 94–107.

3. A call for better understanding and research about ASOs was part of the research agenda articulated by the American Assembly in its report *The Arts and the Public Purpose* (New York: American Assembly, Columbia University, 1997).

4. Frank R. Baumgartner and Beth L. Leech, *Basic Interests: The Importance of Groups in Politics and in Political Science* (Princeton, NJ: Princeton University Press, 1998), 188.

5. National Endowment for the Arts, *Five-Year Planning Document, 1986–1990* (Washington, DC: U.S. Government Printing Office, 1984), 109.

6. Ibid., 112.

7. On the development and activities of ASOs representing nonprofit arts organizations, see Margaret Jane Wyszomirski, "The Politics of Arts Policy: Subgovernment to Issue Network," in *America's Commitment to Culture: Government and the Arts in the United States,* ed. Kevin V. Mulcahy and Margaret J. Wyszomirski (Boulder: Westview, 1995), 47–76; see also Joseph Wesley Zeigler, "Friendly Persuasion: The Arts Arrive on Capitol Hill," *American Arts* (July 1983): 22–26.

8. The term "patrons of political action" comes from Jack A. Walker Jr., "The Origins and Maintenance of Interest Groups in America," *American Political Science Review* 77, no. 2 (1983): 390–406.

9. Wyszomirski, "Political Communities and Policy Influence."

10. The identification of these gaps among arts and cultural interest groups has been based on a reading of general interest groups research, notably Jeffrey M. Berry, *The Interest Group Society* (Boston: Little, Brown, 1984); Jack L. Walker, *Mobilizing Interest Groups in America* (Ann Arbor: University of Michigan Press, 1991); Robert H. Salisbury, "An Exchange Theory of Interest Groups," *Midwest Journal of Political Science* 13 (1969): 1–32; Kay Lehman Schlozman and John T. Tierney, *Organized Interest and American Democracy* (New York: Harper and Row, 1986); Norman J. Ornstein and Shirley Elder, *Interest Groups, Lobbying and Policymaking* (Washington, DC: Congressional Quarterly, 1978).

11. On the role of ASOs in devising content restrictions, see Joni Maya Cherbo, "The Associational Infrastructure for the Culture Industries: Private Policy Making in Arts Service Organizations" (paper presented at the Twenty-Sixth Annual Conference of Social Theory, Politics, and the Arts, Washington, DC, October 12–15).

12. Ken Kollman, *Outside Lobbying: Public Opinion and Interest Group Strategies* (Princeton, NJ: Princeton University Press, 1999); Paul A. Sabatier, "An Advocacy Coalition Framework of Policy Change and the Role of Policy Oriented Learning Therein," *Policy Studies* 21 (1988): 129–68; see also Baumgartner and Leech, *Basic Interests*.

13. Baumgartner and Leech, *Basic Interests*, especially Chapter 8.

14. Elizabeth J. Reid, "Nonprofit Advocacy and Political Participation" (paper presented at the conference on Nonprofit Organizations and the Government: The Challenge of Civil Society, at the Urban Institute Center on Nonprofits and Philanthropy, Washington, DC, June 8–9, 1998).

VII

Postscript: Trends in the Production of Research on the Arts Sector

18

Twenty-Five Years of the Conference
of Social Theory, Politics, and the Arts

Carrie Lee

The Social Theory, Politics, and the Arts (STP&A) conference has been a focus of scholarly research on the arts sector for more than two decades. Indeed, 1999 marked the twenty-fifth anniversary of STP&A, providing a good opportunity to take a look back on how STP&A has evolved over time.

In his 1990 manuscript *Social Theory, Politics and the Arts Reminiscences, Facts, Circumstantial Evidence, Anecdotes, Opinions and Other Materials for a History*, Arnold Foster notes that this yearly conference was originally conceived "as a group of artists and sociologists helping each other to learn more about society through the agency of the arts and/or about the arts through the instrument of sociology."[1] The early years of the conference were also well attended by artists and even featured a photography exhibit in 1975.

Foster marks 1983 as the beginning of a new era in the history of the conference. In 1983, the name of the conference changed from Art and Social Theory to Social Theory, Politics, and the Arts. (See Table 18.1.) Since then, those who study the link between politics and policy have become more involved with the conference. Not only were issues of art policy and patronage addressed, there was now also a focus on the influence of society on art (e.g., how the definition of "art" changes in conjunction with shifts in social structure). The variety of topics addressed by the conference has only increased and diversified. Needless to say, the number of participants and paper presentations in the conference has grown as well. Foster suggests an inevitable downside to this growth: that the spontaneity that marked the early years of the conference has been lost.

This retrospective look back on STP&A can give us some sense of the trends in research on the arts sector and might also serve as a foundation for future research goals and directions. I looked at all the conference programs and

Table 18.1
Organizers of the Social Theory, Politics, and the Arts Conference

Year	Place of Conference	Chairs
1974	Oswego, NY	Bob Leighninger and Derral Cheatwood
1975	Fredonia, NY	Derral Cheatwood
1976	Albany, NY	Arnold Foster et al.
1977	Pomona, NJ	Kenneth R. Donow, Bruce Jennings and Arthur Paris
1978	Syracuse, NY	Barry Glassner and Catherine Valentine
1979	Wayne, NJ	Rosanne Martorella
1980	Chicago, IL	Charles Stevens
1981	St. Paul, MN	Michel McCall and Gary Alan Fine
1983	Rutgers, NJ	Judith Balfe and Margaret Wyszomirski
1984	College Park, MD	John P. Robinson
1985	New York, NY	Vera Zolberg and Sally Ridgeway
1986	San Diego, CA	Chandra Mukerji and Bennett Berger
1987	Albany, NY	Jeffrey Halley
1988	Washington, DC	Valerie B. Morris and David B. Pankratz
1989	Toronto, Canada	Joseph G. Green
1990	New York, NY	Judith Balfe
1991	Jacksonville, FL	Andrew Buchwalter
1992	Philadelphia, PA	Larry Gross
1993	Boston, MA	Ann Galliger
1994	Baton Rouge, LA	Kevin Mulcahy
1995	Santa Barbara, CA	Denise D. Bielby and Connie McNeely
1996	Montreal, Canada	Maria Beaulac and Francois Colbert
1997	Cocoa Beach, FL	Charles Dorn and Kevin Mulcahy
1998	Philadelphia, PA	Cecelia Fitzgibbon
1999	Nashville, TN	Richard A. Peterson and Robert L. Mode

tabulated the presentations by a range of categories of research, based on presentation titles on the programs.[2] In the following sections, I present my definitions for each category and illustrative examples of titles for that category so that readers are able to judge for themselves how well these categories hold (see Table 18.2).[3]

CATEGORIES OF TOPICS PRESENTED AT STP&A

[A] Carving out the Area of Study

The presentations in this category were mainly concerned with the issue of trying to define the parameters surrounding the study of the arts. Examples of titles include *Towards an Aesthetic of Gospel Music* (1977), *Towards a Definition of Bureaucratic Art* (1985), a session titled *Reflections on Disciplinary Boundaries and Culture Studies* (1990), and *Towards a Sociology of Tap Dancing* (1999). Some of the presentations in this category also tried to make an argument for conceiving of various practices as art forms and for studying them as such. For example, a presentation in 1993 was titled *The Need for a Sociological Study of the Performing Arts*. Other papers, like *Theoretical Speculations on Social Aesthetics: An Application of Habermas' Critical Theory to the Arts* (1978), dealt with different theoretical approaches to the study of the arts.

The highest concentration of presentations for this category was in the early years of the conference, where organizers and participants were trying to define the parameters of the conference itself. As the conference and the study of the arts gained ground in the mid-1980s, the percentage of presentations in this category correspondingly fell. Brief resurgences in 1990 and in 1999 perhaps reflected periodic needs to redefine the parameters of the study of the arts.

[B] The Social Construction of Meaning

Paper presentations in this category dealt with the concepts and parameters of how we talk about and perceive the concepts of reality, symbolism, memory, and representation. Representative titles include *The Theory of Expressive Symbolism: Basic Premises, Strategies and Problems* (1976) and *Lessons on Collective Memory* (1993). The highest percentage of presentations in this category were in 1980, 1976, and 1987. For most years, this category was represented in smaller percentages or not at all.

As for subtypes in this category, there were many abstract presentations grappling with the larger theme of reality and symbolism (e.g., *Social Reality, Death and the State of Nature: A Sociological Case Study in the Symbolic*

Table 18.2
Categories of Research in Social Theory, Politics, and the Arts Conference Presentations

	1974	1975	1976	1977	1978	1979	1980	1982	1983	1984	1985	1986	1987	1988	1989	1990	1991	1992	1993	1994	1995	1996	1997	1998	1999
[A] Carving out the Area of Study	20.0	22.7	0	17.6	22.2	28.6	0	0	4.1	5.4	5.5	0	0	0	1.4	8.3	2.3	0	1.5	0	0	0	0	0	4.1
[B] The Social Construction of Meaning	67.0	0	17.2	0	0	0	25.0	0	2.0	3.6	3.6	5.3	13.3	3.8	13.9	0	2.3	2.1	4.5	12.5	13.8	0	2.2	0	9.3
[C] How We Should Read Texts	33.3	18.1	13.8	11.8	0	0	0	0	6.1	16.1	5.5	7.0	6.7	7.5	16.7	4.2	11.6	2.1	4.5	7.5	0	0	0	0	1.0
[D] Link between Art and Politics	13.3	9.0	24.1	17.6	0	0	37.5	0	0	7.1	10.9	8.8	6.7	12.3	12.5	10.4	20.9	10.6	15.2	22.5	20.7	29.2	23.9	11.1	7.2
[E] Social Theories of Art	13.3	18.1	0	0	44.4	0	0	0	0	1.8	0	0	0	0.9	0	0	0	0	0	0	0	0	0	0	0
[F] Art As a Mirror	6.7	0	17.2	35.3	33.3	7.1	0	0	12.2	5.4	5.5	3.5	16.7	9.4	12.5	10.4	7.0	12.8	10.6	2.5	20.7	15.7	4.3	11.1	15.5
[G] Links between Art and Society	6.7	0	10.3	0	0	7.1	12.5	15.2	4.1	7.1	1.8	0	0	0.9	4.2	7.3	0	4.3	3.0	5.0	10.3	10.1	4.3	3.7	1.0
[H] The Organization of Art Worlds	0	4.5	0	0	0	12.5	12.5	0	12.2	7.1	9.1	22.8	3.3	6.6	4.2	13.5	11.6	12.8	6.0	12.5	9.2	5.6	17.4	14.8	11.3
[I] Art World Interaction	0	9.0	0	0	0	7.1	0	15.2	8.2	1.8	1.8	3.5	3.3	4.7	0	5.2	0	0	1.5	2.5	0	3.4	0	9.3	5.2
[J] Audiences: Tastes and Practices	0	4.5	0	11.8	0	7.1	0	0	10.2	7.1	1.8	1.8	10.0	6.6	4.2	2.1	2.3	4.3	9.0	2.5	3.4	3.4	15.2	13.0	8.2
[K] Readings of Texts	0	0	0	5.9	0	0	12.5	15.2	0	5.4	27.3	15.8	10.0	6.6	8.3	4.2	2.3	4.3	1.5	2.5	0	0	0	3.7	2.0
[L] Patronage of the Arts	0	0	0	0	0	7.1	0	15.2	8.2	16.1	5.5	8.8	10.0	5.7	2.8	122	7.0	12.8	18.2	10.0	5.7	4.5	13	11.1	5.2
[M] Art As a Career	0	13.6	10.3	0	0	0	21.2	10.2	0	0	5.5	0	3.3	2.8	0	0	0	4.3	6.0	2.5	4.6	0	0	0	1.0
[N] Artists As Texts	0	0	6.9	0	0	7.1	0	0	10.2	7.1	7.3	5.3	6.7	9.4	4.2	5.2	7.0	8.5	3.0	7.5	5.7	6.7	4.3	3.7	4.1
[O] Arts Administration and Policy	0	0	0	0	0	28.6	0	18.2	12.2	10.7	9.1	5.7	10.0	22.6	15.3	16.7	25.6	21.3	15.2	10.0	5.7	21.3	15.2	18.5	24.7
Total	15	22	29	17	9	14	8	33	49	56	55	57	30	106	72	96	43	47	66	40	87	89	46	54	97

Representation of Experience [1976]). A second subtype of presentation, which became more common in the later years of the conference, dealt with the issue of collective memory and how communities and societies created meaning and reality for themselves. Illustrative titles include *National Memories: The Case of the Pantheon* (1994) and *Americans Define Their Collective Experience* (1995). Finally, there were also presentations that dealt with industries that were in the business of producing and constructing meaning and experience (e.g., *Controversial Public Art: A Discussion of Selected Cases and Problems of Meaning and Cultural Authority* [1988]). Despite differences, these subtypes are all concerned with the theme of power and authority and who gets to define reality and meaning.

[C] How We Should Read Texts

Titles in this category tried to wrestle, on a theoretical and conceptual level, with the issue of how to interpret texts. Most of the titles appeared to be concerned with the issue of which theoretical perspective was most appropriate for interpreting and reading texts and practices. Representative titles include *Feminist/Multicultural Reading of the Sociology of Culture* (1993) and *Historical Structuralism and Literature: Toward a Marxist Synthesis* (1977). There were also presentations that actually read and interpreted particular texts. The highest percentages of presentations in this category were in 1989, 1976, and 1977.

[D] Link between Art and Politics

These presentations were concerned, both theoretically and conceptually, with the interaction between art and politics, that is, how the arts were influenced by politics, or vice versa. Presentations utilized a broad definition of "politics," including such diverse topics as social movements, nationalism, and colonialism. Titles in this category include *Art vs. Ideology: Political Rhetoric and Theatrical Truth* (1984), *Depoliticizing Social Problems: The Growing Power of Popular Culture* (1986), *Canon Formation and Nationalistic Impulses* (1990), and *Feminist Postmodernism and the Field of Cultural Production* (1996). There were also presentations that explored the interaction between the arts and politics on an empirical level utilizing particular case studies.

This was a popular category, topping out at 37.5 percent (1980), 29.2 percent (1996), and 22.5 percent (1994). Unlike the previous categories where presentations all but disappeared for extended periods of time, the percentages for this category mostly wavered around 10 percent (10.9 percent in 1985, 12.5 percent in 1989, and 7.2 percent in 1999). Once again, as with category [B], the theme of power and authority was present in the presentations here.

[E] Social Theories of Art

Presentations in this category tried to argue for a conceptualization of the arts as an institution, in contrast to thinking of the arts simply in terms of material objects (e.g., novels and paintings) or practices (e.g., dancing and symphony performances). Examples of presentation titles include *Art As Institution* (1978), *On the Institutional Theory of Art* (1978), and *The Institutional Theory of Art As a Model for Research and Education* (1988). Presentations in this category were not very common—for most years, there were no or very few such titles. The decline in the number of presentations in this category in later years could be due to the fact that the early focus on conceptualizing the arts as an institution had taken hold and did not need to be dealt with in detail thereafter.

[F] Art As a Mirror

This category is the empirical counterpart of [D], as noted earlier. This category also explores the interaction between the arts and politics. However, these titles presented particular case studies, which were used as data and evidence. Examples include *The Role of Doctrinaires in the Evolution of Liberal Romanticism in France, 1820–30* (1978), *Between Art and Politics: Young Theatre in Poland* (1985), and *Innovation and Discontinuity in American Contemporary Art: Perceptions of the 1980's Art "Bust"* (1994). Paper titles in this category were more common in the early years of STP&A: 35.3 percent in 1977 and 33.3 percent in 1978. Percentages fell as low as 3.5 in the mid-1980s, but enjoyed a renaissance of sorts again in 1995, where 20.7 percent of the presentations that year fell under this category.

Like earlier categories, the theme of power and authority was common among these presentations and, like category [D], the concept of "politics" is broad and diverse as well. Furthermore, the case studies in these papers covered a wide range of different historical periods and contexts, as can be seen from the title examples.

[G] Links between Art and Society

Presentation titles in this category dealt with how the arts interact with and impact larger societal and cultural contexts. Conversely, they also addressed how larger societal contexts and social statuses interact with and impact the arts. Examples of paper titles include *On Some of the Sociocultural Factors Affecting the Western Musical Styles during the Low Middle Ages* (1979), *Art and Social Structure* (1982), and *Social and Political Forces behind the Scandal of Debussy's "Pelleas et Melissande"* (1985). The number of presentation titles in this category topped out around 10 to 15 percent in the years it did appear: 12.5 percent in 1980 and 15.2 percent in 1982. In some years, they did not appear at all, but reappeared at rates of 10.3 percent in 1995 and 10.1 percent in 1996.

Again, like the earlier categories, the theme of power and authority was common and there was a broad range in the data and case studies utilized.

[H] The Organization of Art Worlds

Presentation titles in this category dealt with how art worlds were organized. Like the concept of "politics" in categories [D] and [F], "art" is broadly defined, including such diverse institutions as theaters, symphonies, and museums. Examples of presentation titles include *The Apaches and Other Turn-of-the-Century Parisian Art World* (1986), *The Arts in Cleveland: A Major Institution Examines Its Role and Image* (1988), and *The Museum Volunteer: In the Crack between Democratization and Elitism* (1994). In the early years of this conference, there were no presentation titles in this category. Presentation titles in this category first appeared in 1980 where 12.5 percent of the presentation titles fell under this category. In recent years, despite years of few titles in this category, the number of presentations have "balanced out" around 10 to 15 percent.

Once again, presentation titles in this category dealt with a wide range and variety of historical and political phenomena. And like the earlier categories, the presentation titles in this category were concerned with the themes of power, authority, and stratification. For instance, papers addressed questions such as: Why is an art world organized in a particular way, and who gets to make these decisions? and Why are these decisions made and what is the role of particular individuals within these organizations? Answers to these questions frequently dealt with the implications of power and authority in art worlds.

[I] Art World Interactions

Presentations in this category seemed to deal with how different art worlds interact with, impact, and influence each other. In contrast to category [H], which dealt with a single art world and the ties and linkages within that one art world, these presentations dealt with the ties and linkages between different art worlds. Examples include *Art Groups and Interaction* (1982), *Imagining Reality: Some Considerations of the Impact and Function of TV and Photo-Journalism* (1985), and *Literature and Film* (1988). In 1982, 15.2 percent of the presentation titles fell under this category. By 1990, the percentage had dipped down to 5.2 percent and dipped even lower to 1.5 percent in 1993. However, it had climbed back to 9.3 percent in 1998.

Given the growing pervasiveness of increasing globalization and technological innovation, it behooves researchers on the arts sector to pay more attention to the increasing interactions between different art worlds, forms, and practices. Furthermore, since audiences usually consume different art forms and not just one particular art form, it might be informative to keep this perspective in order to help us shed more light on the consumption practices of audiences and consumers.

[J] Audiences: Tastes and Practices

Presentation titles in this category were concerned with audiences' taste cultures and their practices and consumption of the arts. In addition, some presentation titles were interested in the demographics of the audience. Examples include *The Art Audience* (1983), *Naïve Artists and Savvy Supporters* (1986), *The Social Meaning of Cultural Participation* (1987), *Arts Audiences, Adults and Arts Education* (1987), *1992 Local Arts Participation Surveys* (1993), and *Participation in the Arts: Socioeconomic, Age and Race Patterns* (1995). In 1977, the percentage of presentation titles that fell under this category was 11.8 percent. Generally speaking, that number has ranged from 1.8 to 15.2 percent.

Most of these presentations dealt with issues of audience taste cultures and demographics. However, some addressed actual practices of audiences and consumers themselves, that is, how audiences and consumers incorporated and interpreted the art forms themselves. Still others dealt with the power of individual human agency and considered how individuals can interpret and incorporate different art forms to their own liking and use.

[K] Readings of Texts

These presentations represent the empirical application of category [C]. Here, presentations analyzed particular cultural texts. Examples are *New Observations on Political Content in Jacques Louis David's Prerevolutionary Painting* (1985), *America in Poetry and Art: Changing Perspectives* (1988), and *American Number One Songs 1955–1988: Code and Context* (1990). In 1985, 27.3 percent of the presentation titles for that year fell under this category. Otherwise, for most years, the percentage of presentation titles that fell under this category for a given year wavered between 0 and 5.9 percent.

In comparison to category [F], the presentation titles in this category were relatively few in number. This is an indication that STP&A presenters were more inclined toward utilizing specific historical and political events rather than objects of material culture such as data and evidence.

[L] Patronage of the Arts

The presentation titles in this category engaged issues of patronage and the funding of the arts in general. Examples include *The Corporation and the Arts* (1983), *Federal Assistance for Arts Research and Scholarship* (1984), *Orches-*

trating Public Support for the Arts: The Case of Major Symphony Orchestras (1988), *Art Supply and Demand and the Role of the NEA in Funding* (1990), and *"Friends of ... " Individual Arts Patronage in Museums* (1991). In the late 1970s, there were few presentation titles dealing with issues of patronage. But starting in 1982, presentation titles in the category were present in every year the conference was held, reaching a high of 16.1 percent in 1984.

Much like the other categories, these presentations were concerned, at least implicitly, with issues of power, authority, and stratification. Here, the issues of power and authority are manifested through funding responsibilities for the arts. Who should fund the arts? What are the consequences of certain forms of funding? What are the benefits of corporate funding as compared to state and federal funding?

[M] Art As a Career

Presentation titles in this category explored different career paths and prospects in different occupations within the arts. Again, like the previous categories, "the arts" are defined broadly. Some presentations adopted a "how to succeed" perspective on the topic. Examples include *Ballet As a Career: How to Dance Your Way to Fame* (1976), *Theater Careers in the New Periphery* (1983), and *Selling Deviant Pictures: Tattooing As a Career and Occupation* (1985). Despite years such as 1982 (21.2 percent) and 1983 (10.2 percent), titles in this category were not very common in most STP&A conferences, and simply not present for most years.

[N] Artists As Texts

In this category, artists themselves take center stage as the objects of study and examination. The definition of "artists" is broad and all-encompassing, ranging from dancers to symphony conductors. Titles in this category include *The Social Identity of the Artist As a Product of the Institutionalized Matrix of the Art World* (1976), *Arts Occupation I: Social Psychological Issues* (1983), and *The Changing World of the Fashion Designer: New Approaches to the Sociology of Fashion* (1988). Presentation titles in this category were present every year since 1983, with the high percentage of 10.2 percent in 1983.

Presentations in this category dealt with three different types of issues. First, there was much concern about the social psychological identity issues that artists faced. This concern reflects the fact that artists, working within art worlds, often work within larger structural constraints and therefore face many stresses that impact their social psychological identities. Papers also addressed practices of artists, from symphony conductors' different styles of conducting to diverse styles of dance performances. Finally, presentation titles also analyzed the diverse meanings of these styles.

[O] Arts Administration and Policy

Examples of presentation titles in this category include *Allocating Identities: The Contours of Cultural Policy in Regional Integration* (1993), *Preliminary Comparisons of US and Japanese Cultural Policies and Administration* (1994), and *Public Television, Political Television: Public Broadcasting and Politics in the United States* (1995). Other than the first four years of the conference, presentation titles in this category comprised a large percentage of the presentation titles, ranging from 28.6 percent in 1979 to 10 percent in 1987. In the 1999 conference, 24.7 percent of the presentation titles fell under this category.

Issues of arts administration and policy inevitably deal with issues of power, authority, and stratification. In that sense, these presentations have a lot in common with those in other categories. Also of note, titles did not restrict their study of policy and administration issues in the United States. Furthermore, there is a wide range of subject matter in this category as well, focusing on policies governing public broadcasting to those affecting art museums.

SUMMARY

Foster argues that beginning in 1983 the STP&A conference began to lose touch with the people from the arts and the humanities even as it broadened out to incorporate issues of arts policy, administration, and patronage. Indeed, most of the presentation titles in the years of the conference have indeed had a more "sociological" bent, as opposed to literary analysis of particular cultural texts. Presentation titles have also dealt more with macrostructures and macroinstitutions, encompassing such diverse topics as political ideology, the feminist movement, and arts education. In particular, there has been more focus on issues of arts patronage, policy, and administration, which are becoming more salient in the context of recent debates over public funding for the arts.

However, some elements of STP&A have remained constant, even while the focus of some topics has changed. There has always been a wide variety in the topics presented and discussed at the conference. These topics cover different countries, art forms, institutions, and time periods. Topics have covered a wide range of historical phenomena, from contemporary political situations to social movements in nineteenth-century France.

Finally, the focus on issues of power, authority, and stratification has remained salient throughout the twenty-five years of the conference. In an era where it is tempting to conceive of everything as texts in their own right, presentation titles continue to maintain their focus on how the arts embody issues of power, authority, and stratification.

NOTES

1. Arnold Foster, Social Theory, Politics and the Arts: Reminiscences, Facts, Circumstantial Evidence, Anecdotes, Opinions and Other Materials for a History (Unpublished manuscript, 1990), 6.

2. The total number of presentations for the year are at the bottom of each column. The cell entries represent percentages of the total number of presentations for each category.

3. For this study, I did not include forums or discussion panels. I only considered regular paper sessions. To my understanding, these forums and discussion panels were more likely to deal with the more practical concerns of artists and arts administrators. Also, for particular years, the only information available to me was the title of the session and the names of the presenters. In such cases, I categorized the paper session title and counted each presenter as one presentation for that category.

Select Bibliography

Academy of Television Arts and Sciences Foundation. *A Framework for Teaching and Learning through the Arts and Technologies of Television*. North Hollywood, CA: Academy of Television Arts and Sciences Foundation, 2001.

Acheson, Keith, and Christopher Maule. *Much Ado about Culture: North American Trade Disputes*. Ann Arbor: University of Michigan Press, 1999.

Adams, Don, and Arlene Goldbard. *Creative Community: The Art of Cultural Development*. New York: The Rockefeller Foundation.

————. "Grass Roots Vanguard." *Art in America* 70, no. 4 (April 1982).

Almond, Gabriel A., and Sidney Verba. *The Civic Culture: Political Attitudes and Democracy in Five Nations*. Boston: Little, Brown, 1965.

Alper, Neil, and Gregory Wassall. *More Than Once in a Blue Moon: Multiple Job Holdings by American Artists*. Santa Ana, CA: National Endowment for the Arts and Seven Locks Press, 2000.

Alper, Neil, Gregory Wassall, and Anne Galligan. ""The Career Matrix: The Pipeline for Artists in the United States."

————. "Characteristics of Performing Artists: A Baseline Profile of Sectoral Crossovers."

Alper, N., H. Butcher, H. Chartrand, R. Greenblatt, J. Jeffri, A. Kay, and G. Wassall. *Artists in the Workforce: Employment and Earnings, 1970–1990*. Santa Ana, CA: National Endowment for the Arts and Seven Locks Press, 1994.

Alvarez, Jose Louis, and Silviya Svejenova. "Symbolic Careers in Movie Making: Pedro and Augustin Almodovar." Paper presented at the Creative Careers Conference of the London Business School, March 2000.

American Assembly. *The Arts and the Public Purpose*. New York: American Assembly, Columbia University, 1997.

————. *Deals and Ideals: For-Profit and Not-for-Profit Arts Connections*. New York: American Assembly, Columbia University, 1999.

Americans for the Arts. *Arts Link* 3, no. 6 (July–August 1999).

———. *Arts Link* 3, no. 9 (November–December 1999).

———. *Monographs: Local Arts Agencies Facts*. Washington, DC: Americans for the Arts, 1998.

American Symphony Orchestra League. *The Financial Condition of Symphony Orchestras*. Washington, DC: American Symphony Orchestra League, 1992.

Anand, N., and Richard A. Peterson. "When Market Information Constitutes Fields: Sensemaking of Markets in the Commercial Music Industry." *Organization Science* 11 (2000): 270–84.

Anheier, Helmut K., and Stefan Toepler. "Commerce and the Muse: Are Art Museums Becoming Commercial?" In *To Profit or Not to Profit: The Commercial Transformation of the Nonprofit Sector*, ed. Burton A. Weisbrod. New York: Cambridge University Press, 1998.

Arian, Edward. *The Unfulfilled Promise: Public Subsidy of the Arts in America*. Philadelphia: Temple University Press, 1989.

Arthurs, Alberta, Frank Hodsoll, and Steven Lavine. "For-Profit and Not-for-Profit Arts Connections: Existing and Potential." *Journal of Arts Management, Law, and Society* 29, no. 2 (summer 1999): 80–96.

Arthurs, Alberta, and Glenn Wallach, eds. *Crossroads: Art and Religion in American Life*. New York: New Press, 2001.

Backer, Thomas E. *Strengthening Nonprofits: Capacity-Building and Philanthropy*. Miami, FL: John S. and James L. Knight Foundation, 2000.

Balfe, Judith Huggins, ed. *Paying the Piper: Causes and Consequences of Art Patronage*. Champaign–Urbana: University of Illinois Press, 1993.

Balfe, Judith Huggins, and Monnie Peters. "Public Involvement in the Arts." In *The Public Life of the Arts in America*, ed. Joni Maya Cherbo and Margaret J. Wyszomirski. New Brunswick, NJ: Rutgers University Press, 2000.

Balfe, Judith Huggins, and Margaret J. Wyszomirski. "The Arts in New Jersey: Political and Social Issues." *l of Regional Cultures* 5, no. 1 (1985): 205–22.

———. "An Ecology of Arts Institutions: A Community Case Study of Montclair NJ, 1985." Unpublished, College of Staten Island, City University of New York.

Barber, Benjamin. *Serving Democracy by Serving the Arts*. Washington, DC: President's Committee on the Arts and Humanities, 1996.

Barksdate, Kelly. *A State Arts Agency Performance Measurement Toolkit*. Washington, DC: National Assembly of State Arts Agencies, 1996.

Barlow, John Perry. "The Economy of Ideas: A Framework for Rethinking Patents and Copyrights in the Digital Age." *Wired* (March 1999).

Barry, Dan. "Gaelic Comes Back on Ireland's Byways and Airwaves." *New York Times*, 25 July 2000.

Bartis, Peter, and Paddy A. Bowman. *A Teacher's Guide to Folklife Resources for K–12 Classrooms*. Washington, DC: American Folklife Center, Library of Congress, 1994.

Bassin, Joel. "Dancing with the Devil: An Analysis of the Negative Impact of Federal Arts Support on the American Not-for-Profit Theatre." Ph.D. diss., City University of New York, 2000.

Batstone, David, and Eduardo Mendieta, eds. *The Good Citizen*. New York: Routledge, 1999.

Baumgartner, Frank R., and Beth L. Leech. *Basic Interests: The Importance of Groups in Politics and in Political Science*. Princeton, NJ: Princeton University Press, 1998.

Baumol, William J., and William G. Bowen. "The Performing Arts: The Economic Dilemma." *Twentieth Century Fund Report* (1965).

———. *Performing Arts: The Economic Dilemma*. Cambridge: MIT Press, 1966.

Baxter, Christie I. *Program-Related Investments: A Technical Manual for Foundations*. New York: Wiley, 1997.

Beardsley, John. *Gardens of Revelation: Environments by Visionary Artists*. New York: Abbeville, 1995.

Becker, Howard. *Art Worlds*. Berkeley: University of California Press, 1982.

Benedict, Stephen, ed. *Public Money and the Muse*. American Assembly. New York: Norton, 1991.

Bergonzi, Louis, and J. Smith. *Effects of Arts Education on Participation in the Arts*. Santa Ana, CA: National Endowment for the Arts and Seven Locks, 1996.

Berry, Jeffrey M. *The Interest Group Society*. Boston: Little, Brown, 1984.

Beyer, Landon E. "Schools, Aesthetic Meanings, and Social Change." *Educational Theory* 4 (1977): 274–82.

Bille-Hansen, Trine. "The Willingness-to-Pay for the Royal Theatre in Copenhagen As a Public Good." *Journal of Cultural Economics* 21, no. 1 (1997): 1–28.

Blandy, Doug, and Kristin G. Congdon. "Arts in Other Places: A Conference Critique." *The Bulletin of the Caucus on Social Theory and Art Education* 7 (1987): 75–79.

———. "Community-Based Aesthetics As an Exhibition Catalyst and a Foundation for Community Involvement in Art Education." *Studies in Art Education* 29, no. 4 (1988): 243–49.

———, eds. *Pluralistic Approaches to Art Criticism*. Bowling Green, OH: Popular, 1987.

———. "Viewers Sound Off: A Feminist Analysis of Vernacular Art Criticism of 'All My Children' and 'Another World' on Electronic 'Boards.'" *Journal of Gender Issues in Art and Education* (forthcoming).

Blau, Judith. *The Shape of Culture: A Study of Contemporary Cultural Patterns in the United States*. New York: Cambridge University Press, 1986.

Booth, Wayne. *For the Love of It: Amateuring and its Rivals*. Chicago: University of Chicago Press, 2000.

Bourdieu, Pierre, and James S. Coleman, eds. *Social Theory for a Changing Society*. Boulder, CO: Westview, 1991.

Bourdieu, Pierre, with Alain Darbel. *The Love of Art: European Art Museums and Their Public*. Trans. Caroline Beattie and Nick Merriman. Stanford, CA: Stanford University Press, 1990.

Bowen, William G., et al. *The Charitable Nonprofits*. San Francisco: Jossey-Bass, 1994.

Bradford, Gigi, Michael Gary, and Glenn Wallach, eds. *The Politics of Culture: Policy Perspectives for Individuals, Institutions, and Communities*. New York: New Press, 2000.

Brooks, Arthur C. *Arts, Markets, and Government: A Study in Cultural Policy Analysis*. Santa Monica, CA: RAND, 1997.

Brooks, Arthur, and Roland Kushner. *A Cultural District for Downtown Atlanta*. Atlanta: Research Atlanta, Inc., Georgia State University, 2000.

Brustein, Robert. "Requiem." *New Republic*, 27 March 2000, 29.

Buchwalter, Andrew. *Culture and Democracy*. Boulder, CO: Westview, 1992.

Bucuvalas, Tina, Peggy A. Bulger, and Stetson Kennedy. *South Florida Folklife.* Jackson: University Press of Mississippi, 1999.

Burgin, Victor. *The End of Art Theory: Criticism and Postmodernity.* Atlantic Highlands, NJ: Humanities Press International, 1986.

Cannon, Steve, Kellie Jones, and Tom Finkelpearl. *David Hammons: Rousing the Rubble.* Cambridge: MIT Press, 1991.

Carroll, Glenn R. "Concentration and Specialization: Dynamics of Niche Width in Populations of Organizations." *American Journal of Sociology* 90 (1985): 1262–83.

Carroll, Glenn R., and Michael T. Hannan. *The Demography of Corporations and Industries.* Princeton, NJ: Princeton University Press, 2000.

Castells, Manuel. *The Rise of the Network Society.* Vol. 1, *The Information Age: Economy, Society and Culture.* 3 vols. Berkeley: University of California Press, 1996.

Center for Arts and Culture. *America's Cultural Capital.* Washington, DC: Center for Arts and Culture, 2000.

Center on Philanthropy and Public Policy. *What's "New" about New Philanthropy?* Los Angeles: University of Southern California, 2001.

Cha, Ariana Eunjung. "E-Power to the People." *Washington Post,* 18 May 2000.

Chapman, Dan. "Article Title" *Atlanta Journal-Constitution,* 9 April 2000, C1–C2.

Chartrand, Harry. "Toward an American Arts Industry." In *The Public Life of the Arts in America,* ed. Joni Maya Cherbo and Margaret J. Wyszomirski. New Brunswick, NJ: Rutgers University Press, 2000.

Cherbo, Joni Maya. "The Associational Infrastructure for the Culture Industries: Private Policy Making in Arts Service Organizations." Paper presented at the Twenty-Sixth Annual Conference of Social Theory, Politics, and the Arts, Washington, DC, October 12–15, 2000.

———. "Creative Synergy: Commercial and Not-for-Profit Live Theater in America." *Journal of Arts Management, Law, and Society* 28, no. 2 (summer 1998): 129–43.

———. "A Department of Cultural Resources: A Perspective on the Arts." *Journal of Arts Management, Law, and Society* 22 (winter 1992): 44–62.

Cherbo, Joni Maya, and Monnie Peters. *American Participation in Opera and Musical Theatre, 1992.* Santa Ana, CA: National Endowment for the Arts and Seven Locks Press, 1995.

Cherbo, Joni Maya, and Margaret J. Wyszomirski, eds. *The Public Life of the Arts in America.* New Brunswick, NJ: Rutgers University Press, 2000.

Cleveland, William. *Art in Other Places: Artists at Work in America's Community and Social Institutions.* Amherst: University of Massachusetts Arts Extension Service, 2000.

Clotfelter, Charles T., ed. *Who Benefits from the Private Sector?* Chicago: University of Chicago Press, 1992.

Collaborative Economics. The Creative Community: Leveraging Creativity and Cultural Participation for Silicon Valley's Economic and Civic Future. San Jose, CA: Cultural Initiatives Silicon Valley, 2001.

Colonna, Carl M. "The Economic Contributions of Volunteerism toward the Value of Our Cultural Inventory." *Journal of Cultural Economics* 19 (1995): 341–50.

Commission on the Humanities. *Report.* New York: American Council of Learned Societies, 1964.

Communications Industry Forecast. New York: Veronis, Suhler and Associates, 1996.

Cook, Derrick. *Theater News* (January 2000).

Cowen, Tyler. *In Praise of Commercial Culture.* Cambridge, MA: Harvard University Press, 1998.

Crane, Diana, ed. *Emerging Theoretical Perspectives in the Sociology of Culture.* London: Blackwell, 1994.

———. *The Transformation of the Avant-Garde: The New York Art World, 1940–1985.* Chicago: University of Chicago Press, 1987.

"Cross Talk." *Inter@ctive Week,* 24 April 2000, 110.

Cuccia, Tiziana, and Giovanni Signorello. "A Contingent Valuation Study of Willingness to Pay for Visiting a City of Art: The Case Study of Noto, Italy." Paper presented at the Eleventh Biennial Conference of the Association for Cultural Economics, International, Minneapolis, Minnesota, May 28–31, 2000.

Cummings, Milton C., Jr., and Richard S. Katz, eds. *The Patron State: Government and Arts in Europe, North America, and Japan.* New York: Oxford University Press, 1987.

Cummings, Milton C., Jr., and J. Mark Davidson Schuster, eds. *Who's to Pay for the Arts.* New York: American Council for the Arts, 1989.

Dale, Martin. *The Movie Game: The Film Business in Britain, Europe and America.* London: Casell, 1997.

DeNora, Tia. *Beethoven and the Construction of Genius: Musical Politics in Vienna, 1792–1803.* Berkeley: University of California Press, 1995.

de Sola Pool, Ithiel. *Technologies without Boundaries: On Telecommunications in a Global Age.* Cambridge, MA: Harvard University Press, 1990.

Dewhurst, C. Kurt, and Marsha MacDowell. "Gathering and Interpreting Tradition." *Journal of Museum Education* 24, no. 3 (1999): 7–10.

DiMaggio, Paul J. "Cultural Boundaries and Structural Change: The Extension of the High Culture Model to Theater, Opera and the Dance, 1900–1940." In *Cultivating Differences: Symbolic Boundaries and the Making of Inequality,* ed. Michele Lamont and Marcel Fournier. Chicago: University of Chicago Press, 1992.

———. "Cultural Entrepreneurship in Nineteenth-Century Boston." In *Nonprofit Enterprise in the Arts: Studies in Mission and Constraint,* ed. Paul J. DiMaggio. New York: Oxford University Press, 1986.

———. "Cultural Entrepreneurship in Nineteenth-Century Boston, Part II: The Classification and Framing of American Art." *Media, Culture and Society* 4 (1982): 303–22.

———, ed. *Nonprofit Enterprise in the Arts: Studies in Mission and Constraint.* New York: Oxford University Press, 1986.

———. "Social Structure, Institutions, and Cultural Goods: The Case of the United States." In *Social Theory for a Changing Society,* ed. Pierre Bourdieu and James S. Coleman. Boulder, CO: Westview, 1991.

DiMaggio, Paul J., and Francie Ostrower. *Race, Ethnicity, and Participation in the Arts.* Washington, DC: National Endowment for the Arts and Seven Locks Press, 1992.

Dissanayake, Ellen. *Homo Aestheticus: Where Art Comes from and Why.* New York: The Free Press, 1992.

Dorian, Frederick. *Commitment to Culture.* Pittsburgh: University of Pittsburgh Press, 1964.

Doss, Erika. *Elvis Culture: Fans, Faith, and Image.* Lawrence: University Press of Kansas, 1999.

Dreezen, Craig. *Community Cultural Planning*. Washington, DC: Americans for the Arts, 1998.

Drucker, Peter. *Managing the Nonprofit Organization*. New York: HarperCollins, 1990.

Druker, Donald. "E-Culture." Panel discussion hosted by the Center for Arts and Culture, Washington, DC, April 11, 2000.

Dwyer, Christine M., and Susan L. Frankel. Reconnaissance Report of Existing and Potential Uses of Arts and Culture Data: A Product of the Arts and Culture Indicators in Community Building Project. Washington, DC: Urban Institute, 1997.

Filicko, Therese. "In What Spirit Do Americans Cultivate the Arts: A Review of Survey Questions on the Arts." *Journal of Arts Management, Law, and Society* 26 (1997): 221–46.

Filicko, Therese, and Sue Anne Lafferty. *Defining the Arts and Cultural Universe: Early Lessons for the Profiles Project*. Columbus: Arts Policy and Administration Program, Ohio State University, 1999.

Fitzgibbon, Cecelia, ed. *Looking Ahead: A Collection of Papers from the International Social Theory, Politics and the Arts Conference*. Philadelphia: Drexel University Press, 1999.

Focke, Anne. *Financial Supports for Artists*. Seattle, WA: Grantmakers in the Arts, 1996.

Foster, Arnold. Social Theory, Politics and the Arts: Reminiscences, Facts, Circumstantial Evidence, Anecdotes, Opinions and Other Materials for a History. Unpublished manuscript, 1990.

Freeman, Everette J., and Neil Bania. "A Different Tempo: African American Attendance at Performances of the Cleveland Orchestra." *Journal of Arts Management, Law, and Society* 25, no. 2 (summer 1995): 127–40.

Freeman, Roland L. *A Communion of the Spirits: African American Quilters, Preservers, and their Stories*. Nashville: Rutledge, 1996.

Frey, Bruno S. *Arts and Economics: Analysis and Cultural Policy*. New York: Springer-Verlag, 2000.

———. "Evaluating Cultural Property: The Economic Approach." *International Journal of Cultural Property* 6, no. 2 (1997): 231–46.

Frohnmayer, John. *Leaving Town Alive: Confessions of an Arts Warrior*. Boston: Houghton Mifflin, 1993.

Galligan, Ann M., and Neil O. Alper. "The Career Matrix: The Pipeline for Artists in the United States." In *The Public Life of the Arts in America*, ed. Joni Maya Cherbo and Margaret J. Wyszomirski. New Brunswick, NJ: Rutgers University Press, 2000.

———. "Characteristics of Performing Artists: A Baseline Profile of Sectoral Crossovers." *Journal of Arts Management, Law, and Society* 28, no. 2 (summer 1998): 155–77.

Gans, Herbert J. *Popular Culture and High Culture: An Analysis and Evaluation of Taste*. New York: Basic, 1999.

Gapinski, James H. "Economic Structure and Impact of the Arts: Comparisons with the Nonarts." In *Economic Impact of the Arts: A Sourcebook*, ed. Anthony J. Radich. Denver, CO: National Conference of State Legislators, 1987.

Gildea, Robert. *France since 1945*. New York: Oxford University Press, 1996.

Gilmore, Samuel. "Schools of Activity and Innovation." *Sociological Quarterly* 29 (1988): 202–19.

Glaeser, Edward L. "Are Cities Dying?" *Journal of Economic Perspective* 12, no. 2 (spring 1998): 139–60.

Goetz, Edward, and Terrence Kayser. "Competition and Cooperation in Economic De- velopment: A Study of the Twin Cities Metropolitan Area." *Economic Develop- ment Quarterly* 7, no. 1 (1993): 63–78.

Goldbard, Arlene. "Postscripts to the Past: Notes towards a History of Community Arts." *High Performance* 64 (winter 1993).

Goodall, Howard. *Big Bangs: The Story of Five Discoveries that Changed Music His- tory.* London: Ghatto and Windus, 2000.

Gould, Samuel B. *The Arts and Education: A New Beginning in Higher Education.* New York: Rockefeller Brothers Fund, 1968.

Gray, Charles M. *Turning on and Tuning In: Public Participation in the Arts via Media in the United States.* Santa Ana, CA: National Endowment for the Arts and Seven LocksPress, 1995.

Greenfeld, Liah. *Different Worlds.* New York: Cambridge University Press, 1989.

Griswald, Wendy. "American Character and the American Novel." *American Journal of Sociology* 86 (1981): 740–65.

———. *Renaissance Revivals: City Comedy and Revenge Tragedy in the London The- atre, 1576–1980.* Chicago: University of Chicago Press, 1986.

———. "The Writing on the Mud Wall: Nigerian Novels and the Imaginary Village." *American Sociological Review* 57 (1992): 709–24.

Guernsey, Lisa. "MP3 Trading Service Can Clog Networks on College Campuses." *New York Times,* 20 January 2000, <http://www.nytimes.com>.

Haas, Nancy. "The Secret of His Excess." *Art News* 98, no. 6 (1999): 96–99.

Halle, David. *Inside Culture: Arts and Class in the American Home.* Chicago: University of Chicago Press, 1994.

Hammersley, Ben. "Out to Destroy Copyright Killers." *The Times* (London), 15 May 2000.

Hannan, Michael, and Glenn Carroll. *Organizational Demography.* Princeton, NJ: Princeton University Press, 2000.

Hansmann, Henry. "Nonprofit Enterprise in the Performing Arts." In *Nonprofit Enter- prise in the Arts: Studies in Mission and Constraint,* ed. Paul J. DiMaggio. New York: Oxford University Press, 1986.

Hauser, Arnold. *The Social History of Art.* New York: Vintage, 1985.

Hebel, Sarah. "Public Colleges Feel Impact of the Economic Downturn." *Chronicle of Higher Education,* 20 July 2001, A21.

Heckathorn, Douglas D. "Respondent Driven Sampling: A New Approach to the Study of Hidden Populations." *Social Problems* 44 (1997): 174–99.

Heckathorn, Douglas D., and Joan Jeffri. "Finding the Beat: Using Respondent-Driven Sampling to Study Jazz Musicians." *Poetics* (November 2000).

Heilbrun, James, and Charles Gray. *The Economics of Art and Culture: An American Perspective.* New York: Cambridge University Press, 1993.

Heinz Endowments. "Bringing the Arts to Life." Pittsburgh, PA (1999): 3.

Hendon, William S., ed. *The Arts and Urban Development: Critical Comment and Dis- cussion.* Monograph Series in Public and International Affairs no. 12. Center for Urban Studies, University of Akron, August 1980.

———. "Evaluating Cultural Policy through Benefit-Cost Analysis." In *Economic Im- pact of the Arts: A Sourcebook,* ed. Anthony J. Radich. Denver, CO: National Conference of State Legislators, 1987.

Hendon, William S., and James L. Shanahan, eds. *Economics of Cultural Decision.* Cam- bridge, MA: Abt Associates, 1983.

Hickey, Dave. *Air Guitar: Essays on Art and Democracy.* Los Angeles: Art Issues, 1997.

Hobbs, J. A. "Popular Art versus Fine Art." *Art Education* 37, no. 3 (1984): 11–14.

Hofferbert, Richard I., and John K. Urice. "Small-Scale Policy: The Federal Stimulus versus Competing Explanations for State Funding of the Arts." *American Journal of Political Science* 471, no. 29 (1985): 308–29.

Holmes, Helen, and David Taras. *Seeing Ourselves: Media Power and Policy in Canada.* 2nd ed. Toronto: Harcourt Brace, 1996.

Hufford, Mary. *American Folklife: A Commonwealth of Cultures.* Washington, DC: American Folklife Center, Library of Congress, 1991.

Humphreys, Jeffrey M., and Michael K. Plummer. *The Economic Impact on the State of Georgia of Hosting the 1996 Olympic Games.* Prepared for the Atlanta Committee for the Olympic Games. University of Georgia, August 1992.

Hyman, James B. Exploring Social Capital through a Proposed Collective Efficacy Framework: A Concept Paper. Washington, DC: Urban Institute, 2000.

Ihlanfeldt, Keith. "The Importance of the Central City to the Regional and National Economy: A Review of the Arguments and Empirical Evidence." *Cityscape: A Journal of Policy, Development, and Research* 1, no. 2 (August 1995): 125–50.

Independent Commission. *A Report to Congress on the National Endowment for the Arts.* Washington, DC: Independent Commission, 1990.

Independent Committee on Arts Policy. *The Nation and the Arts: A Presidential Briefing Paper.* New York: Independent Committee on Arts Policy, 1988.

Ingram, Paul, and Peter W. Roberts. "Friendships among Competitors in the Sydney Hotel Industry." *American Journal of Sociology* (2000).

Ivey, William J. "Bridging the For-Profit and Not-for-Profit Arts." *Journal of Arts Management, Law, and Society* 29, no. 2 (summer 1999): 97–100.

Jackson, Maria-Rosario. Arts and Culture Indicators in Community Building Project: January 1996–May 1998, a Report to the Rockefeller Foundation. Washington, DC: Urban Institute, 1998.

Jacob, Mary Jane, ed. *Culture in Action.* Seattle, WA: Bay Press, 1995.

Jacob, Mary Jane, with Michael Brenson. *Conversations at the Castle: Changing Audiences and Contemporary Art.* Cambridge: MIT Press, 1998.

Jeffri, Joan, ed. *Information on Artists.* New York: Research Center for the Arts and Culture, Columbia University, 1989.

———. *Information on Artists II.* New York: Research Center for the Arts and Culture, Columbia University, 1997.

Jones, David W. *The Life of Beethoven.* Cambridge: Cambridge University Press, 1998.

Jones, Kellie. "The Structure of Myth and the Potency of Magic." In *David Hammons: Rousing the Rubble,* by Steve Cannon, Kellie Jones, and Tom Finkelpearl. Cambridge: MIT Press, 1991.

Jones, Suzie, ed. *Webfoots and Bunchgrassers: Folk Art of the Oregon Country.* Eugene: Oregon Arts Commission, 1980.

Kalleberg, Arne J., David Knoke, Peter Marsden, and Joe L. Spaeth. *Organizations in America: Analyzing Their Structures and Human Resources Practices.* Thousand Oaks, CA: Sage, 1996.

Kammen, Michael. *American Culture American Tastes: Social Change in the 20th Century.* New York: Knopf, 1999.

Kangas, Anita, and Jill Onsér-Franzén. "Is There a Need for a New Cultural Policy Strategy in the Nordic Welfare State?" *International Journal of Cultural Policy* 3, no. 1 (1996): 15–26.

Kaplan, Ann E., ed. *Giving USA: The Annual Report on Philanthropy for the Year 1998.* New York: AAFRC Trust for Philanthropy, 1999.

Kaple, Deborah, Hugh Louch, Ziggy Rivkin-Fish, Lori Morris, and Paul DiMaggio. "Comparing Sample Frames for Research on Arts Organizations: Results of a Study in Three Metropolitan Areas." *Journal of Arts Management, Law, and Society* 28 (1998): 41–66.

Kaple, Deborah A., Lori Morris, Ziggy Rivkin-Fish, and Paul DiMaggio. *Data on Arts Organizations: A Review and Needs Assessment, with Design Implications.* Princeton, NJ: Center for Arts and Cultural Policy Studies, Princeton University, 1996.

Kernan, Michael. "Making Art Accessible." *Smithsonian* 29, no. 12 (1999): 24–28.

Kindleberger, Charles P., and Bruce Herrick. *Economic Development.* International student ed. London: McGraw-Hill, 1977.

Kingdon, John. *Agendas, Alternatives, and Public Policies.* 2nd ed. New York: HarperCollins, 1995.

Kling, Robert, et al. "Estimating the Public Good Value of Preserving a Local Historic Landmark: The Role of Non-substitutability and Information in Contingent Valuation." Paper presented at the Eleventh Biennial Conference of the Association for Cultural Economics, International, Minneapolis, Minnesota, May 28–31, 2000.

Kollman, Ken. *Outside Lobbying: Public Opinion and Interest Group Strategies.* Princeton, NJ: Princeton University Press, 1999.

Kotkin, Joel, and Ross DeVol. *Knowledge-Value Cities in the Digital Age.* Santa Monica, CA: Milken Institute.

Kotler, Philip, and Joanne Scheff. *Standing Room Only: Strategies for Marketing in the Arts.* Boston: Harvard Business School Press, 1997.

Kramer, Jane. *Whose Art Is It Anyway?* Durham, NC: Duke University, 1994.

Kriedler, John. "Leverage Lost: Evolution in the Nonprofit Arts Ecosystem." In *The Politics of Culture: Policy Perspectives for Individuals, Institutions, and Communities,* ed. Gigi Bradford, Michael Gary, and Glenn Wallach. New York: New Press, 2000.

Krugman, Paul. "Space: The Final Frontier." *Journal of Economic Perspective* 12, no. 2 (spring 1998): 161–74.

Kumpf, Hilary Anne Frost. *Cultural Districts: The Arts As a Strategy for Revitalizing Our Cities.* Washington, DC: American Council for the Arts, 1998.

Kurin, Richard. "The New Study and Curation of Culture." In *The Politics of Culture: Policy Perspectives for Individuals, Institutions, and Communities,* ed. Gigi Bradford, Michael Gary, and Glenn Wallach. New York: New Press, 2000.

———. *Reflections of a Culture Broker: A View from the Smithsonian.* Washington, DC: Smithsonian Institution Press, 1997.

Kurzweil, Raymond. *The Age of Intelligent Machines.* Cambridge: MIT Press, 1990.

Lachapelle, Guy. *Quebec under Free Trade: Making Public Policy in America.* Sainte-Foy, Quebec: Presses de l'Universite du Quebec, 1995.

Lainsbury, Andrew. *Once upon An American Dream: The Story of EuroDisneyland.* Lawrence: University of Kansas Press, 2000.

Lamont, Michele, and Marcel Fournier, eds., *Cultivating Differences: Symbolic Boundaries and the Making of Inequality.* Chicago: University of Chicago Press, 1992.

Lavine, Steven. *The Artist at the Beginning of the 21st Century.* Unpublished manuscript, 2000.

Le Blanc, Jamal, and Victoria Bernal. "The Role of the Arts in Bridging the Digital Divide." Benton Foundation, 28 April 2000, <http://www.benton.org>.

Letts, Christine, Allen Grossman, and William Ryan. *High Performance Nonprofit Organizations: Managing Upstream for Greater Impact.* New York: Wiley, 1999.

Levine, Judy. "New York City Department of Cultural Affairs: Art As Municipal Service." In *Paying the Piper: Causes and Consequences of Art Patronage,* ed. Judith Huggins Balfe. Champaign–Urbana: University of Illinois Press, 1993.

Levine, Lawrence. *Highbrow/Lowbrow: The Emergence of Cultural Hierarchy in America.* Cambridge, MA: Harvard University Press, 1988.

Lijphart, Arend. *Democracy in Plural Societies.* New Haven, NJ: Yale University Press, 1977.

Lincoln, James. "Intra- and Inter-organizational Networks." *Research in the Sociology of Organizations* 1 (1982): 1–38.

Lippard, Lucy. *Mixed Blessings: New Art in a Multicultural America.* New York: Pantheon, 1990.

Lipset, Seymour Martin. *Continental Divide: The Values and Institutions of the United States and Canada.* New York: Routledge, 1990.

Litt, Paul. *The Muses, the Masses, and the Massey Commission.* Toronto: University of Toronto Press, 1992.

Loomis, O. "Buckaroos." In *Webfoots and Bunchgrassers: Folk Art of the Oregon Country,* ed. Suzie Jones. Eugene: Oregon Arts Commission, 1980.

Loosley, David. *The Politics of Fun: Cultural Policy and Debate in Contemporary France.* Oxford: Berg, 1995.

Lopes, Paul D. "Innovation and Diversity in the Popular Music Industry, 1969–1990." *American Sociological Review* 57 (1992): 56–71.

MacIntosh, Robert, and Arthur Francis. *The Market, Technological and Industry Contexts of Business Process Re-engineering in UK Business.* Glasgow: Business Processes Resource Center, 1997.

Maines, David R., and Carl Couch, eds. *Information, Communication and Social Structure.* Springfield, IL: Charles C. Thomas, 1988.

Mangset, Per. "Risks and Benefits of Decentralisation: The Development of Local Cultural Administration in Norway." *International Journal of Cultural Policy* 2, no. 2 (1995): 67–86.

Markusen, Ann. "Should We Target Occupations Rather Than Industries? An Illustration from the Arts." Paper presented at the Eleventh Biennial Conference of the Association for Cultural Economics, International, Minneapolis, Minnesota, May 28–31, 2000.

Marsden, Peter V., and Joseph F. Swingle. "Conceptualizing and Measuring Culture in Surveys: Values, Strategies and Symbols." *Topical Report* no. 26, the National Opinion Research Center (1993), <http://www.icpsr.umich.edu/GSS/rnd1998/reports/t-reports/topic26.htm>.

Martin, Fernand. "Determining the Size of Museum Subsidies." *Journal of Cultural Economics* 18 (1994): 255–70.

Mathews-DeNatale, G. "Folk Arts: Art in Everyday Life." <http://www.carts.org/folkarts.html>.

McAnany, Emile G., and Kenton T. Wilkinson, eds. *Mass Media and Free Trade: NAFTA and Cultural Industries.* Austin: University of Texas Press, 1996.

McCarthy, Kevin F., and Kimberly Jinnett. *A New Framework for Building Participation in the Arts.* Santa Monica, CA: RAND, 2001.

McCarthy, Kevin F., Arthur Brooks, Julia Lowell, and Laur Zakaras. *The Performing Arts in a New Era.* Santa Monica, CA: RAND, 2001.

McCosh, John. "Downtown Atlanta Gets Boost." *Atlanta Journal-Constitution,* 27 April 2000, E1, E4.

McCulloch-Lovell, Ellen. *Can We Have a Cultural Policy?* Columbus: Arts Policy and Administration Program, Ohio State University, 1998.

McPherson, J. Miller. "An Ecology of Affiliation." *American Sociological Review* 48 (1983): 519–32.

Meisel, John. "Extinction Revisited: Culture and Class in Canada." In *Seeing Ourselves: Media Power and Policy in Canada,* ed. Helen Holmes and David Taras. 2nd ed. Toronto: Harcourt Brace, 1996.

———. "Government and the Arts in Canada." In *Who's to Pay for the Arts,* ed. Milton C. Cummings Jr. and J. Mark Davidson Schuster. New York: American Council for the Arts, 1989.

Meisel, John, and Jean Van Loon. "Cultivating the Bushgarden: Cultural Policy in Canada." In *The Patron State: Government and Arts in Europe, North America, and Japan,* ed. Milton C. Cummings Jr. and Richard S. Katz. New York: Oxford University Press, 1987.

Melzer, Arthur M., Jerry Weinberger, and M. Richard Zinman. *Democracy and the Arts.* Ithaca, NY: Cornell University Press, 1999.

Mirikitani, Cora. "The Role of Philanthropy in the Intersection between Culture and Commerce." *Journal of Arts Management, Law, and Society* 29, no. 2 (summer 1999): 128–31.

Moriarty, Erin. "Teamwork: Sports and Arts; City Makes Big Pitch with All-Star Game Promotion." *Atlanta Business Chronicle,* 28 April–4 May 2000, 3A, 21A.

Morrison, William G., and Edwin G. West. "Subsidies for the Performing Arts: Evidence on Voter Preferences." *Journal of Behavioral Economics* 15 (fall 1986): 57–72.

Mulcahy, Kevin V. "The Abused Patron of Culture: Public Culture and Cultural Patronage in the United States." *Boekmancahier* 44 (June 2000): 169–81.

———. "Cultural Imperialism and Cultural Sovereignty: US–Canadian Cultural Relations." *American Review of Canadian Studies* 30, no. 2 (2000): 181–206.

———. "Cultural Patronage in the United States." *International Journal of Arts Management* 2 (fall 1999): 53–58.

———. "The Government and Cultural Patronage: A Comparative Analysis of Cultural Patronage in Canada, Norway, France and the United States." In *The Public Life of the Arts in America,* ed. Joni Maya Cherbo and Margaret J. Wyszomirski. New Brunswick, NJ: Rutgers University Press, 2000.

———. "Public Culture and Political Culture." In *Quebec under Free Trade: Making Public Policy in America,* ed. Guy Lachapelle. Sainte-Foy, Quebec: Presses de l'Université du Quebec, 1995.

———. "Public Culture and Political Culture: La Politique Culturelle du Quebec." *Journal of Arts Management, Law, and Society* 25 (fall 1995): 225–49.

———. "The Public Interest in Arts Policy." In *America's Commitment to Culture: Government and the Arts in the United States,* ed. Kevin V. Mulcahy and Margaret J. Wyszomirski. Boulder, CO: Westview, 1995.

———. "The Public Interest in Public Culture." *Journal of Arts Management and Law* 21 (spring 1991): 5–27.

———. Review of *The Muses, the Masses, and the Massey Commission,* by Paul Litt. *Governance* 7 (winter 1994): 102–3.

Mulcahy, Kevin V., and Margaret J. Wyszomirski, eds. *America's Commitment to Culture: Government and the Arts in the United States.* Boulder, CO: Westview, 1995.

National Assembly of State Arts Agencies. *Advancing America's Creativity.* Washington, DC: National Assembly of State Arts Agencies, 2001.

———. *State Arts Agency Funding Sourcebook.* Washington, DC: National Assembly of State Arts Agencies, 2000.

National Endowment for the Arts. *Artists in American Life.* Washington, DC: National Endowment for the Arts, 2000.

———. *Five-Year Planning Document, 1986–1990.* Washington, DC: U.S. Government Printing Office, 1984.

———. The National Endowment for the Arts 1965–2000: A Brief Chronology of Federal Support for the Arts. Washington, DC: National Endowment for the Arts, 2000.

———. "Non-profit Gateway." <http://www.arts.endow.gov/gateway>.

———. "Research Division Note #70." In *1997 Survey of Public Participation in the Arts.* Washington, DC: National Endowment for the Arts, 1998.

———. "Summary Report." In *1992 Survey of Public Participation in the Arts.* Washington, DC: National Endowment for the Arts, 1992.

———. "Summary Report." In *1997 Survey of Public Participation in the Arts.* Washington, DC: National Endowment for the Arts, 1997.

Neelamegham, Ramya, and Dipak Jain. "Consumer Choice Process for Experience Goods: An Econometric Model and Analysis." *Journal of Marketing Research* (August 1999).

Netzer, Dick. "Arts and Culture." In *Who Benefits from the Private Sector?,* ed. Charles T. Clotfelter. Chicago: University of Chicago Press, 1992.

New England Council. The Creative Economy Initiative: A Blueprint for Investment in New England's Creative Economy. Boston: New England Council, 2001.

———. The Creative Economy Initiative: The Role of the Arts and Culture in New England's Economic Competitiveness. Boston: New England Council, 2000.

Noll, Roger G., and Andrew Zimbalist. "The Economic Impact of Sports Teams and Facilities." In *Sports, Jobs and Taxes,* ed. Roger G. Noll and Andrew Zimbalist. Washington, DC: Brookings Institution Press, 1997.

Nunley, John W., and Judith Bettelheim, eds. *Caribbean Festival Arts: Each and Every Bit of Difference.* Seattle: University of Washington Press, 1998.

Nye, Russel B. *The Unembarrassed Muse: The Popular Arts in America.* New York: Dial, 1970.

Olson, Ruth, and Anne Pryor. "Talk Stage: Using Stories in Living Cultural Exhibits." *Journal of Museum Education* 24, no. 3 (1999): 17–20.

Ornstein, Norman J., and Shirley Elder. *Interest Groups, Lobbying and Policymaking.* Washington, DC: Congressional Quarterly, 1978.

Pankratz, David. *Multiculturalism and Public Arts Policy.* Westport, CT: Bergin and Garvey, 1993.

———. "R&D and the Arts Sector: Components and Criteria for Development." In *Building Creative Assets: New Ways for the Entertainment and Not-for-Profit Arts Industries to Work Together,* by Americans for the Arts. White papers for a November 12, 1998, forum, Los Angeles, California.

Pankratz, David B., Milton C. Cummings Jr., Monnie Peters, C. Richard Swaim, and Margaret Jane Wyszomirski. "Arts Policy Research for the 1990s and Beyond." In *The Future of the Arts: Public Policy and Arts Research,* ed. David B. Pankratz and Valerie B. Morris. New York: Praeger, 1990.

Pankratz, David B., and Valerie B. Morris, eds. *The Future of the Arts: Public Policy and Arts Research.* New York: Praeger, 1990.

Perret, Jacques, and Guy Saez. *Institutions et Vie Culturelles.* Paris: La Documentation Française, 1996.

Peters, Monnie, and Joni Maya Cherbo. "The Missing Sector: The Unincorporated Arts." *Journal of Arts Management, Law, and Society* 28, no. 2 (summer 1998): 115–28.

Peterson. Richard A. "Culture Studies through the Production Perspective." In *Emerging Theoretical Perspectives in the Sociology of Culture,* ed. Diana Crane. London: Blackwell, 1994.

———. "From Impresario to Arts Administrator: Formal Accountability in Nonprofit Cultural Organizations." In *Nonprofit Enterprise in the Arts,* ed. Paul J. DiMaggio. New York: Oxford University Press, 1986.

———. "Globalization and Communalization of Popular Music in the Production Perspective." In *The Globalization of Popular Music,* ed. Andreas Gebesmair. Forthcoming.

———, ed. *The Production of Culture.* Beverly Hills, CA: Sage, 1976.

———. "The Production of Culture: A Prolegomenon." In *The Production of Culture,* ed. Richard A. Peterson. Beverly Hills, CA: Sage, 1976.

———. "The Rise and Fall of Highbrow Snobbery As a Status Marker." *Poetics* 25 (1997): 75–92.

———. "Six Constraints on the Production of Literary Works." *Poetics* 14 (1985): 45–67.

———. "Snob to Omnivore: The Implication of Shifting Tastes for the Arts and Cultural Industries." Paper presented at the Long-Term Developments in the Fine Arts and Culture Industries Conference, Rotterdam, 2000.

———. "Why 1955? Explaining the Advent of Rock Music." *Popular Music* 9 (1990): 97–116.

Peterson, Richard A., and David G. Berger. "Cycles in Symbol Production: The Case of Popular Music." *American Sociological Review* 40 (1975): 158–73.

Peterson, Richard A., and Roger Kern. "Changing High-Brow Taste: From Snob to Omnivore." *American Sociological Review* 61 (1996): 900–7.

Peterson, Richard A., and Darren E. Sherkat. "Effects of Age on Arts Participation." In *Age and Arts Participation, with a Focus on the Baby Boom Cohort.* National Endowment for the Arts, Research Division Report no. 34. Santa Ana, CA: Seven Locks Press, 1996.

Peterson, Richard A., and Albert Simkus. "How Musical Taste Groups Mark Occupational Groups." In *Cultivating Differences: Symbolic Boundaries and the Mak-*

ing of Inequality, ed. Michele Lamont and Marcel Fournier. Chicago: University of Chicago Press, 1992.

Peterson, Richard A., Pamela Hull, and Roger Kern. *Aging Arts Audiences.* Santa Ana, CA: Seven Locks, 2000.

Peterson, Richard A., Darren E. Sherkat, Judith Huggins Balfe, and Rolf Meyerson. *Age and Arts Participation with a Focus on the Baby Boom Cohort.* Santa Ana, CA: Seven Locks Press for the National Endowment for the Arts, Research Division Report no. 34, 1996.

Petherbridge, Jonathan. "Escape from the Black Box." *artsbusiness,* 24 April 2000, 5–6.

Pettit, Becky. Resources for Studying Public Participation in the Arts, and Inventory and Review of Available Survey Data on North Americans' Participation in and Attitudes towards the Arts. Working Paper no. 2. Princeton, NJ: Princeton University Center for Arts and Cultural Policy Studies, 1997.

Pine, B. Joseph, II, and James H. Gilmore. *The Experience Economy: Work Is Theatre and Every Business a Stage.* Cambridge, MA: Harvard Business School Press, 1999.

———. "Welcome to the Experience Economy." *Harvard Business Review* 76, no. 4 (July–August 1998): 97–105.

Port Authority of New York and New Jersey. *The Arts As an Industry: Their Economic Importance to the New York–New Jersey Metropolitan Region.* New York: Port Authority of New York and New Jersey, 1993.

Powell, Walter W., and Paul J. DiMaggio, eds. *New Institutionalism in Organizational Analysis.* Chicago: University of Chicago Press, 1991.

President's Committee on the Arts and Humanities. *Creative America: A Report to the President.* Washington, DC: President's Committee on the Arts and Humanities, 1997.

Putnam, Robert. *Bowling Alone: The Collapse and Revival of American Community.* New York: Simon and Schuster, 2000.

Quigley, John M. "Urban Diversity and Economic Growth." *Journal of Economic Perspective* 12, no. 2 (spring 1998): 127–38.

Raboy, Marc, Ivan Bernier, Florian Sauvageau, and Dave Atkins. "Cultural Development and the Open Economy: A Democratic Issue and a Challenge to Public Policy." *Canadian Journal of Communication* 19, no. 3–4 (summer–autumn 1994): 291–315.

Radich, Anthony J., ed. *Economic Impact of the Arts: A Sourcebook.* Denver, CO: National Conference of State Legislators, 1987.

Rakoff, David. "The Way We Live Now: Questions for Michael Hirschorn and Kurt Andersen." *New York Times Magazine,* 16 April 2000, 14.

Rees, Matthew. "The Best of Times, the Best of Times." *Philanthropy* (May–June 1999).

Reid, Elizabeth J. "Nonprofit Advocacy and Political Participation." Paper presented at the conference on Nonprofit Organizations and the Government: The Challenge of Civil Society. Urban Institute Center on Nonprofits and Philanthropy, Washington, DC, June 8–9, 1998.

Remond, Rene. *Nôtre Siecle de 1918 à 1991.* Paris: Fayard, 1991.

Renz, Loren, and Steven Lawrence. *Arts Funding: An Update on Foundation Trends.* New York: Foundation Center, 1998.

———. *Arts Funding 2000.* New York: Foundation Center, 2000.

Renz Loren, and Cynthia W. Massarsky. *Program-Related Investments: A Guide to Funders and Trends.* New York: Foundation Center, 1995.

"RIAA Sues Napster, Claiming 'Music Piracy.'" SonicNet.com, 7 December 1999, <http://www.sonicnet.com>.

Riley, Tom. "Who's Afraid of Giving to the Arts? Are the Arts Missing out on the Next Boom?" *Philanthropy* (January–February 2000).

Robinson, P. John. *Arts Participation in America, 1982–1992: A Report for the National Endowment for the Arts*. NEA Report no. 27. Prepared by Jack Faucett Associates (October 1993).

Rockefeller Panel Report. The Performing Arts: Problems and Prospects—Rockefeller Panel Report on the Future of Theatre, Dance, Music in America. New York: McGraw-Hill, 1965.

Rothenbuhler, Eric W. "Live Broadcasting, Media Events, Telecommunication, and Social Form." In *Information, Communication and Social Structure*, ed. David R. Maines and Carl Couch. Springfield, IL: Charles C. Thomas, 1988.

Ryan, John. *The Production of Culture in the Music Industry*. New York: University Press of America, 1985.

Ryan, John, and William M. Wentworth. *Media and Society: The Production of Culture in the Mass Media*. Boston: Allyn and Bacon, 1999.

Sabatier, Paul A. "An Advocacy Coalition Framework of Policy Change and the Role of Policy Oriented Learning Therein." *Policy Studies* 21 (1988): 129–68.

Salamon, Lester M. *Holding the Center: America's Nonprofit Sector at a Crossroads*. New York: Nathan Cummings Foundation, 1997.

Salisbury, Robert H. "An Exchange Theory of Interest Groups." *Midwest Journal of Political Science* 13 (1969): 1–32.

Santagata, Walter. "Cultural Districts for Sustainable Economic Growth." Paper presented at the Eleventh Biennial Conference of the Association for Cultural Economics, International, Minneapolis, Minnesota, May 28–31, 2000.

Scheppele, Kim L. *Legal Secrets: Equality and Efficiency in the Common Law*. Chicago: University of Chicago Press, 1988.

Schlozman, Kay Lehman, and John T. Tierney. *Organized Interest and American Democracy*. New York: Harper and Row, 1986.

Scott, Allen J. *The Cultural Economy of Cities*. Newbury Park, CA: Sage, 2000.

Seaman, Bruce A. "Arts Impact Studies: A Fashionable Excess." In *Economic Impact of the Arts: A Sourcebook*, ed. Anthony J. Radich. Denver: National Conference of State Legislators, 1987.

Sharp, Elaine. *Culture Wars and Local Politics*. Lawrence: University of Kansas Press, 1999.

Simpson, Charles R. *SoHo: The Artist in the City*. Chicago: University of Chicago Press, 1981.

Singh, Jitendra V., ed. *Organizational Evolution: New Directions*. Newbury Park, CA: Sage, 1990.

Siporin, Steve. *American Folk Masters: The National Heritage Fellows*. New York: Harry N. Abrams, 1992.

Smith, Allan. *Canada—An American Nation? Essays on Continentalism, Identity, and the Canadian Frame of Mind*. Montreal: McGill-Queen's University Press, 1994.

Smith, James Allen. *The Idea Brokers: Think Tanks and the Rise of the New Policy Elite*. New York: The Free Press, 1991.

Smith, Ralph A., and Ronald Berman, eds. *Public Policy and the Aesthetic Interest*. Urbana: University of Illinois Press, 1992.

Soh, Byung Hee, and Yong Joong Yoon. "Economic Development and Public Support for the Arts and Culture in Korea." Paper presented at the Eleventh Biennial Conference of the Association for Cultural Economics, International, Minneapolis, Minnesota, May 28–31, 2000.

Southern Legislative Conference. *More Than a Song and Dance: The Economic Impact of the Arts in the Southern Legislative Conference States.* Atlanta, GA: Southern Office, the Council of State Governments, 2000.

Starr, Paul. "The Edge of Social Science." *Harvard Educational Review* 44 (1974): 393–415.

Stern, Mark J. *Is All the World Philadelphia? A Multi-city Study of Arts and Cultural Organizations, Diversity and Urban Revitalization.* Working Paper no. 9. Social Impact of the Arts Project, University of Pennsylvania School of Social Work, May 1999.

Stern, Mark. J., and Susan C. Seifert. "Cultural Organizations in the Network Society." Working Paper no. 11. Social Impact of the Arts Project, University of Pennsylvania School of Social Work, February 2000.

Stevens, Louise K. *California Arts Audience Research Project.* Vol. 1 (November 1999).

———. "The Earnings Shift: The New Bottom Line Paradigm for the Arts Industry in a Market Driven Era." *Journal of Arts Management, Law, and Society* 26, no. 2 (summer 1996): 101–13.

———. "Impacts, Measurement, and Art Policy: Starting the Change Process." *Journal of Arts Management, Law, and Society* 28, no. 3 (fall 1998): 225–28.

———. *The Performing Arts in California: Rebuilding, Repositioning, Re-emerging.* Bozeman, MT: ArtsMarket, 2000.

Taylor, E. Andrew. "The Experience Brokers: The New Role for Arts Administrators in the Information Age." In *Looking Ahead: A Collection of Papers from the International Social Theory, Politics and the Arts Conference,* ed. Cecelia Fitzgibbon. Philadelphia: Drexel University Press, 1999.

———. "Rethinking the Performing Arts for the Media Age." *Journal of Arts Management, Law, and Society* 25, no. 3 (fall 1995): 206–24.

Thompson, Eric C. "Contingent Valuation in Arts Impact Studies." *Journal of Arts Management, Law, and Society* 28, no. 3 (fall 1998): 206–10.

Thomson, Robert Farris. *Face of the Gods: Art and Altars of Africa and the African Americans.* New York: Museum for African Art, 1993.

Throsby, David C., and Glenn A. Withers. "Measuring the Demand for the Arts As a Public Good: Theory and Empirical Results." In *Economics of Cultural Decision,* ed. William S. Hendon and James L. Shanahan. Cambridge, MA: Abt Associates, 1983.

United Nations Educational, Scientific, and Cultural Organization. *Final Report: Intergovernmental Conference on Cultural Policies for Development, Stockholm, Sweden, March 30–April 2, 1998.* Paris: United Nations Educational, Scientific, and Cultural Organization, 1998.

United States Census Bureau. *Statistical Abstract of the United States, 1999.* Washington, DC: U.S. Government Printing Office, 1999.

United States Conference of Mayors Special Committee on Historic Preservation. *With Heritage So Rich.* New York: Random House, 1966.

United States Department of State. International Understanding through the Performing Arts: A Report on the Cultural Presentations Program. Washington, DC: U.S. Government Printing Office, 1965.

Urice, John K. "Government Support for the Arts in the United States, 1990–2015: A Forecast." In *The Future of the Arts: Public Policy and Arts Research,* ed. David B. Pankratz and Valerie B. Morris. New York: Praeger, 1990.

———, ed. "Information Systems and the Arts." *Journal of Arts Management, Law, and Society* (Special Issue) 14, no. 1 (spring 1984).

Van Camp, Julie. "Freedom of Expression at the National Endowment for the Arts: An Opportunity for Interdisciplinary Education." *Journal of Aesthetic Education* 30 (fall 1996): 43–65.

Venture Philanthropy Partners. *Venture Philanthropy: Landscape and Expectations.* Reston, VA: Morino Institute, 2000.

———. Venture Philanthropy 2001: The Changing Landscape. Reston, VA: Morino Institute, 2001.

Venturelli, Shalini. *From the Information Economy to the Creative Economy.* Washington, DC: Center for Arts and Culture, 2001.

Voith, Richard P. "City and Suburban Growth: Substitutes or Complements?" *Business Review* (Federal Reserve Bank of Philadelphia) (September–October 1992): 21–33.

———. Does City Income Growth Increase Suburban Income Growth, House Value Appreciation, and Population Growth? Working Paper no. 93–27. Federal Reserve Bank of Philadelphia, 1993.

Walker, Jack A., Jr. "The Origins and Maintenance of Interest Groups in America." *American Political Science Review* 77, no. 2 (1983): 390–406.

Walker, Jack L. *Mobilizing Interest Groups in America.* Ann Arbor: University of Michigan Press, 1991.

Wallis, Brian, Marianne Weems, and Philip Yenawine. *Art Matters: How the Culture Wars Changed America.* New York: New York University Press, 1999.

Wasserman, Stanley, and Katherine Faust. *Social Network Analysis: Methods and Applications.* New York: Cambridge University Press, 1994.

Weisbrod, Burton A., ed. *To Profit or Not to Profit: The Commercial Transformation of the Nonprofit Sector.* New York: Cambridge University Press, 1998.

West, Cornel. "The Moral Obligations of Living in a Democratic Society." In *The Good Citizen,* ed. David Batstone and Eduardo Mendieta. New York: Routledge, 1999.

Western States Arts Federation. *Cultural Policy in the West.* Denver: Western States Arts Federation, 2000.

White, David Manning. *Popular Culture (The Great Contemporary Issues).* North Stratford, NH: Ayer, 1975.

White, Harrison C. *Careers and Creativity: Social Forces in the Arts.* Boulder, CO: Westview, 1993.

White, Harrison C., and Cynthia A. White. *Canvases and Careers.* New York: Wiley, 1965.

Willette, Jeanne. "Stitching Lives: Fabric in the Art of Betye Saar." *Fiberarts* (March–April 1997): 44–48.

Wilson, K. E. "Crafting Community-Based Museum Experiences: Process, Pedagogy, and Performance." *Journal of Museum Education* 24, no. 3 (1999): 3–6.

Wilton, J. "Toward an Understanding of Skin Art." In *Pluralistic Approaches to Art Criticism,* ed. Doug Blandy and Kristin G. Congdon. Bowling Green, OH: Popular, 1987.

Wolf, Michael J. *The Entertainment Economy: How Mega-media Forces Are Transforming Our Lives.* New York: Times Books/Random House, 1999.

Wolman, Harold, and David Spitzley. "The Politics of Local Economic Development." *Economic Development Quarterly* 10, no. 2 (May 1996): 115–50.

Wyszomirski, Margaret Jane. "The Arts and Performance Review, Policy Assessment, and Program Evaluation: Focusing on the Ends of the Policy Cycle." *Journal of Arts Management, Law, and Society* 28, no. 3 (fall 1998): 191–200.

———. "Creative Assets and Cultural Development: How Can Research Inform Nonprofit–Commercial Partnerships?" *Journal of Arts Management, Law, and Society* 29, no. 2 (summer 1999): 132–41.

———. "From Accord to Discord: Arts Policy during and after the Culture Wars." In *America's Commitment to Culture: Government and the Arts in the United States,* ed. Kevin V. Mulcahy and Margaret J. Wyszomirski. Boulder, CO: Westview, 1995.

———, ed. Going Global: Negotiating the Maze of Cultural Interactions—The 2000 Barnett Arts and Public Policy Symposium at Ohio State. Columbus: Arts Policy and Administration Program, Ohio State University, 2000.

———. "Policy Communities and Policy Influence: Securing a Government Role in Cultural Policy for the 21st Century." *Journal of Arts Management, Law, and Society* 25, no. 3 (fall 1995): 192–205. Reprinted in Gigi Bradford, Michael Gary, and Glenn Wallach, eds., *The Politics of Culture: Policy Perspectives for Individuals, Institutions, and Communities.* New York: New Press, 2000.

———. "The Politics of Arts Policy: Subgovernment to Issue Network." In *America's Commitment to Culture: Government and the Arts in the United States,* ed. Kevin V. Mulcahy and Margaret J. Wyszomirski. Boulder, CO: Westview, 1995.

———. *Public Policy at the Intersection on the Arts, Technology and Intellectual Property.* Columbus: Arts Policy and Administration Program, Ohio State University, 2000.

———. "Raison d'Etat, Raisons des Arts: Thinking about Public Purposes." In *The Public Life of the Arts in America,* ed. Joni Maya Cherbo and Margaret J. Wyszomirski. New Brunswick, NJ: Rutgers University Press, 2000.

———. *Revealing the Implicit: Searching for Measures of the Impact of the Arts.* Washington, DC: The Independent Sector Conference on Measuring the Impact of the Non-profit Sector on Society, 1996.

Wyszomirski, Margaret J., and Pat Clubb, eds. *The Cost of Culture: Patterns and Prospects of Private Arts Patronage.* New York: American Council for the Arts, 1989.

Wyszomirski, Margaret J., and Kevin V. Mulcahy. "The Organization for Public Support for the Arts." In *America's Commitment to Culture: Government and the Arts in the United States,* ed. Kevin V. Mulcahy and Margaret J. Wyszomirski. Boulder, CO: Westview, 1995.

Yudice, George. "Civil Society, Consumption, and Govermentality in an Age of Global Restructuring." *Social Text* 45 (1995): 1–26.

Zaltman, Gerald. "Thoughts and Feelings about the Arts." Harvard Business School (1998).

Zeigler, Joseph Wesley. *Arts in Crisis: The National Endowment for the Arts Versus America.* Chicago: A Cappella, 1994.

———. "Friendly Persuasion: The Arts Arrive on Capitol Hill." *American Arts* (July 1983): 22–26.

Zeitlin, Steve J. "I'm a Folklorist and You're Not: Expansive versus Delimited Strategies in the Practice of Folklore." *Journal of American Folklore* 113, no. 447 (2000): 3–19.

Zimmer, Annette, and Stefan Toepler. "Cultural Policies and the Welfare State: The Cases of Sweden, Germany, and the United States." *Journal of Arts Management, Law, and Society* 26 (fall 1996): 167–93.

Zimmerman, Dennis. "Subsidizing Stadiums: Who Benefits, Who Pays?" In *Sports, Jobs and Taxes,* ed. Roger G. Noll and Andrew Zimbalist. Washington, DC: Brookings Institution Press, 1997.

Zolberg, Vera L. *Constructing a Sociology of the Arts.* New York: Cambridge University Press, 1990.

Zolberg, Vera L., and Joni Maya Cherbo. *Outsider Arts: Contesting Boundaries in Contemporary Culture.* New York: Cambridge University Press, 1996.

Index

About the Editors and Contributors

VALERIE B. MORRIS is Dean of the School of the Arts at the College of Charleston in South Carolina. The school contains Departments of Art History, Music, Studio Art, and Theater, with programs in arts management and in historic preservation and community planning. She is actively involved in the arts community in Charleston and in the state, serving on the board of directors of the Charleston Symphony Orchestra, the South Carolina Arts Alliance, and the South Carolina Alliance for Arts Education, and on the advisory committee for the Arts in Basic Curriculum program, which develops systems to make arts education a central part of primary and secondary curricula. She also works with the annual Spoleto and Piccolo Spoleto arts festivals, held in Charleston. She has served as Executive Editor of the *Journal of Arts Management, Law, and Society* since 1982. Her writings appear in a number of scholarly publications, and she is an active spokesperson for the arts and education throughout the country. She served as coeditor, with David B. Pankratz, of *The Future of the Arts* (1989).

DAVID B. PANKRATZ is an arts research consultant based in southern California. He has served in senior positions for ARTS, Inc.: The Arts and Business Council of Greater Los Angeles, the J. Paul Getty Trust, the Independent Commission on the National Endowment for the Arts, and Urban Gateways: The Center for Arts in Education. For ARTS, Inc., he served as the Los Angeles research manager for the National and Local Profiles of Cultural Support research project, and coordinated public forums and disseminated information on policy issues and cross-sector partnership opportunities in the arts and culture. He teaches graduate courses and workshops in arts and arts education policy for

Ohio State University and the University of Oregon and is the author of *Multiculturalism and Arts Policy* (1993) and *Current Research in Arts Education: A Research Compendium* (2001). A coeditor of *The Future of the Arts* (1989) and *The Challenge to Reform Arts Education* (1989), he has also contributed to public reports by the American Assembly (on for-profit/nonprofit arts partnerships), Americans for the Arts, the Center for Arts and Culture, and the University of Southern California. He is a long-time consulting editor for the *Journal of Arts Management, Law, and Society* and *Arts Education Policy Review.*

ALBERTA ARTHURS is an associate of MEM Associates, a nonprofit consulting group in New York City and was Director for Arts and Humanities at the Rockefeller Foundation, where she oversaw national and international programming in culture and scholarship. She was Codirector for the 1997 American Assembly "The Arts and the Public Purpose," and has served on many boards and advisory committees, including Technoserve, the Kenan Institute for the Arts, and the Center for Arts and Culture.

JUDITH HUGGINS BALFE (deceased) was Professor of Sociology at the City University of New York's Graduate Center and at its College of Staten Island. She had been an active contributor to annual Social Theory, Politics, and the Arts conferences and served as Executive Editor of the *Journal of Arts Management, Law, and Society.* Her many publications include "Age and Arts Participation: With a Focus on the Baby Boom Cohort" (2000) and the coedited book *Paying the Piper: Causes and Consequences of Art Patronage* (1993).

DOUG BLANDY is the current Director of the Arts and Administration Program and the Institute for Community Arts Studies at the University of Oregon. His published research attends to issues of community arts, civil society, curriculum development, program accessibility, and art education, with special interests in relationships between the arts, education, community, and place. He is coeditor of *Art in a Democracy* (1987) and *Pluralistic Approaches to Art Criticism* (1987).

GIGI BRADFORD has served as Director of the Literature Program for the National Endowment for the Arts and as Executive Director of the Center for Arts and Culture, an independent research organization based in Washington, DC, that promotes research and dialogue on issues shaping cultural life. She is coeditor of *The Politics of Culture: Policy Perspectives for Individuals, Institutions, and Communities* (2000), to which she contributed a chapter on defining culture and cultural policy.

JONI M. CHERBO is an independent scholar and arts consultant based in New York City who teaches, researches, and writes frequently on the sociology of art, arts issues, and cultural policy. A Senior Research Fellow at Ohio State University's Arts Policy and Administration program and Research Director for the American Assembly forum "The Arts and the Public Purpose," she coedited *The Public Life of the Arts in America* (2000), for which she cowrote "Mapping the Public Life of the Arts in America."

KRISTIN G. CONGDON is Professor of Art and Philosophy at the University of Central Florida in Orlando, where she coordinates the art history program and teaches classes on theory and criticism, women and art, and twentieth-century art. A recent President of the Florida Folklore Society, she has published extensively on the study of folk arts, feminist criticism, and community arts and has coedited *Art in a Democracy* (1987), *Pluralistic Approaches to Art Criticism* (1987), and *Histories of Community-Based Art Education* (1997).

PAUL DIMAGGIO is Professor of Sociology at Princeton University, serves as Research Coordinator of Princeton's Center for Arts and Cultural Policy Studies at the Woodrow Wilson School, and is an advisor to the Center for Arts and Culture's Network project. He has written widely on organizational analysis, focusing especially on nonprofit and cultural organizations, patterns of participation in the arts, and cultural conflict, and has served as principal investigator for research on arts and culture data.

MARIAN A. GODFREY is Director of the Culture Program at the Pew Charitable Trusts. Under her leadership, grant making in the arts and culture at Pew has sought to foster broader public appreciation of the arts and their role in society and, through the Optimizing America's Cultural Policies initiative, has explored and advanced new research and policy frameworks for the arts and culture. She has also served as Chair for Grantmakers in the Arts and on the board of Theatre Communications Group.

MARIA-ROSARIO JACKSON is Director for the Arts, Culture, and Communities Program at the Urban Institute, where she currently serves as the principal investigator on the Arts and Culture Indicators in Community Building Project and Investing in Creativity, a study of support for artists in the United States. A frequent presenter at conferences worldwide, she is the author of numerous articles and publications in the areas of community development, cultural policy, and arts and culture at the community level.

CARRIE LEE is a graduate student and doctoral candidate in the Department of Sociology at Vanderbilt University. She assisted in coordination of the Twenty-Fifth Annual Conference on Social Theory, Politics, and the Arts held in 1999 at Vanderbilt University, and analyzed how and in what ways this annual conference has evolved as a focus of scholarly research on the arts sector for more than two decades.

ERIN V. LEHMAN is Program Manager of the Arts and Culture Initiative at the Hauser Center for Nonprofit Organizations based within the Kennedy School of Government at Harvard University. Her publications include an edited monograph for the National Endowment for the Arts, "The Effect of Age on Arts Participation in the U.S." (1997), a cross-national study of symphony orchestras, and a study of the management practices and organizational effectiveness of self-governing orchestras.

KEVIN V. MULCAHY is Professor of Political Science and the Humanities at Louisiana State University and Executive Editor of the *Journal of Arts Management, Law, and Society.* The coauthor of *Public Policy and the Arts* and *America's Commitment to Culture: Government and the Arts* (1995), he has written extensively on comparative cultural policy, drawing on scholarship and teaching in France, Norway, Sweden, and Canada and service on advisory boards of state and local arts agencies.

RICHARD A. PETERSON for many years served as Professor of Sociology at Vanderbilt University, and now writes and lectures widely on the sociology of cultural production, popular music, and arts audiences. He is a founding member of the Sociology of Culture section of the American Sociological Association, served as the host of the Twenty-Fifth Annual Conference on Social Theory, Politics, and the Arts, and his many publications include *The Production of Culture* (1976) and *Creating Country Music* (1997).

BRUCE A. SEAMAN is Associate Professor of Economics at Georgia State University (GSU) and Senior Associate in the GSU Policy Research Center who has also served as President of the Association of Cultural Economics International. The author of "An Assessment of Recent Applications of Economic Theory to the Arts" (1981), among many other publications, his research interests span public regulation law, forensic economics, cultural economics, and the economics of nonprofit and public sector economies.

LOUISE K. STEVENS is Founder, President, and Executive Consultant of ArtsMarket, a national consulting firm in strategic planning, research, cultural education, and building audiences. A widely published author and in-demand speaker, she has provided counsel and research to hundreds of organizations, corporations, and agencies, encompassing audience/funder research and target-market development, stabilization, and cultural and educational planning and evaluation.

ANDREW TAYLOR is Director of the Bolz Center for Arts Administration at the University of Wisconsin–Madison School of Business. The author of articles on communications technology and the management, marketing, and support of the arts, his current projects include advising the $100 million Overture Project to benefit the cultural arts in downtown Madison and the Bolz Center Idea Portal project to enable on-line knowledge sharing in the arts.

JOHN K. URICE is Professor of Theater and Arts Administration at Illinois State University, having joined Illinois State as Vice President and Provost in 1994 after service as Dean of the College of Arts and Sciences at Oakland University. The author of numerous articles on public policy, higher education, and demographic and economic trends in the arts, he was a former Executive Editor for the *Journal of Arts Management, Law, and Society.*

GLENN WALLACH has taught history and American studies at Yale and Georgetown Universities and served as Deputy Director of the Center for Arts and Culture, an independent research organization based in Washington, DC, that promotes research and dialogue on issues shaping cultural life. He is co-editor of *The Politics of Culture: Policy Perspectives for Individuals, Institutions, and Communities* (2000), to which he contributed a chapter on culture and policy in local and global contexts.

MARGARET J. WYSZOMIRSKI is Professor of Public Policy and Director of the Arts Policy and Administration Program at Ohio State University. The author of books and many journal articles on public purposes and the arts, cultural policy communities and leadership, policy evaluation, and government roles in arts and culture, she has served as Staff Director for the Independent Commission on the National Endowment for the Arts and as Director of the National Endowment for the Arts Office of Policy Planning, Research, and Budget.